RITUAL, POLITICS, AND POWER

Ritual,
Politics,
and
Power

David I. Kertzer

Yale University Press
New Haven and London

Designed by James J. Johnson
and set in Palatino type by The Composing Room of Michigan.
Printed in the United States of America by
Vail-Ballou Press, Binghamton, N.Y.

Library of Congress Cataloging-in-Publication Data

Kertzer, David I., 1948–
  Ritual, politics, and power / David I. Kertzer.

  Bibliography: p.
  Includes index.
  1. Political customs and rites—Cross-cultural studies.
  2. Power (Social sciences)—Cross-cultural studies.
  3. Symbolism in politics—Cross-cultural studies. I. Title.
GN492.3.K47 1988
306'.2—dc19   87–16122
ISBN 0–300–04007–5 (cloth)
     0–300–04362–7 (pbk.)

The paper in this book meets the guidelines for
permanence and durability of the Committee on
Production Guidelines for Book Longevity of the
Council on Library Resources.

10 9 8 7 6 5

For Susan

Contents

	Preface	ix
1	The Power of Rites	1
2	Flaming Crosses and Body Snatchers	15
3	Legitimacy and Mystification	35
4	The Virtues of Ambiguity	57
5	The Ritual Construction of Political Reality	77
6	Rite Makes Might: Struggling for Power through Ritual	102
7	Conflict and Crisis	125
8	Rituals of Revolution	151
9	The Rites of Power	174
	Notes	185
	References	205
	Index	223

Preface

Although the political rites examined in these pages encompass many centuries and almost all parts of the world, the impetus for this book comes from my own experiences: political observations made primarily in the United States and Italy, but also in all too brief visits to Sri Lanka and China, to Ethiopia, Kenya, and the Ivory Coast, to Brazil and Colombia. Even for the transient visitor, it is difficult to avoid encounters with the rites and symbols of politics. From making my way across an Addis Ababa boulevard clogged with demonstrators supporting the new Ethiopian military conscription law in 1983 to being the object of a banquet toast in Beijing to a future under the wise guidance of the Central Committee, I found myself puzzling at the symbolic forms politics take.

But the genesis of this book is to be found closer to home. My most vivid childhood political memories are of political rites, and in this I think myself no different from others. What remains most memorable to me about John Kennedy's presidential campaign of 1960 comes from a festively decorated motorcade of the then candidate down the main highway of Long Island. Loudspeakers boomed the campaign theme song ("Vote for Kennedy, vote for victory . . . ") while the crowds lining the streets waved multicolored banners and life-size pictures of the candidate. Three years later, the Kennedy funeral rites provided me, along with so many others, with a dramatic ritual close to the brief Kennedy era. The rites brought Americans together to a degree not seen since.

From college, during the civil rights and Vietnam war protests, of all the political activities to which my fellow students and I devoted so much time, the most salient memories come from the mass demonstrations— marching through the streets of New York, marching from the Capitol to the Pentagon and symbolically blocking the entrances, and sitting in during a recruitment visit by the Central Intelligence Agency on campus. In Italy in the 1970s I encountered a different, yet familiar, series of political rites, from the neighborhood festivals organized by the Communist party, in effect doing ritual battle with the Roman Catholic Church, to the rites surrounding the kidnapping and bodyless burial of Aldo Moro, president of the Christian Democratic party.

The origins of this book spring from all these sources. I was struck by the ubiquity of political rites and perplexed that scholars had attributed so little significance to them. For an anthropologist like myself, nothing could be more normal than tracing the relationships between ritual and politics. Yet, to date, anthropological studies have too often been dismissed as bearing only on the political organization of "primitives" living in small-scale societies. Historians, especially in the past couple of decades, have provided many valuable descriptions of political rites, but these too are commonly dismissed by readers as the quaint customs of a bygone era. Some political scientists have questioned the assumptions of the classic "political man" model of the rational bases of modern political action, but studies of political rites remain underdeveloped and largely ignored by the mainstream of the discipline.

In searching out the universal principles behind the political uses of ritual, I take a broad view of humanity, which ranges from mountain tribesmen in New Guinea to construction workers in Ohio, from the rites of chiefs in precolonial Chad to the rites of modern presidents and prime ministers. I go back to the ancient Chinese dynasties and to the Roman Empire, to European kings of past centuries and to the sacred rulers of the Sandwich Islands. Although this historical and anthropological eclecticism may raise the hackles of some areal and period specialists, it is only by taking such an expansive view that I can make my point. Only by looking at peoples around the world and back in time can we make out the common threads that unite us.

This book has benefited, though I have occasionally suffered, from its long gestation. It was begun in 1982–83, a year I spent at the Center for Advanced Studies in the Behavioral Sciences at Stanford, supported by the Center and by grants from the John D. and Catherine T. MacArthur

Foundation and the Bowdoin College Faculty Research Fund. The Center offered an ideal ambience for this work. Constant contact with colleagues from a variety of disciplines and excellent library facilities were a tremendous help. I would like in particular to thank James Fernandez, Elizabeth Eisenstein, Thomas Trobasso, Sherry Ortner, Samuel Barnes, and Ray Kelly for their help as sounding boards and valuable sources of bibliographical suggestions. I would also like to thank Margaret Amara, the Center librarian, for all her help.

Following three years of sporadic labors, aided by the library assistance of Kate Dempsey and the Bowdoin College library staff, a grant from the John Simon Guggenheim Memorial Foundation, together with supplementary funding from Bowdoin College, gave me the freedom to spend 1986–87 completing the manuscript. I chose to spend the year in Bologna, Italy, to allow me to learn more about European politics and through geographical distance to gain some valuable perspective on American political life. Arturo Parisi, Marzio Barbagli, Massimo Marcolin, and Egeria di Nallo helped make this an enjoyable and productive year by aiding with my local arrangements. Arturo Parisi and Pier Cesare Bori also provided kind assistance with scholarly sources.

Comments on a draft of this manuscript by Emily Boochever, Daniel Wathen, Myron Aronoff, James Fernandez, Arturo Parisi, Bernardo Bernardi, and Mary Hegland helped me strengthen the final version. Julie Hodgkins and Jean Lee provided excellent secretarial support, transatlantically and transcontinentally. I would like to thank Alfred Fuchs, Dean of the Faculty at Bowdoin College, who has done much to support my research activities over the past years. I would also like to thank Ellen Graham, senior editor at Yale University Press, for all her help and encouragement.

Finally, thanks are due Susan, Molly, and Seth, who were uprooted from Maine first to spend a year in California and then another year in Italy so that I could write this book. Indeed, I could only complete this manuscript by dispossessing Seth of his bedroom in Bologna every day for many months so that I could have a quiet place to work. If I too often snapped at Molly when she interrupted me to ask questions about Dante or Verga for her Bologna public school homework, or at Seth for his interruptions to ask who was the shortest player to dunk a basketball, I take this occasion to apologize. I dedicate this book to Susan, with apologies for the fact that copies of this book are not nestled next to the *National Enquirer* at the checkout shelf of Shop-&-Save.

RITUAL, POLITICS, AND POWER

On September 15, 1810, the Creole priest Miguel Hidalgo summoned his parishioners to the village church and called on them to rise up against the oppressive government of the Spanish colony of Mexico, thus catalyzing a bloody revolt. Over a century and a half later, on each September 15 at exactly 11:00 P.M.—the hour when Hidalgo issued his call to rebellion—the president of Mexico steps onto the balcony of the National Palace in Mexico City, bearing the nation's tricolored flag. Above a central plaza packed with celebrating citizens, he bellows the ceremonial shout: "Viva La Independencia! Viva Hidalgo! Viva Morelos! Viva Juarez! Viva Mexico!" A thunderous "Viva!" from the euphoric crowd greets each phrase as his amplified voice resounds through the plaza. Stepping aside, the president rings the palace bells, which are soon joined by those of the National Cathedral. Fireworks light the heavens; the final glowing colors in the sky form the face of Father Hidalgo as he shouted his original "Viva!" in that obscure church so many years ago.[1]

From national party convention to presidential inauguration, from congressional committee hearing to the roar of the football stadium crowd belting out the national anthem, ritual is a ubiquitous part of modern political life. Through ritual aspiring political leaders struggle to assert their right to rule, incumbent power holders seek to bolster their authority, and revolutionaries try to carve out a new basis of political allegiance. All of these political figures, from leaders of insurrections to champions of the status quo, use rites to create political reality for the people around them. Through participation in the rites, the citizen of the modern state identifies with larger political forces that can only be seen in symbolic form. And through political ritual, we are given a way to understand what is going on in the world, for we live in a world that must be drastically simplified if it is to be understood at all.

Yet few people recognize how important ritual is in modern politics. Because ritual is usually identified with religion and, since modern Western societies have presumably separated political affairs from religious life, there is an assumption that ritual remains politically significant only in less "advanced" societies.[2]

But is industrial society really any different in its sacralization of power? Are politics now the product of rational activities by bureaucrats, are political allegiances decided by cost-benefit analysis, and are leaders regarded by the public as essentially no different from themselves? In Polynesia, temporal rulers were viewed as descendants of the gods and, as such, they radiated *mana*, or supernatural power. Being so powerful, they were surrounded by a web of rituals that governed all interaction with their subjects.[3] Although no such supernatural rationalization of secular power prevails today in the United States or in other industrial states, the politically powerful nonetheless are still surrounded by rites that govern their interaction with the public and with each other when they are in the public eye. Political ritual, as Shils quips, has been given a "bad name" by Western intellectuals raised in utilitarian traditions.[4] Blinded by their rational model of the political universe, these intellectuals ignore the ritual that envelops political action and political power.[5]

In these pages I try to show why ritual is important in *all* political systems and to point out the many ways ritual is employed in politics. In doing this I argue against the common view that political ritual merely serves to bolster the status quo. Ritual is much more important to politics than this. True, kings use ritual to shore up their authority, but revolutionaries use ritual to overthrow monarchs. The political elite employ ritual to legitimate their authority, but rebels battle back with rites of delegitimation. Ritual may be vital to reaction, but it is also the life blood of revolution.

Politics, Symbolism, and Ritual

Politics is expressed through symbolism. Rather little that is political involves the use of direct force, and, though material resources are crucial to the political process, even their distribution and use are largely shaped through symbolic means. To understand the political process, then, it is necessary to understand how the symbolic enters into politics, how political actors consciously and unconsciously manipulate symbols, and how this symbolic dimension relates to the material bases of political power.[6]

Symbolism is involved in politics in many ways. In these pages I focus on just one, ritual. Anthropologists have long been associated in the public view with the search for quaint rites and seemingly illogical behavior. My goal, however, is not to exhume the exotic but to challenge some comfortable assumptions about the bases of our own political systems. Although many political observers in the United States and other industrial nations have noted the ritual behavior associated with politics, few have ever taken it seriously. They view ritual as mere embellishment for more important, "real" political activities. But, in fact, ritual is an integral part of politics in modern industrial societies; it is hard to imagine how any political system could do without it.

The ubiquity of political ritual is reflected in the range of political systems that appears in these pages. I draw on cases from small-scale nonliterate societies of Africa, Asia, Oceania, and the Americas, but given my central theme, I pay special attention to the use of ritual in the politics of state societies in Europe and North America. Besides trying to provide a global perspective by drawing on societies from all over the world, I also dig into the historical literature to examine political uses of ritual in societies of past times. From all this, a common pattern emerges, a legacy from which modern bureaucratic nations are not exempt.

The Power of Symbols

Since my argument rests on the importance of symbolism in politics, it makes sense to begin with some general observations about the role of symbolism in human societies and in people's lives. Thurman Arnold, a witty legal scholar of a half-century ago, observed that all human conduct and all institutional behavior are symbolic. Arnold attempted to puncture the common conceit that people in modern societies behave in pragmatic, goal-oriented ways. On the contrary, he declaimed, "Society is generally more interested in standing on the side lines and watching itself go by in a whole series of different uniforms than it is in practical objectives." Scholars, chided Arnold, cannot bear the idea that people are more influenced by symbolic forms than by utilitarian calculations. As a consequence, the "chief interest of the intellectual is to prove that such irrational conduct is inherently rational—or else the product of some form of group sinning."[7]

But let me back up a bit here and begin by considering the individual's relation to his or her culture. Human reality is not provided at birth by the physical universe, but rather must be fashioned by individuals out of the culture into which they are born and the experiences they have, experiences that bring them into contact with other people and with various parts of nature. The world out there confronts each individual with an infinite number of stimuli, yet no one can deal with all of them. We must be selective in our perceptions, and those aspects of the world that are selected must be further reduced and reordered in terms of some system of simplification (or categorization) that allows us to make sense of them. This order is largely provided by the symbol system we learn as members of our culture, a system that allows for both social creativity and individual idiosyncrasy.

Such symbol systems provide a "shield against terror."[8] They are a means, indeed the primary means, by which we give meaning to the world around us; they allow us to interpret what we see, and, indeed, what we are. Perhaps the most striking aspect of this symbolic process is its taken-for-granted quality.[9] People are not generally aware that they themselves endow the world with their own symbolically constructed version of reality. On the contrary, people believe the world simply presents itself in the form in which it is perceived. This may be naive, but it is nevertheless necessary. We could not get out of bed in the morning if we did not subscribe to this view, for if we fully recognized the extent to which our notions of reality are the product of an artificially constructed symbol system, it would be, as Kenneth Burke pointed out, "like peering over the edge of things into an ultimate abyss."[10]

Through symbols we confront the experiential chaos that envelops us and create order. By objectifying our symbolic categories, rather than recognizing them as products of human creation, we see them as somehow the products of nature, "things" that we simply perceive and recognize. Indeed, the very distinction we make between the objective world and the subjective world is itself a product of humanly created symbols that divide the world of fact from the world of opinion.[11]

That people perceive the world through symbolic lenses does not mean that people or cultures are free to create any symbolic system imaginable, or that all such constructs are equally tenable in the material world. There is a continuous interaction between the ways people have of dealing with the physical and social universe and the actual contours of that universe. When symbolic systems collide with refractory social or physical forces, the potential for change in the symbolic system is ever present. Moreover, symbols do not simply arise spontaneously, nor is the continuing process of redefinition of the symbolic universe a matter of chance. Both are heavily influenced by the distribution of resources found in the society and the relationships that exist with other societies. Though symbols give people a way of understanding the worlds, it is people who produce new symbols and transform the old.

Symbolism in Politics

In a playful passage, Thomas Carlyle asks us to envision a pompous ceremonial gathering in Britain, replete with dukes, colonels, generals, and others of lofty status. Imagine, he says, that with a wave of the wand their clothes were all to vanish and they were left entirely naked. What would happen to the dignity of the occasion? Pursuing the point, Carlyle asks, "Lives there a man that can figure a naked Duke of Windlestraw addressing a naked House of Lords? Imagination, choked as in mephitic air, recoils on itself, and will not forward with the picture." Carlyle's clothes are one example of how all objects function in human society, for they all act as symbols, endowed with special meaning. To say that a person is clothed with authority is something more than metaphorical.[12]

Through symbolism we recognize who are the powerful and who are the weak, and through the manipulation of symbols the powerful reinforce their authority. Yet, the weak, too, can try to put on new clothes and to strip the clothes from the mighty. In Kessler's words, "The symbolic is not a residual dimension of purportedly real politics; still less is it an insubstantial screen upon which real issues are cast in pale and passive form. The symbolic is real politics, articulated in a special and often most powerful way."[13] Political reality is in good part created through symbolic means, as many a candidate for political office has recognized. Creating a symbol or, more commonly, identifying oneself with a popular symbol can be a potent means of gaining and keeping power, for the hallmark of power is the construction of reality.[14]

Some political observers have gone so far as to say that people live in a "dream world," a world of "illusion." They contrast the "real" world with this phantom realm of the symbol. In a stirring passage written in the shadow of Hitler's preparations for war, Max Lerner, horrified by the adulatory allegiance evoked by the Fuehrer, warned that while the power of dictators derives from the "symbols that they manipulate, the symbols depend in turn upon the entire range of associations that they invoke." He concluded: "The power of these symbols is enormous. Men possess thoughts, but symbols possess men."[15] Yet, just as Hitler's skillful manipulation of symbols was inspiring the German people to war, so a different set of symbols was being powerfully framed by Churchill, Roosevelt, and others to mobilize the opposition.[16]

Modern wars depend on a sense of national allegiance, but the nation itself has no palpable existence outside the symbolism through which it is envisioned. As Walzer puts it, "The state is invisible; it must be personified before it can be seen, symbolized before it can be loved, imagined before it can be conceived."[17] People subscribe to the "master fiction" that the world is divided into a fixed number of mutually exclusive nations; they see these units as part of the nature of things, and assume an antiquity that the nations in fact lack. This symbolic conception of the universe leads people to believe that everyone "has" a nationality, in the same sense that everyone has a gender. It is in this light that Benedict Anderson defined a nation as "an imagined political community." Far from being window dressing on the reality that is the nation, symbolism is the stuff of which nations are made.[18]

Symbols instigate social action and define the individual's sense of self. They also furnish the means by which people make sense of the political process, which largely presents itself to people in symbolic form. When Americans form their opinions regarding the activities of the president or the Congress, they do so mainly on the basis of the manipulation of symbols by these officeholders, in conjunction with their own material experiences, which are themselves perceived in good part through a symbolic filter. For this reason one observer of the American presidency concluded that "Politics is primarily the art of understanding the symbols actually operative in society and learning how to make them issue forth in action. . . . It is the art of governing not rationalists, but people." In electing a president, we elect "the chief symbol-maker of the land. . . ."[19]

The strength of people's allegiance to political symbols was certainly evident in Ohio during the days of inflamed patriotic zeal accompanying the captivity of the American embassy personnel in Iran. When the workers at a construction site were ordered by their boss to remove the American flag decals they sported on their hard hats, they staunchly refused. As one worker explained, "The hat says who you are . . ."—and, of course, so did the miniaturized stars and stripes.[20]

As this example of national allegiance shows, modern politics depends on people's tendency to reify political institutions. Entities such as "government," "party," or the "state" are not viewed as symbolic constructions. Rather, they are thought of as objects that exist independently of people and their symbolic universe. Children find it easier to conceive of authority in terms of a person like the president (or a teacher) rather than a collectivity such as Congress. Similarly, adults use the metaphor of a "body" to conceive of Congress, which allows them to treat a variegated group of people as a single entity.

Perhaps this can be made clearer by recounting the story of the Indian who came to see the "government" in Ottawa. The Indian grew increasingly frustrated as he was led from one office to the next, meeting one man after another who claimed responsibility for government affairs, yet never confronting the "government" itself, who, he thought, did a good job of keeping himself hidden.[21]

Many of the most potent political symbols have a palpable quality to them, making it easier for people to treat concepts as things. This is evident in the metaphors that help define the political universe. For numerous Americans, an "iron curtain" lies across Europe, separating those on the other side from the "free world." Similarly, a flag is not simply a decorated cloth, but the embodiment of a nation; indeed, the nation is defined as much by the flag as the flag is defined by the nation.

Studies of politics in modern states, with a few important exceptions, pay little attention to the role of the symbolic in the political process.[22] In many studies, politics is examined as a give-and-take in which people simply follow their material interests. These material interests are often taken to be self-evident. In other studies, people are viewed as consumers in a public relations market, or as empty slates socialized to reproduce the political views of their parents, peers, or neighbors.

The lack of systematic studies of the symbolic dimension of politics in contemporary Western societies is no doubt also due to the difficulty all people face in examining their own symbol systems. Since people perceive the world through symbolic lenses, it is difficult for them to be conscious of just what those symbols consist of and what influence they have.[23]

The underdevelopment of studies on the symbolic dimension of modern politics is also due to the kinds of empirical methods emphasized in modern social science. Symbols cannot be satisfactorily studied in quantitative terms, nor through surveys or electoral analyses. In emphasizing such methods, analysts have a tendency to assume that those aspects of politics that cannot be easily quantified must be unimportant. To complete the vicious circle, the resulting empirical studies then reinforce the view that modern politics is determined by rational action.[24] Clifford Geertz points out some of the flaws in such approaches:

The main defects of the interest theory are that its psychology is too anemic and its sociology too muscular. Lacking a developed analysis of motivation, it has been constantly forced to oscillate between a narrow and superficial utilitarianism that sees men as impelled by rational calculation of their consciously recognized personal advantage and a broader, but no less superficial, historicism that speaks with a studied vagueness of men's ideas as somehow "reflecting," "expressing," "corresponding to," "emerging from," or "conditioned by" their social commitments.[25]

In short, people are not merely material creatures, but also symbol producers and symbol users. People have the unsettling habit of willingly, even gladly, dying for causes that oppose their material interests, while vociferously opposing groups that espouse them. It is through symbols that people give meaning to their lives; full understanding of political allegiances and political action hinges on this fact.[26]

To argue that symbolism and ritual play important roles in the political process in Western societies flies in the face of much received wisdom. Yet, far from arguing that politics becomes less encrusted in symbol and myth as a society grows more complex, I suggest that a case could be made that just the reverse is true. Living in a society that extends well beyond our direct observation, we can relate to the larger political entity only through abstract symbolic means. We are, indeed, ruled by power holders whom we never encounter except in highly symbolic presentations. And what political environment could be more dependent on symbolism than one in which our decision whether to pat a person on the back or to shoot him in the back depends on the color of the uniform he wears? With the increase in the size of the state and the growth of bureaucracy, Michael Walzer observes, politics is transformed "from a concrete activity into what Marx once called the fantasy of everyday life."[27]

Defining Ritual

Before examining the role of ritual in politics, I should clarify what "ritual" means. Here, I take a middle path between an overly restrictive definition, which would limit ritual to the religious sphere and identify it with the supernatural, and an overly broad definition, labeling as ritual any standardized human activity. In defining ritual, I am not, of course, trying to discover what ritual "really" is, for it is not an entity to be discovered. Rather, ritual is an analytical category that helps us deal with the chaos of human experience and put it into a coherent framework. There is thus no right or wrong definition of ritual, but only one that is more or less useful in helping us understand the world in which we live. My own use of the term reflects my goal of shedding light on how symbolic processes enter into politics and why these are important.

Until a generation ago, anthropologists typically defined ritual as culturally standardized, repetitive activity, primarily symbolic in character, aimed at influencing human affairs (or at least allowing humans to understand better their place in the universe), and involving the super-natural realm.[28] Durkheim offered the most influential early social scientific view of ritual, relating it to religious practices, which, he believed, divide the world into two classes: the sacred and the profane. Rites, he asserted, are the "rules of conduct which prescribe how a man should comport himself in the presence of these sacred objects."[29]

Although on the surface Durkheim's view seems to link ritual behavior to the supernatural realm, a closer look leads to a different conclusion. For Durkheim, worship of a god is the symbolic means by which people worship their own society, their own mutual dependency. Thus, the sacred ultimately refers not to a supernatural entity, but rather to people's emotionally charged interdependence, their societal arrangements. What is important about rituals, then, is not that they deal with supernatural beings, but rather that they provide a powerful way in which people's social dependence can be expressed.

I follow this perspective in defining ritual as symbolic behavior that is socially standardized and repetitive.[30] This is, in fact, the way in which many anthropologists now use the concept.[31] In doing so, some have been at pains to distinguish between religious and secular ritual.[32] I think, however, that such a distinction is more a hindrance than a help in understanding the importance of ritual in political life. I thus use the term *ritual* in the more general sense.[33]

Characteristics of Ritual

Ritual action has a formal quality to it. It follows highly structured, standardized sequences and is often enacted at certain places and times that are themselves endowed with special symbolic meaning.[34] Ritual action is repetitive and, therefore, often redundant, but these very factors serve as important means of channeling emotion, guiding cognition, and organizing social groups.[35]

I have defined ritual as action wrapped in a web of symbolism. Standardized, repetitive action lacking such symbolization is an example of habit or custom and not ritual.[36] Symbolization gives the action much more important meaning. Through ritual, beliefs about the universe come to be acquired, reinforced, and eventually changed. As Cassirer puts it: "Nature yields nothing without ceremonies." Ritual action not only gives meaning to the universe, it becomes part of the universe.[37] As one observer noted, "Through ritualized action, the inner becomes outer, and the subjective world picture becomes a social reality."[38]

Ritual helps give meaning to our world in part by linking the past to the present and the present to the future. This helps us cope with two human problems: building confidence in our sense of self by providing us with a sense of continuity—I am the same person today as I was twenty years ago and as I will be ten years from now—and giving us confidence that the world in which we live today is the same world we lived in before and the same world we will have to cope with in the future. "By stating enduring and underlying patterns," Myerhoff writes, "ritual connects past, present, and future, abrogating history and time."[39]

One of the perennial problems people face is coping with the frustrating indeterminacy of the world. People respond by doing what they can to fix a single, known reality so that they can know what behavior is appropriate and so that they can understand their place in the world.[40] The very fixity and timelessness of ritual are reassuring parts of this attempt to tame time and define reality.

But even though there are certain psychological and even physiological bases of ritual, understanding its political importance depends on recognizing the ways ritual serves to link the individual to society.[41] Through ritual the individual's subjective experience interacts with and is molded by social forces.[42] Most often, people participate in ritual forms that they had nothing to do with creating. Even where individuals invent new rituals, they create them largely out of a stockpile of preexisting symbols, and the rituals become established not because of the psychic processes of the inventor but because of the social circumstances of the people who participate in the new rite.[43]

The power of ritual, then, stems not just from its social matrix, but also from its psychological underpinnings. Indeed, these two dimensions are inextricably linked. Participation in ritual involves physiological stimuli, the arousal of emotions; ritual works through the senses to structure our sense of reality and our understanding of the world around us.[44]

These psychological attributes are evident in another characteristic of ritual: its frequently dramatic character. Indeed, Arnold argued that people relate to the world through a series of dramatic productions:

Every individual, for reasons lying deep in the mystery of personality, constructs for himself a succession of little dramas in which he is the principal character. No one escapes the constant necessity of dressing himself in a series of different uniforms or silk hats, and watching himself go by.[45]

Perhaps it is in this light that the proposal made by a local socialist newspaper at the end of the nineteenth century should be seen. It called for construction of a little platform along the line of march at Vienna's May Day demonstration so that marchers could step up momentarily to see the huge crowd of demonstrators of which they were a part.[46]

Ritual provides one of the means by which people participate in such dramas and thus see themselves as playing certain roles. The dramatic quality of ritual does more than define roles, however, it also provokes an emotional response. Just as emotions are manipulated in the theater through the "varied stimuli of light, colour, gesture, movement, voice," so too these elements and others give rituals a means of generating powerful feelings.[47]

Ritual dramas are widely found in politics.[48] In the United States, as elsewhere, election campaigns involve the staging of such dramas by candidates as well as the attempts to get the mass media to broadcast these dramatic productions into people's homes. Indeed, candidates often try to limit all contact with the public and the mass media that does not take place through carefully arranged dramatic productions, heavily laden with well-choreographed symbols.[49]

Symbols provide the content of ritual; hence, the nature of these symbols and the ways they are used tell us much about the nature and influence of ritual. Three properties of symbols are especially important; condensation of meaning, multivocality, and ambiguity.

Condensation refers to the way in which individual symbols represent and unify a rich diversity of meanings. The symbol, whether verbal or iconic—that is, manifest in a physical form such as a bible or a flag— somehow embodies and brings together diverse ideas. At a subconscious, and hence more powerful, level, these various ideas are not just simultaneously elicited but also interact with one another so that they become associated together in the individual's mind.[50]

Closely tied to the condensation of meaning in ritual symbols is their *multivocality*, the variety of different meanings attached to the same symbol. Where condensation refers to the interaction of these different meanings and their synthesis into a new meaning for an individual, multivocality suggests another aspect, the fact that the same symbol may be understood by different people in different ways. This trait is especially important in the use of ritual to build political solidarity in the absence of consensus.[51]

Given the properties of condensation and multivocality, it should hardly be surprising that ritual symbolism is often *ambiguous:* the symbol has no single precise meaning. Put in more positive terms, this means that symbols are not arcane ways of saying something that could be more precisely expressed in simple declarative form. The complexity and uncertainty of meaning of symbols are sources of their strength.[52]

I have emphasized the fact that rituals have a standardized form and are presented to individuals by society rather than generated from individual psychological activity. But this does not mean that ritual is an inherently conservative force. Rituals do change in form, in symbolic meaning, and in social effects; new rituals arise and old rituals fade away. These changes come through individual creative activity. People, in short, are not just slaves of ritual, or slaves of symbols, they are also molders and creators of ritual. It is because people create and alter rituals that they are such powerful tools of political action.[53]

Yet even though ritual does have this creative potential, it also has a conservative bias. Ritual forms do tend to be slower to change than many other aspects of culture, as any student of Western religions knows. Indeed, their ability to give people a sense of continuity derives in good part from their constancy of form over time. The impact of a particular enactment of a ritual is a product of its past performances. Memories associated with those earlier ritual experiences color the experience of a new enactment of the rites.[54] Rites thus have both a conservative bias and innovatory potential. Paradoxically, it is the very conservatism of ritual forms that can make ritual a potent force in political change.

The Political Importance of Ritual

According to mainstream Western ideology, ritual occupies at best a peripheral, if not irrelevant, role in political life. Serious political analysts, we are led to believe, would hardly waste their time by distracting attention from the real nitty-gritty of politics—interest groups, economic forces, and power relations—in order to turn a critical eye to ritual.[55]

But this image of "political man" as a rational actor who carefully weighs his or her objective circumstances and decides on a course of action based on an instrumental calculation of self-interest leaves out culture and all that makes us human. Though we are rooted in the physical world and much affected by material forces, we perceive and evaluate them through our symbolic apparatus. We communicate through symbols, and one of the more important ways in which such symbolic understandings are communicated is through ritual. Mary Douglas puts this starkly: "Social rituals create a reality which would be nothing without them. For it is very possible to know something and then find words for it. But it is impossible to have social relations without symbolic acts."[56]

Each society has its own mythology detailing its origins and sanctifying its norms. Some of these revolve around great men (in Western society female cultural heroes are less common), while others revolve around notable events that, whether having a historical basis or not, are defined through a web of symbolically constructed meaning. In the United States, children grow up learning about the Puritans, the Indians, the slaves, life on the plantation, the melting pot, George Washington, Abraham Lincoln, Daniel Boone, John Kennedy, and Martin Luther King. Indeed, their conceptions of society are in good part based on understandings passed on through such symbols. They learn both what are the valued norms of conduct and what are the criteria of success. More to the point here, these symbols provide a way to understand such abstract political entities as the nation and a means (indeed the compulsion) of identifying with them. Lance Bennet, a political scientist, observes:

Myths condition the public to the powerful symbols used by politicians. Myths underwrite the status quo in times of stability and they chart the course of change in times of stress. In the day-to-day business of politics myths set the terms for most public policy debate. When mythical themes and myth-related language are stripped away from policy discourse, very little of substance remains. Most political controversy centers around disagreement over which myth to apply to a particular problem.[57]

Ritual practices are a major means for propagating these political myths. The symbols at the heart of ritual observances are part of the tissue of myth that helps structure an understanding of the political world and the public's attitude to the various political actors that populate it.

Once constructed, such symbolic understandings of the political order are resistant (though not immune) to change. Here again, there is a conflict between the view of humans as rational actors and a view that stresses a more complex interaction of the symbolic with the material. In the former view, changing a person's political opinion is a matter of logical argumentation and the marshaling of facts. But the resistance of beliefs to change through such rational debate has long been recognized. In China many centuries ago, Chuang Tzu wrote: "Suppose I am arguing with you and you get the better of me. Does the fact that I am not a match for you mean that you are really right and I am really wrong? Or if I get the better of you, does the fact that you are not a match for me mean that I am really right and you are really wrong?"[58]

The Confucian philosophers understood the importance of ritual for efficient government. People's behavior, they realized, is not a simple product of consciously weighing options, but rather takes shape through the rituals in which they take part. Rulers should always avoid giving commands, opined one of these philosophers, for commands, being direct and verbal, always bring to the subject's mind the possibility of doing the opposite. He continued:

But since rituals are non-verbal, they have no contraries. They can therefore be used to produce harmony of wills and actions without provoking recalcitrance; if a man finds himself playing his appointed part in *li* [ritual] and thus already—as it were *de facto*—in harmony with others, it no more occurs to him than it occurs to a dancer to move to a different rhythm than that being played by the orchestra.[59]

Not only does ritual have this cognitive effect on people's definition of political reality, it also has an important emotional impact. People derive a great deal of satisfaction from their participation in ritual. Rulers have for millennia (indeed, for as long as there have been rulers) attempted to design and employ rituals to arouse popular emotions in support of their legitimacy and to drum up popular enthusiasm for their policies. But, by the same token, rituals are also important for revolutionary groups who must elicit powerful emotions to mobilize the people for revolt. Trotsky recognized the need for such ritual forms in the early years of the Soviet state. He was especially disturbed by the church monopoly on everyday rites, arguing that "rationalistic" appeals to the masses were not sufficient. We must recognize, Trotsky insisted, "man's desire for the theatrical," his "strong and legitimate need for an outer manifestation of emotions."[60]

To explain the political importance of ritual I consider in the next four chapters how political ritual works: how ritual helps build political organizations; how ritual is employed to create political legitimacy; how ritual helps create political solidarity in the absence of political consensus; and, how ritual molds people's understandings of the political universe. I then examine how political competitors struggle for power through ritual, how ritual is employed in both defusing and inciting political conflict, and how ritual serves revolution and revolutionary regimes. Finally, I ask what all this has to do with the nature of political life. How important is ritual in politics today?

2

Flaming Crosses and Body Snatchers

With a half moon lighting their path, two thousand Georgians puffed their way to the treeless plateau on top of Stone Mountain. They had come in hopes of witnessing a dramatic ceremony, and they would not be disappointed. Up the side of the mountain came the Grand Dragon, in his rich green robe, leading seven hundred white-hooded figures, their sheets reaching the ground. Beyond them marched hundreds of other men, their uncovered heads and dark suits in stark contrast to the white masks and white robes that preceded them. The initiates marched in lock step, single file, each man's arms on the shoulders of the man in front, in a style recalling the old Georgia chain gangs. In the eerie light of the towering flaming cross—three hundred feet tall and two hundred wide—the initiates kneeled and bowed their heads before two white knights, one bearing a cross, the other an American flag. They repeated the oath by which Klansmen were made: "I most solemnly swear that I will forever keep sacredly secret the signs, words and grip and any and all other matters and knowledge of the klan. . . . I will die rather than divulge same, so help me God." It was May 9, 1946. The ceremonies had been postponed many times, leaders explained, because of the wartime shortage of sheets.[1]

No organization—whether Ku Klux Klan or General Motors—can exist without symbolic representation, for organizations can be "seen" only through their associated symbols.[2] Indeed, people tend to think of organizations as physical units, part of the material world. Ritual is one of the important means by which these views of organizations are constructed and through which people are linked to them. Just how ritual accomplishes these tasks, especially how it contributes to the organizational life of politics, is the subject of this chapter.

Belonging to a Political Organization

Since organizations themselves can only be represented symbolically, it follows that a person's allegiance to an organization can be expressed only through symbolism. I wear certain clothing, I say an oath, I sing a song, I cut my hair in a certain way, I address people with certain terms, and by doing so I consider myself and am considered by others to belong to a particular organization, whether it be the Boy Scouts, the Nazis, or the Kiwanis Club. Through such symbolism, in which ritual plays a major role, the relationships between individuals and organizations are objectified.[3]

People make themselves, that is, they establish their own self-image, in part through their symbolic identification with these groupings. This is what Burke meant in writing that "The so-called 'I' is merely a unique combination of partially conflicting 'corporate we's.'"[4] By identifying with a larger group, the individual can assert his importance in a more effective and socially acceptable fashion than if he were to boast of his own virtues more directly. By praising such an organization, he is praising himself.[5]

Organizations, in turn, do what they can to take advantage of this fact. In 1973, for example, the Soviet Communist Party, in an attempt to reinvigorate its membership, issued new membership cards. To inflate the significance of these slips of paper, they conducted a solemn ceremony in which card #1 was issued to Lenin and card #2 to Brezhnev. Lenin, unlike Babe Ruth, did not live long enough to see his jersey retired.[6]

If a person's identification with an organization can only be assured through symbolism, it follows that successful organizations depend on symbolic behavior. It is through such symbolism that people formulate their ideas about an organization. Some scholars have marveled at the fact that small children often make no distinction between the abstract organization and its symbolic representation. Thus, the flag does not simply stand for the country, but flag and country are thought of as the same thing.[7] Yet, how different is it when they grow up and proclaim their willingness to die for the flag?[8]

Such symbolic representations consist not only of inanimate objects such as flags, but also of individuals who symbolize the political unit. Recent attempts to establish new nations out of former colonial territories often involve just such creation of heroic political leaders, whose portraits adorn every wall, every coin, and every stamp. The famous (though probably apocryphal) pronouncement by Louis XIV, *L'état, c'est moi*, should be seen in this light. For the French masses, the state was too abstract an entity to inspire the kind of identification and allegiance sought by the rulers. By personifying France, by identifying it with a single figure, people were able to conjure up the notion of the French state and treat it as part of their universe.[9]

Not only does the individual come to feel a part of the political organization by adopting the symbols associated with it, but, just as importantly, he also comes to be recognized as a fellow member by others in the organization. Through symbols the individual is integrated into the organization and treated as a privileged member. This is seen most dramatically in rituals of membership induction, where incorporation into the group is often invested with powerful emotions. Why should the Ku Klux Klan bother with such elaborate rites as those I just described? A major goal, certainly, is to get the recruit to redefine his identity, to see himself as a Klansman with new loyalties and new priorities. A corollary organizational advantage of the rite is that it signals to other members that the recruit is now to be considered part of the group and treated accordingly.

This emphasis on rites of induction in heterodox political organizations is nothing new. In France in the 1850s, democrats organized into Montagnard societies to prepare for republican uprising. To become a member, the recruit was blindfolded and an officiant held a cold metal weapon against his head. The recruit then recited an oath: "I swear to arm myself against tyranny, to defend the Democratic and Social Republic; I swear to kill a traitor if fate chooses me; I swear to die the most infamous death if I become a traitor or turncoat; I swear to help a brother in need." Finally, the officiant pronounced, "I baptize you Montagnard." The symbolism of rebirth could scarcely be more clear.[10]

Even in organizations where membership is compulsory, such as the military, great emphasis may be placed on rituals of induction. In these situations, the major goal is to change the individual's definition of himself from his previous allegiances and roles to his new ones. The greater the transition, in general, the more elaborate the rites.[11]

Organizational Distinctiveness

In order to have members, or even adherents, an organization must have some way of representing itself, and it carves out a distinct identity through both mythic and ritual means. Organizations propagate myths regarding their origin and purpose, while members engage in symbolic practices that serve to mark them off from nonmembers. These myths often assert the group's superiority. Associated with these beliefs are rituals of purity and pollution, a system of taboos and other ritual observances that separate the members from the rest of the world.[12] One effect of this organizational ritual is to make the group appear to other people as a solidarity unit. It is, according to Arnold, a "unifying force . . . as mysterious as the law of gravitation."[13]

In its heyday in the 1920s, the Ku Klux Klan had millions of members. What defined the members was their participation in the rites and symbols of the organization. In Colorado in 1925, the KKK not only boasted a large male membership, but it also had thousands of women in its klaverns. In August of that year, ten thousand of these women, clad in white sheets, paraded through the streets of a Denver suburb, marching with military precision. But shortly thereafter, dissatisfied with the direction of the KKK, Minnie Love, the local commander, persuaded the majority of female members to drop the white sheets and wear Betsy Ross outfits instead. The organizational reaction was swift: the Imperial Commander suspended Love and revoked the charter of the Denver Klan.[14]

An organization maintains its identity and its continuity through its symbolic representations. Since over time the people making up an organization, including its leaders, change, it is only through symbols that we think of the organization as being the same. Thus, it is crucial to organizations that they have a clear symbolic identity. Where a political leader has become an important symbol of organizational unity, the leader's death can threaten this unity. One solution is to keep the symbolism connected with the leader alive even after his demise. The temples containing the bodies of Lenin in Moscow and Mao in Beijing are among the more impressive examples of this political immortality, but similar examples can be found throughout history.[15]

The symbols of organizational identity are important in all kinds of societies. Indeed, in nonliterate societies, where no written organizational charters exist, rituals are especially important. Among the Tallensi of West Africa, for example, the political system was organized around a system of clans and lineages. These clans and lineages were themselves defined in terms of common ritual practices: members of a lineage worshipped at a common ancestral shrine, separate from the members of all other lineages. Relationships among clans and lineages were made concrete through regular ritual celebrations in which each group had a specified place. Indeed, as with so many peoples, the very notion of being a Tallensi, one of "us," was defined by participation in common ritual.[16]

Similarly, among the Bemba of what was once northeastern Rhodesia, it was ritual connected with the paramount chief that brought the people together and maintained them as a single society with a unifying political organization.[17]

In New Guinea, where societies sometimes consist of but a few hundred people, there are graphic examples of this establishment of political identity through ritual. In the Strickland-Bosavi area, dotted by tiny indigenous polities, each distinguishes itself from the others on the basis of the male initiation rites it performs. From an outsider's perspective what is most striking is one similarity in these rites among the groups: they all believe that boys cannot become adults unless they are inseminated. What differs is the method of insemination found in the different societies: anal intercourse among the Kaluli, fellatio among the Etoro, and the smearing of semen on the initiates among the Onbabasulu. Each of the groups finds the customs of the other disgusting and, indeed, these sentiments not only reinforce notions of group allegiance, but can be whipped up to provoke hostilities among the groups.[18]

In modern states, written constitutions and other such documents are used as symbols of organizational distinctiveness, and mass media broadcast verbal symbols of organizational identity to all parts of the population. In nonliterate societies, the whole notion of a separate, distinguishable sphere of political life of specifically political organizations is generally absent. Politics occurs through societal mechanisms that are not themselves seen as political in nature. Primary among these are kinship systems and the organization of ritual, and both of these typically connect the temporal order with what can be called the supernatural realm.

For many people in nonstate societies, common ritual observances defined the boundaries of their polity. Just as the smaller political units— such as lineages and clans—were defined by a common set of ritual practices, from observance of certain taboos to worship at a certain shrine, what tied the larger society together was participation in a common set of rituals, often combined with an ideology of common descent from a founding ancestor.[19] When such societies confronted European colonialists, the rituals that bound them together became a means for organizing politically on a larger scale than was previously known. Lacking formal political institutions, and under pressure to react in a more coordinated fashion to the perils posed by colonial expansion, these societies relied on key ritual specialists to lead their political and military response.[20]

In centralized societies, where rites also play a major role in furnishing organizational distinctiveness, rulers who seek to distance their regimes from those of their predecessors must create new rites to replace the old. This was recognized many centuries ago when the T'ang dynasty arose in China on the embers of the vanquished Sui. Fu I, the Grand Astrologer of the new regime, urged the immediate creation of a new calendar, new color for court dress, new names for bureaucratic offices, new music, and new court rites.[21] Indeed, the identification of a new regime with a new way of symbolizing time—evident in the creation of a new system for reckoning time—was found repeatedly not only in ancient China, but also in Rome from the emperors of old to Mussolini, and in France during the Revolution.[22] By controlling time, rulers identified their political creation with the rhythms of nature.

More recently, the emancipation of European colonies has given rise to another round of attempts to replace the old political rites and symbols with new ones. Typical in this regard—but not in others—was the postwar experience in South Africa, where images of local heroes replaced British monarchs on stamps, coins, and paper currency. Awards such as the Cape of Good Hope Decoration replaced British honors like the Victoria Cross, and Settlers' Day and the Day of the Covenant replaced Empire Day and the Queen's Birthday. A new national flag and a new national anthem gave rise to further ritual change. A new political entity without new rites and symbols was inconceivable.[23]

The importance of ritual in providing organizational distinctiveness is not limited to the societal level. The Monhegan Indians of New England, who have been struggling since the 1930s to maintain their own organization, provide a good example.[24] As a result of European colonization and warfare, there was little left of traditional Monhegan society by the nineteenth century. In 1880, when the state legislature legally disbanded the tribe, observers assumed that the end of the Monhegans as a distinctive group was at hand. Yet Monhegan identity did not fade away. The effort to renew tribal identity began with the creation of a legally incorporated tribal organization in the 1930s, and from this a renaissance occurred.

The problem faced by the Monhegans was how to assert their distinctiveness in the face of a skeptical citizenry. For centuries, the Monhegans had intermarried with neighboring whites and blacks, so that they possessed no clear physical features that could mark them as Indians in terms of popular stereotype. Moreover, they no longer spoke their own language, and in all other respects they shared in the larger American culture in which they lived. As one Monhegan bitterly lamented, unless you rode to work on a horse and lived in a teepee, people would not believe you were an Indian. Somehow, a way had to be found to establish this identity. Yet there was a thin line between successfully asserting one's Indian identity and appearing ridiculous in neighbors' eyes.

The Monhegans solved this problem of organizational distinctiveness by stressing rites and symbols that identify them as Indians and as Monhegans. The most important of these rites is the annual powwow. Each year widespread publicity goes out to announce the event. The hosts invite Indians from other, better-established tribes to join with them and, before a large crowd of non-Indian neighbors and tourists, the Monhegans perform native dances, parade in Indian clothing, display Indian crafts, and recount their history.

The importance of these rites in carving out a distinctive organizational identity is poignantly reflected in the comments of the Monhegan chief at one of these powwows. Asked about the origin of the large headdress he was wearing, the chief immediately admitted that it was not Monhegan but of Plains Indian origin. He had ordered it through a Sears catalogue. With a resigned sigh, he explained that the public had come to expect such attire from Indian chiefs.

Relating the Local to the National

One problem that all large-scale organizations face is how to integrate local activity into the higher organizational level. The question might be put as follows: How can the actions of a group of villagers or townsmen be seen as an expression of national-level organizational life? Identification of the local with the national can take place only through the use of symbols that identify the one with the other.

This is why Minnie Love's switch from white sheets to Betsy Ross garb was so threatening to the Ku Klux Klan. What identified the action of a crowd of women parading through the streets of Denver with the action of a bunch of men in Chicago or Alabama was their use of a common symbolism, a common ritual. The common rites served not only to make these far-flung individuals feel part of a larger organization; they also made the public interpret the actions of the different groups of people as part of the same organization, the same political group. The Montagnard secret societies in nineteenth-century France confronted a related problem. When their organization was made illegal, there could be no direct public recognition of their existence from any higher organizational level or from other local units. What united the secret groups was the ritual. Without the ritual, there was no Montagnard rebel organization.

Just as ritual has been an important means of defining the boundaries of societies that lacked formal political institutions, so it has been impor-

tant in coordinating the actions of different local groupings in such societies. A good example is provided in Bali, where coordination of the
irrigation works was a supralocal task of great importance. Yet this was
not accomplished through bureaucracy, but rather by a system of ritual
obligations that regularly brought the scattered people together, facili-
tated the needed division of labor, and coordinated the timing of the
distribution of water to the various fields.[25]

But though many nonliterate societies made use of ritual to coordi-
nate action beyond the local level, it was with the centralization of government that the problem of identifying local activities with higher-level
political organizations became especially important. With the spread of
the Roman Empire, problems of political integration arose that had never
before been confronted on such a vast scale. What was it that made a town
in Asia Minor part of the empire rather than an autonomous political
unit? How were people encouraged to think of themselves as part of such
a nebulous and distant concept as the Roman Empire, when all they
actually saw were occasional soldiers and tax collectors, the latter often
local residents themselves? Part of the solution was to construct monuments that served as perpetual reminders of imperial ties. Equally significant, popular participation in rites of allegiance became a regular feature
of community life.[26]

In many cases, rulers preferred to renew bonds of dependence
through the more dramatic—and hence more effective—rites of royal
entry. By staging large-scale rites in localities scattered throughout the
realm, people were better able to identify with the power of the ruler,
and, at the same time, the subservience of local authorities to the central
ruler was made clear.

In southeast Asia the dazzling procession of a fourteenth-century
Javanese king, as described by Geertz, further shows how widespread
this political device was. This royal caravan passed through 210 communities during a two-and-a-half-month trek. Hundreds of ox-drawn carts
were accompanied by elephants, horses, and even imported camels to
magnify the splendor. The royal retinue, officials, attendants carrying the
royal regalia, and beasts lurched along "like some archaic traffic jam . . .
over the narrow and rutted roads lined with crowds of astonished
peasants."[27]

European monarchs were not to be outdone in this parade of
power. In a climate of religious unrest and political intrigue, Charles IX
officially took over the powers of king of France in 1563 at the age of 13.
Given the tenuousness of the new king's authority, his mother,
Catherine de'Medici, thought it important for Charles to tour the kingdom with the entire court. Her hope was that he would be able to con-

solidate his rule and so counter the rising forces of rebellion. Thus began a royal procession that lasted two years and involved rites of royal entry at over one hundred cities and towns.[28]

Such ritualized attempts to tie the periphery to the center were especially important where other aspects of the political infrastructure were weak and where the possibility of disintegration of the realm was ever present. In the warrior monarchies of Morocco, from the seventeenth century to the nineteenth, this practice was common. Indeed, as Geertz tells us, the last of these kings spent half of each year in such processions through the kingdom, "demonstrating sovereignty to skeptics."[29]

This use of ritual to tie local communities to the center of state power also assumes urgency when new nations are established. Such was the case, for example, in Tanzania, a political entity created by colonialism and encompassing a large number of cultural groups, each with a separate language, religion, and social organization. The government of the new state was eager to portray itself as the expression of the people. This was done by establishing local party sections in all the towns throughout the country. Regular meetings were held in each community in order to foster a sense of unity with the national party and thus put the villagers "in touch with that unseen and unseeable entity, the state." These common public displays, with their standardized presentations at local ward meetings, not only relate the local people to the government, but also provide a symbolic means for the local people to identify with Tanzanians living elsewhere in the new nation. In the past, many of these people had been considered foreigners; but now, as they are all busy performing the same rites, they have been redefined as fellow countrymen.[30]

One of the most potent, and widely found, mechanisms for tying local groups to a national entity is the simultaneity of symbolic action. The Mexican celebrations of Hidalgo's revolt offer a good example of this, with participation in the same sequence of ritual action at the exact same time in town plazas throughout the country giving people the impression they are part of a larger social unit. Leaders of the French Revolution showed a similar compulsion, indeed what Ozouf termed an "obsession," in ensuring that the oath of allegiance to the new regime be spoken "together and at the same moment" by all the people of France. In simultaneity lies political communion.[31]

This use of symbolism and ritual to relate local groups to national political movements is not by any means limited to official or governmental organizations. People seeking political change also express their relationship to the larger movement with which they identify by using symbol and ritual.

The Black Power movement in the United States in the 1960s shows just such use of common rites and symbols to create national unity. This case is especially interesting as an example of how far-flung, often un-coordinated, local activities can be formed into a national political entity in the absence of any national organization at all. What bound together these scattered local groups, and made their participants and the public see them as expressions of a common political force, was a system of symbols and rituals. This involved rallies, marches, demonstrations, and confrontations that incorporated such distinguishing features as stylized chants and songs, symbolic gestures, and clothing. By reacting at the same time and with the same rituals to events such as the as-sassination of Martin Luther King or the indictment of Huey Newton, these widely dispersed local groups further asserted their identity as part of a larger association.[32]

Likewise, in Iran, shortly after the revolution, a group of villagers was eager to lay claim to the large land holdings of the local elite family. To do this successfully, they sought to show that the expropriation was not an individual act of greed or aggression, but rather the local-level execution of a national policy. They did not simply move onto the land and begin to farm it; instead they staged a complex ritual to identify themselves as the local executors of the decrees of Khomeini and the Revolutionary Council. They gathered at a local mosque and hoisted the Islamic flag. Singing revolutionary songs and shouting praise to Allah, they marched off in procession to occupy the land that was rightfully theirs.[33]

Investing and Divesting Power

Political organizations and, more generally, political systems require a division of labor. In all state societies this entails a hierarchy of status and power. In order to invest a person with authority over others, there must be an effective means for changing the way other people view that per-son, as well as for changing the person's conception of his right to impose his will on others. Authority, the belief that a person has the right to exercise influence over others' behavior, is itself an abstraction, and peo-ple can conceive of who has authority and who does not only through symbols and rituals.[34] That the same person one moment has no such authority and at a subsequent moment acquires it must be represented through ritual performances. This is why formal ceremonies of induction are universal for public power holders in government.[35] Through these rituals, a distinction is made between the individual and the role of au-thority with which he or she is being invested, but at the same time the individual becomes identified with the role. Ritual mobilizes societal authority for this investiture, while powerful symbols help make the general population emotionally receptive to the creation of such power over them.[36]

"In rites of initiation," Cassirer claims, "a man is given a new name because what he receives in the rite is a new self."[37] A man becomes a king because he comes to be treated as a king. Ritual is used to constitute power, not just reflect power that already exists. This becomes most evident where authority is under attack. In 1485, the Tudors were struggling in England against their rivals' armies and it was not clear just who would win. The ritual coronation of Henry VII at Westminster in that year, and his subsequent marriage to Elizabeth, symbolically uniting the rival houses of York and Lancaster, were important parts of his victorious political campaign.[38]

A more contemporary example is the simultaneous celebration at two different locations of the 1986 inauguration rites for the president of the Philippines. In one mass rite Ferdinand Marcos took the oath of office, while in another Corazon Aquino solemnly took the oath. Who thus became president of the Philippines? Although these rites were only one part of the political battle raging in Manila, their significance is clear if one considers what would have happened if Marcos had put off the ceremonies and Aquino had held hers on the appointed day. His already precarious position would have been further undermined.[39]

The stability of hierarchical political systems, paradoxically, depends on the investment of authority in particular individuals at the same time that it depends on being able to replace them. This is a tricky proposition, especially where a ruler is proclaimed as the embodiment of the divine on earth. Religions may be able to wait millennia for a second coming, but more worldly political systems require speedier divine replacement. An example of how to deal with this problem is found among the Shilluk, an East African people ruled by a king. The divine spirit that looks after the people is known as Nyikang, which normally resides in the king. Nyikang, the principle of political and social order, is eternal, but Shilluk kings are not. Though the king embodying Nyikang inevitably dies, Nyikang must live on and somehow be transferred to the new king. It is hard to see how this could be accomplished without ritual.

In fact, when a Shilluk king dies an effigy of Nyikang is taken from its shrine in the north and moved southward. In each area through which it passes, people come to pay their respects and escort the effigy to the next district, for in the interregnum it is the effigy that contains the spirit of Nyikang. When it finally reaches the outskirts of the royal capital,

Nyikang's accompanying "army" of the north meets the king-elect's army of the south in a mock battle. The southern army is defeated and the king is captured by Nyikang and taken by the effigy to the capital. As Evans-Pritchard puts it, "The kingship captures the king." In the capital Nyikang's spirit leaves the effigy and enters the king-elect, who trembles with the spirit's entry, and thus becomes king. Later, the effigy is taken back to its shrine to await the death of the new king.[40]

Lest the Shilluk case be dismissed as an exotic practice of a remote people, it is well to recall the case of the king's two bodies in France and the accompanying maxim: "Le roi ne meurt jamais." In France, as among the Shilluk, the eternal power of the king was represented by an effigy, and this effigy was used in rituals of transition between the old and new kings. Beginning with the funeral procession of 1498, the effigy that accompanied the king's body was referred to as if it were alive, and the procession was organized as if the rites were being lavished on a living king. The effigy consisted of a life-like image of the dead monarch, complete with wax face, wide-awake eyes, and full royal regalia. Thus two bodies of the king were paraded through the streets of Paris, the one mortal, the other defying death and living on.[41]

As in the Shilluk case, the French used these rites to express the immortality of the royal dignity, yet they had to deal at the same time with the king's mortality. In short, the effigy had to be replaced by a living king. This was done by subsequent coronation ceremonies. It is notable, though, that just as the Shilluk effigy of royal power initially vanquished the king-elect in East Africa, the French royal effigy drove out the king-elect in Paris. Since the effigy of the dead king was to be treated as alive in the funeral procession, the new king's status was anomalous. There could not be two kings of France marching in the same procession, each clad in the royal regalia.[42]

In effect, the proper celebration of rites of mourning conflicted with the rites of power. The new king, as an embodiment of the principle of royal power, could not appear in public dressed in the black of mourning, as this would undercut his royal resplendence, his royal dignity.[43] By the same logic, members of the French Parlement, though they marched in the funeral processions of this period, would not compromise the symbols of their authority by wearing black. If the king's life-like effigy wore the striking royal robes, the members of Parlement must march in their scarlet robes, making their independence clear amidst the sea of black-clad mourners.[44]

Rituals express the continuity of positions of authority in the fact of the comings and goings of their occupants. To guard against the ambiguities of the transition period, ritual forms have been developed that shorten the interregnum. This movement toward speedier transitions is nicely illustrated in France itself, if we compare the sixteenth-century rites of the king's two bodies with events that took place on September 1, 1715, when Louis XIV died. At the royal palace on that day, the grand chamberlain, wearing a black plume in his hat, strode onto the balcony of the dead Sun King's bedroom. He called out, "The king is dead!" and retired inside. A few moments later, a white plume now tucked in his hat, the chamberlain reappeared on the balcony and called out, "Long live King Louis XV! Long live King Louis XV! Long live King Louis XV!"[45]

By the same token, there are limits to the flexibility of coronation rites, since their value derives from their ability to assert that the authority of the new ruler is no different from that of his predecessors. The new emperor's clothes are the same as those of the old, even if the incumbent's measurements are different. In this light, it is easier to understand the problem faced by the child-kings of France, who were bound to wear regalia designed for sturdier, adult frames. In 1561, when ten-year-old Charles IX was crowned, his royal vestments weighed so heavily on him that he could not walk by himself and had to be supported. Later, Louis XIII, only eight years old at the time of his coronation and similarly afflicted by the weight of the royal regalia, suffered the embarassment of having to be carried up the steps to the throne.[46]

The coronation of the king itself involved a related paradox. If the person became king through a ritual performed by others, he was dependent on them for his power. But how could it be their power to give? Creation of a truly autocratic ruler, independent from other sources of legitimation, accordingly involved changes in coronation ritual. In the early Middle Ages, beginning in the ninth century, kings in western Europe were crowned in rites administered by church officials, who were then accorded great prestige, and the king became dependent on the church.[47] In the Byzantine East, on the other hand, coronation did not in itself create the king. Although the ceremonies were important in giving the new king the diadem, the symbol of his legitimacy, it was believed that he was directly appointed by divine forces. Hence, coronation was simply recognition of the new emperor's previously acquired right to rule. This is reflected in the rites themselves. While in the west the king prostrated himself when he was about to be inaugurated, the Byzantine emperor never kneeled during the ceremonies, and, unlike his western counterpart, he uttered no coronation oath.[48]

This ritual statement of independent power was further developed in the coronation ceremonies of the Russian tsars. Beginning with Elizabeth's coronation in 1742, the new tsar crowned herself. Here the senior archbishop simply handed the crown to the empress, who then set it atop her head, showing that her authority was not dependent on any outside source.[49]

If assumption of political office is ritually marked, so are attempts to divest an officeholder of his authority. Having been previously ritually joined to the office, the individual must also be separated from his or her authority by further ritual. When the divesting of authority from a person is unscheduled, it is disruptive of the normal symbolic representation of the political order and violates the sacralization of power; at these times, especially powerful symbolism is likely to be employed. This ritual must fuse together strong emotions—often associated with the notion that the power holder has sinned against the community—with the idea that the individual who a moment ago could legitimately exercise power over them can do so no longer.

Just such ritualization was involved in the divesting of Richard Nixon's authority through the congressional hearings on Watergate. Nixon had not only been invested with the office of the presidency in an elaborate ritual display; he had for years been at the center of ceaseless ritualization that expressed and legitimated that authority. For five years, Nixon's every public appearance required a ceremonial entry, accompanied by the stirring chords of "Hail to the Chief." The hearings, with their symbolic drama, their use of highly charged political symbolism, and their emotional quality, provided an effective means for divesting Nixon of his authority. Had there been no such public ritual, had all the investigations been conducted privately, with a Congressional committee chairman releasing the final report, the political situation in the country would have been very different.[50]

Such rites of degradation are by no means limited to divesting authority from current officeholders. They are also important in delegitimizing the authority associated with the symbolism of leaders of the past.

A good case of this is provided by the de-Stalinization campaign in the Soviet Union in the early 1960s, in the wake of Krushchev's revelations about the crimes of the Stalin regime. In order to transform what had been a powerful symbol of political authority into a symbol of the abuse of authority, a variety of ritual changes were introduced. The leadership of the Soviet Union ordered that Stalin's body be removed from the mausoleum, thus putting an end to the mass daily pilgrimages honoring the former hero. Innumerable busts, statues, and portraits of Stalin were removed from public buildings and streets throughout the nation. Places named for Stalin, most notably the city of Stalingrad, were hastily renamed. With the dismantling of the ritual system centered on him, Stalin was posthumously divested of authority, and a blow was struck against those associated with him.[51]

Communication

For organizations to be effective they must have efficient means of internal and external communication, much of which takes place without ritual. But there is an element of ritual found in the communication of all organizations, and since much of what gets communicated is not new, the standardized, repetitive nature of ritual is an advantage. One of the most common uses of ritual within an organization is to socialize new members to the values and expectations that make up its culture.

Ritual is especially valuable to hierarchical organizations in communicating power relationships. Indeed, people can increase their power through the manipulation of ritual, just as they can lose power through ritual neglect or incompetence. This is most dramatically seen where power is most concentrated. Over two thousand years ago, for example, a Chinese peasant, Kao-tsu, rose to power and founded the Han dynasty. Since he had little background in such matters, one of his first acts as emperor was to abolish the court rituals, which he regarded as trivial. But the result of this move was that he was shown little respect by his followers in court, who disrupted court audiences through their drunken deportment. They traded loud insults and hacked on the wooden palace pillars with their swords. Disturbed and threatened by this lack of proper distance between himself and his followers, the emperor authorized a new ritual code. The change was dramatic. The emperor no longer walked into court but was borne in on a litter, with hundreds of banner-carrying officials announcing his arrival. All then rose and toasted him. He was now an emperor, no longer a peasant potentate.[52]

Ritual communicates not only the authority of the head of the state or organization; it is also important in making claims to positions of political importance within that state. Ancient Rome affords a dramatic example, for the military leaders of this bellicose empire asserted their prestige and power through rites of triumphal entrance into the city. These entries were already well developed in Etruscan times. In the sixth century B.C., victorious generals donned purple togas and gold crowns, reddened their faces, and took up eagle-tipped scepters for their chariot-borne entries. The Roman authorities recognized the significance of these triumphal entries in establishing the powerful position of the celebrant, and the Senate sought to exercise control over them. Rules were thus enacted which set the criteria for such an honor. The general must have defeated a foreign enemy and killed at least five thousand men. Before authorizing such a ceremony, the Senate met the claimant outside the city to adjudicate his claim to the rite.

The impact of such ceremonies—a hundred were held in the one hundred fifty years from 220 to 70 B.C.—was great. Magistrates and senators led the long procession into the city, followed by trumpeters and carts bearing some of the spoils of war: arms, gold, silver, art, and other treasures. Paintings and models of the conquered lands followed, as well as the golden crowns presented to the general by the towns he had vanquished. A richly adorned white ox, soon to be sacrificed to Jupiter, was accompanied by priests carrying sacred vessels. Then trudged in the captives, in chains. Behind all these came the victorious general, who stood in his plush chariot amidst a rising screen of incense. Resplendently dressed, the general held a laurel branch in one hand and an eagle-topped scepter in the other. A slave held a golden crown over his head. Accompanied by his children, the general was followed by his officers on horseback or on foot. These, in turn, led the masses of exultant soldiers, who sang praises (or ribald rhymes) to their general. Once in Rome, captives were beheaded, strangled, or sacrificed. After the general had gone to the Capitol and put his laurel branch in the lap of the statue of Jupiter, he was feasted in the temple by the Senate. None of the participants or onlookers at such triumphal entries were likely to forget them.[53]

Ritual is not only used to communicate that a person is to be exalted over others; it is also used to calibrate degrees of power within an organization, whether it be a Chinese empire or a New York law firm, and whether the symbolism involves the location of one's grave or the location of one's office. When the leaders of the Soviet Union gather on the Moscow reviewing stand as the troops pass by, their physical order relative to the central power holder symbolically represents and communicates their place in the hierarchy of authority and power. Yet this is not a new phenomenon: the use of space in rituals to communicate status can be traced back far through human history.[54]

Transmission of messages through ritual dramatization is much more powerful than communication through verbal declaration. Moreover, in many situations, direct verbal expression of status differences is more likely to create overt conflict among those in lower ranks than is ritual expression of the same message. Such use of ritual is also especially important where there is a conflict between official norms regarding the hierarchy of power holders and the actual hierarchy of power relations.

This does not mean, however, that ritual expressions of status never lead to conflict. Officeholders are loathe to give up any of the ritual prerogatives of their position, lest it undermine their authority and power. More than one fist fight has broken out between participants at political rituals over their distance from the ruler. At the imperial coronation of Charles V by Pope Leo X in Bologna in 1530, for example, a violent brawl erupted among the ambassadors from Ferrara, Genoa, and Siena about their seating. As one observer described it, "One of the people from Genoa grabbed the hair of the archbishop of Siena . . . and pulled it backward; one of those from Siena yanked on the beard of the man from Genoa who had the archbishop by his hair." Given the status of the brawlers and the symbolic importance of the occasion, King Charles himself was hurriedly consulted. On his order, all the disputants were tossed out.[55]

Ritual is employed to communicate power relations not just among the political elite, but between the powerful and the powerless as well. This occurs not only in the context of formal organizations, but also in defining political relations among people outside any formal context. In many peasant societies, for example, people depend on the protection offered by a patron, while the patron, in turn, depends for his own power and status on the number of "clients" he is able to accumulate. Though these patron-client relations are crucial to the political system, they have no formal organizational existence, nor any explicit legal basis. For the system to work there must be a means whereby people communicate their pledge of clientage to a particular patron and, likewise, a means by which the patron communicates his acceptance of that role vis-à-vis the prospective client. This does not take place through any written agreements, but by culturally standardized rituals.

In many cases these rites involve the offering of specified gifts by the client to the patron on certain ceremonial occasions, or the use of particular terms of address. When two men greet each other in rural Turkey, for example, they communicate their claim to equality by clasping hands, but one expresses his subservience to the other by taking the hand of the higher-status man, bowing, kissing it, and placing it to his forehead. Should the higher-status man not wish to have this dependent relationship publicly validated, he struggles to transform this ritual of subservience into the ritual of egalitarian greeting.[56]

If ritual serves important communicative purposes within organizations or states, it is equally important for communication among organizations and among states. An organization's political position is often communicated more effectively, and more credibly, through ritual than through simple written platforms or oral addresses. It is in this light that the polemic between Italy's Socialist and Communist parties in October 1986 can be understood. A mass peace demonstration was to be held in Rome, with the Italian Communist Party prominent among the sponsors. The Socialists refused to get involved in the peace march, on the grounds that the Communists did not share the Socialists' even-handed approach to the problems of international aggression. And what was given as the primary evidence of the Communists' guile? The revealing fact, according to a prominent editorial in the Socialist Party newspaper, was that the Communists had never marched against the repression in Czechoslovakia or Poland, against the Russian tanks that rolled into Hungary, against the Soviet invasion of Afghanistan, or against the Vietnamese military role in Cambodia. "We have seen them dissent and criticize, but never have they marched."[57] Here, the true indication of a political party's sympathies is to be found in its rituals, not in its public pronouncements.

The use of ritual for communication between states is, of course, highly developed in the world of international protocol. Should a ruler of another country arrive and certain rites not be performed—his national anthem played, his country's flag displayed with military honors alongside that of the hosts—serious international tensions can result. For example, in 1986, because of scheduling conflicts, Soviet leader Gorbachev was not met by Iceland's head of state on his arrival in Reykjavik for his meeting with President Reagan. Gorbachev was so incensed by this slight, which was blamed on the Soviet ambassador to Iceland, that, on his return to Moscow, he had the ambassador fired.[58] Perhaps the Soviet emissary was unfamiliar with John Lyly's verse:

> For he that mightie states hath feasted, knowes
> Besides theire meate, they must be fedd with shewes.[59]

It is not just deference that is communicated to visiting diplomats and heads of state through ritual. Indeed, such rites are often used to impress foreign powers with the strength and wealth of their host. Four centuries ago, in the mid-sixteenth century, Catherine de'Medici, whose two-year procession through France I have already recounted, sponsored a series of magnificent court fêtes for foreign dignitaries; these were designed to disabuse them of the notion that her country was close to ruin. Catholics and Protestants may be at war with each other, the nation's purse bare, the king a mere inexperienced boy, but to admit to these conditions by scaling down or abandoning court rites would send an important signal of defeat to France's neighbors.[60]

The role of ritual in impressing foreign political powers is also much in evidence in colonial administrations, where great emphasis was placed on ritual display as a means of communicating the authority and power of the rulers. This typically took the form of local ritual display of colonial superiority, but occasionally it involved bringing local indigenous rulers to the colonial homeland for a ritual lesson.

Such was the case in 1937 when Yeta, leader of Barotseland, left what was then Northern Rhodesia to attend the king's coronation in London. First Yeta went to meet Queen Mary. Taken through a large hall, he passed through huge doors to encounter the queen, standing in the middle of a cavernous room. When he subsequently encountered the king, Yeta got down on his knees before the monarch and gave the Barotse royal salute. The celebration of the coronation rites, though on a much more vast and opulent scale than he had ever witnessed, were not beyond his comprehension by any means, for such rites of rulers were as much part of politics in the states of Africa as they were in Europe.[61]

Yeta was not the first African leader to visit British royalty in England, nor the first subject to a ritual lesson in the colonial hierarchy of power. Back in 1919, the Paramount Chief of Basutoland, in southern Africa, came to England for an audience with the king. When the chief asked permission to stop in Rome on his way back home, his English hosts refused. They feared that the potentially greater splendor of the Vatican's reception might lead the chief to conclude that the pope was more important than the king.[62]

It would be difficult, though, to top the Aztecs in the use of ritual to intimidate the emissaries of other peoples. On special occasions, such as the dedication of a new temple, Aztec rulers invited kings and notables from neighboring societies to observe their rites, which always included human sacrifice. Since most of the sacrificial victims were war captives, it was not uncommon for the guests to witness the mass disembowelment of their own warriors.[63] The message about the power of the Aztec state is best conveyed by contemporary descriptions of these rites, many of which have survived.

In the Aztec ceremonial system, the sacrifice of humans to the gods occupied a central place. Atop a long series of stone stairs stood the altar, before which a stone platform lay. One by one, the victims—many wailing as they climbed—were taken up the stairs. They were placed on the platform, facing the sky, with their backs painfully arched, and their hands and feet tied down. Using a flint knife, the officiant slit open the victim's taut chest and quickly cut out his heart. He then struck the heart against the altar, letting it drop on the ground, where it continued to beat. Meanwhile, the body was rolled down the steps, where it was recovered by the soldier who had originally captured the victim. The lucky soldier made off with the corpse, using it to prepare a feast for friends and relatives. Back on the altar, the priest smeared the blood on the lips of the stone depictions of the gods, thus nourishing them.

For rites of special state importance, held in the capital city, the ceremonies were on a spectacular scale, with long lines of victims waiting their turn to pay homage to the Aztec state. There, as on other major occasions, a high-ranking captive was kept for separate ritual purposes. The captive dignitary did not suffer the ignominy of having his body rolled down the altar stairs. Rather, he was flayed so that Montezuma, master of the Aztec empire, could wear his skin in a special dance. Should this ceremony not be sufficient to impress on the invited guests the power of the Aztec empire, subsequent tours of the long racks lined with thousands of skulls of previous sacrificial victims brought the point home. It would be difficult to find a more striking example of ritual overkill.[64]

3

Legitimacy and Mystification

Among the Bunyoro, an agricultural people of Uganda, the Mukama reigned supreme, head of the kingdom and ultimate source of all authority. Upon the Mukama's death, succession norms dictated that one of his sons should take over the kingdom. There was, however, no rule determining in advance just which son this should be. Since the Mukama had many wives and thus many sons, the death of the king led to a period of strife. Brothers lined up allies and fought one another, and the successful prince was likely to win the kingship literally over his brothers' dead bodies. To make a king of the fratricidal prince, a richly developed series of rites was begun.

The Bunyoro preserved the royal corpse by first disemboweling it and then drying it over a slow fire. Later, when the successful heir emerged, he returned to his father's corpse and removed the jawbone. The new king buried it at a special spot where a house was then built for the dead king's regalia. Though the rest of the body was unceremoniously discarded, the tomb housing the royal jawbone would long be venerated.

In the accession rites that followed, the initiate king underwent ceremonial washing, shaving, nail-paring, anointment with special oil, and smearing with white chalk. Animal sacrifices were performed, and the king was handed a variety of symbols of political and military power: spears, bow and arrows, and a dagger. A representative of neighboring regions formerly under Bunyoro rule offered him ivory and copper bracelets as symbolic tribute. Finally, the new king let loose arrows to each of the four cardinal points, uttering, "Thus I shoot the countries to overcome them." Lest his

authority subsequently diminish, he
repeated many of these rites each year.[1]

———————————

It was the anniversary of the Great Trek and
the day in 1838 when 468 Afrikaners
(*voortrekkers*), accompanied by their servants
and sixty African allies, drew their wagons
into a circle and drove off a huge Zulu army.
The battle proved to be a major turning
point in the creation of white rule in Natal.
A century later, while still under British
colonial control, Afrikaner nationalists
foresaw the day when they would rule an
independent South Africa, and so they
resurrected the event, with eight ox-wagons,
each named after a hero of the original trek,
going on different routes, winding their way
through white settlements throughout the
nation. At each village enthusiastic
Afrikaners met the wagons, which would
eventually converge at a hill overlooking
Pretoria.

On December 16, 1938, exactly one
hundred years after the sacred event, one-
hundred thousand Afrikaners—a tenth of
the entire Afrikaner people—gathered for
the laying of the foundation stone of the
Voortrekker Monument. To celebrate the
occasion, men grew beards and women
wore old-fashioned voortrekker dress. As a
journalist described the event: "Men and
women gazed at the cumbersome vehicles
that had cradled a nation, and were silent
with adoration. . . . The Afrikaners on the
Rand had made a pilgrimage to a new
symbol of nationhood." From a fire lit at the
former headquarters of the defeated Zulu
commander, a relay team of boys brought
torches through the countryside. Arriving in

Pretoria, they were surrounded by women who hovered over the flames, burning the fringes of their handkerchiefs and bonnets, to have lasting mementos of the event. At the conclusion of the ceremony, the crowd sang the Afrikaner anthem, *Die Stem van Suid Afrika*, the chords drifting toward the city below. As one Afrikaner political leader explained, "The Great Trek gave our people its soul. It was the cradle of our nationhood. It will always show us the beacons on our path and serve as our lighthouse in our night."[2]

For many observers, the political effects of ritual consist primarily of legitimating the existing system and the power holders in it. This thesis has a long history, but it was with the writings of Durkheim in the early part of this century that it received its modern social scientific form. Durkheim argued that through ritual people project the secular sociopolitical order in which they live onto a cosmological plane. It is through ritual that people symbolize the "system of socially approved 'proper' relations between individuals and groups."[3]

People everywhere tend to sacralize their socio-political environment. We feel uncomfortable in recognizing our society as merely the arbitrary product of cultural history, environmental adaptation, and political struggle. Instead, we attribute cosmological meaning to our political order, believing that our society has somehow been divinely ordained, that it reflects some higher purpose.[4] Anthropologists have long accused westerners of ethnocentrism, of believing that their own society is superior to all others, endowed with a divine mission. However, people everywhere—from hunting and gathering bands to modern nation-states—share this trait. They imagine that their own society represents both the best and the most natural order, and they take part in communal rituals that express and renew this view. Every session of the U.S. Congress begins with an invocation of divine guidance; so did meetings of the Roman senate two millennia ago. Indeed, the Roman senate's assembly hall was a temple, and so is that of Congress.[5]

In rendering their political system sacred through the use of ritual, people also end up legitimizing the power held by political leaders. Bettelheim identifies a general human tendency to invest the political conqueror with semi-divine characteristics. He attributes this to people's fear that the ruler's awesome power will be used against them. Through ritual people express their hope and belief that the ruler is beyond the realm of human caprice. The greater the threat posed to them by the leader's power, "the greater the need to deny it by believing in his virtue."[6]

The glorification of the ruler through ritual often continues after the ruler's death, serving in many cases to legitimize the rulers and the regime that follow. So we have the popular Soviet slogan: "Lenin lived, Lenin lives, Lenin shall live." And indeed he does continue to live, though his body has been under glass for six decades. His mausoleum in Red Square is the symbolic center of Moscow and the nation, with long lines of pilgrims from all parts of the Soviet Union ever ready to pay their respects. Following the precedent of countless others facing more mundane dangers, Yuri Gagarin visited Lenin before being launched into orbit in order to gather strength for his voyage, and after his return he reported back to his immortal leader. Important state holidays all reach their emotional zenith in Red Square, with leaders addressing both a mute Lenin and a more animated audience. The person who makes light of these rituals of obeisance risks provoking an extreme reaction, not only from the political elite, but also from the person in the street. Lenin's body is now an icon of the Soviet regime; disrespect for the ritual that surrounds him is sacrilege.[7]

Does this mean that the political stability of stratified societies depends on popular belief in the legitimacy of the system and its power holders? Durkheim assumed as much: since people worship their society through ritual, political legitimacy is a feature of all stable societies. Ritual, in turn, plays a major role in nurturing and expressing this social consensus.

It is possible to accept Durkheim's thesis regarding the importance of ritual in legitimating political systems and political power holders without accepting the corollary view that rituals simply reinforce whatever political system happens to exist. Indeed, if the latter view were adopted, ritual could only (and mistakenly) be seen as an inherently conservative political force, with no role to play in political conflict or political change.

The best-known alternatives to the social consensus view of political legitimacy are those inspired by Marxian perspectives, or, more broadly, theories based on the view that deep-seated conflicts of interest are built into stratified societies. Even in this camp, though, there is considerable difference of opinion as to the nature and importance of political legitimacy. According to one branch of Marxian theory, the ideas of the ruling class become the ruling ideas of the entire society and thus provide ideological justification for existing power differences. In some ways, this perspective is quite similar to Durkheim's: both envision a broad sharing of a political worldview by members of a society, with rituals employed to express and reinvigorate it. The difference is that this Marxian perspective identifies an agent of change, located in the economic and material infrastructure. Changes in the infrastructure—as occur when new modes of production arise—ultimately account for changes in the political system, its accompanying ideology, and its system of rituals.

Other conflict theorists place much less emphasis on the unifying function of ruling class ideology and look instead to the power relations themselves as the primary means by which popular acquiescence to the political system is obtained. In this view, people go along with their position as exploited workers and powerless citizens not because they believe in the moral virtue of the system, but because they have no practical choice. To feed themselves and their families they must get jobs; since jobs are controlled by the economic elite (the proverbial owners of the means of production), they must meet the conditions of the elite if they are to make a living. Whether they like the system is of little political consequence.[8]

There is much to be said for this position. People do not necessarily behave the way they do because they believe their behavior is right. People often behave in one way because they see the alternatives as having worse consequences for them. Yet, we should be skeptical of the view that most people in complex societies go along with the political system without believing in its legitimacy. For one thing, the evidence suggests that, in the great majority of cases of relatively stable political systems, there is a widely shared ideology of legitimacy. Where the system is perceived to be illegitimate, it is unstable. Thus it is important for the powerful to lend what legitimacy they can to the system and, thereby, to their own privileged position in that system. One of the ways they do this is through ritual.

Whether looking at historical accounts or at the world today, one is most struck not by the rebellions of the oppressed who rise up to destroy the political system that exploits them. Rather it is the overwhelming conformity of the people living in such societies that is most impressive. As Piven has written: "However hard their lot may be, people usually remain acquiescent, conforming to the accustomed patterns of daily life in their community, and believing those patterns to be both inevitable and just." Most people *do* go along with the social arrangements into which they are born, for these generally appear to them as "the only possible reality."[9] Of course, those who most benefit from such inequalities do what they can to encourage this belief in the legitimacy, or at least the inevitability, of the social arrangements. This is true not only of modern nation-states, but of all societies in which some people have power over others. As Bloch put it, "It is precisely through the process of making a power situation appear a fact in the nature of the world that traditional authority works."[10]

One of the reasons why ritual is such a potent means of legitimation is that it offers a way to unite a particular image of the universe with a strong emotional attachment to that image. Rituals are built out of symbols that embody certain views of how the world is constructed. But at the same time, by engaging people in a standardized, often emotionally charged, social action, rituals make these symbols salient and promote attachment to them. As Victor Turner put it, ritual "is precisely a mechanism that periodically converts the obligatory into the desirable." In ritual, "the dominant symbol brings the ethical and jural norms of society into close contact with strong emotional stimuli." Turner continues:

In the action situation of ritual, with its social excitement and directly physiological stimuli, such as music, singing, dancing, alcohol, incense, and bizarre modes of dress, the ritual symbol . . . effects an interchange of qualities between its poles of meaning. Norms and values, on the one hand, become saturated with emotion, while the gross and basic emotions become ennobled through contact with social values. The irksomeness of moral constraint is transformed into the "love of virtue."[11]

This is a powerful way of looking at the political role of ritual, yet its full implications have not been recognized. Social arrangements are not simply validated through ritual, and ritual works not merely to legitimate dominant political arrangements in a society. As Turner notes, ritual is a powerful means of uniting symbols of social reality with the strong emotions that ritual performance can stir. But these ritual symbols can be the symbols of change, indeed of revolution; they need not be symbols of stability.

The political leader who wants to create the public impression that he is champion of justice, equity, and the general good is far more likely to achieve a deeper and more lasting impression by staging a dramatic presentation of this image than he is by simply asserting it verbally. His appearance should be replete with appropriate symbols and managed by a team of supporting actors. In this way, power holders, or aspiring power holders, seek to promulgate the view of the political situation they would like the general population to hold. The drama not only constructs a certain view of the situation, but it also engenders an emotional response that associates notions of right and wrong with the elements in this view. It is, indeed, a moral drama, not just an instructional presentation.[12]

An episode in African colonial history shows just how power holders can consciously employ ritual to manage impressions and legitimate a regime. In 1924, when Sir Herbert Stanley became the first British governor of what was then Northern Rhodesia, he inherited a situation of political unrest. He blamed this on the exploitive history of the British South Africa Company, which previously had had authority over the region. In short, the local people had a poor image of their British rulers. Stanley's plan was to replace this image with one of imperial paternalism: British authority would be based on the glory and magnanimity of the British Crown, not on colonial military might.

Stanley's schemes were boosted by plans to have the future king of England, the Prince of Wales, visit the colony. If properly organized, the visit could project both an image of the vast power of the Empire and the image of a concerned royal father. Stanley took no chances, writing in his instructions for the prince: "It would be appreciated if HRH at the meetings with Natives would wear some uniform more impressive than khaki." Lest the prince miss his point, he continued, "May I further take the liberty of mentioning that the Police, most of whom have seen service, are immensely proud of their medals and interested in the medals and decorations worn by others. It would therefore have an excellent effect if HRH would consent to wear a large number of medals and decorations at the Police Parade."

The royal family had more than a little experience in such matters, and it is unlikely that Stanley's strictures were needed or, for that matter, appreciated. On the prince's first appearance, at which he met local chiefs, he wore the dazzling scarlet uniform of the Welsh Guards, which was shining with medals. According to a colonial report, one of the chiefs, on his return from the ceremonies, exclaimed that the prince "shone so brightly in his uniform that we could not look upon him." Whether such a statement was ever offered shall never be known, but clearly the colonial officials thought the ceremonies arranged for the prince's visit had the desired effect.[13]

Not all rituals that endow political arrangements with legitimacy are the product of conscious design. Indeed, there should also be room in our conception of the political universe for the unconscious forces that drive our lives. Although people do consciously manipulate ritual for political ends, they also sometimes invent, revise, or reinvigorate ritual forms that have political effects without being conscious of what those effects will be.[14]

Perhaps an example would help make this point more clearly. One of the most common means of legitimating a political decision (and, more generally, a political system) is to hold formal meetings at which these decisions are discussed. Since all participants theoretically have the right to say what they want, such meetings give people the impression that the decisions that are taken result from a process in which they, or at least some others much like themselves, are involved. Yet we know that in most cases the subsequent political course has little or nothing to do with the content of the meeting. Moreover, strong symbolic forces are at work at such meetings to limit severely the kinds of criticisms and alternative ideas that can be expressed.

Deal and Kennedy, in their study of the rites and rituals of corporate life, refer to such meetings as "opportunities for managers to stage events that dramatize cultural beliefs and values."[15] Similarly, in the political sphere, Edelman claims that "Formal governmental procedures . . . *are* formalities, vital for inducing general acquiescence in power arrange-ments."[16] But while corporate and governmental power holders may consciously call such meetings to legitimize their own decisions and their own power, no such conscious motive of legitimation need be held. The ruling ideology may well be that of democratic governance and popular participation, or collegial corporation responsibility, and the power hold-ers who call the meetings can believe in this ideology as much as the general population does.

Borrowing Legitimacy

One of ritual's most distinguishing features is its standardization. This, along with its repetitive nature, gives ritual its stability. Stability, in turn, serves to connect ritual to strongly felt emotions: emotions experienced in past enactments of the ritual reemerge at subsequent reenactments. But doesn't this lead to a paradox when we consider the role of ritual in political change? If ritual is by nature a conservative form of symbolic action, wouldn't it simply act as a drag on political change? Oddly enough, ritual can be important to the forces of political change just *because* of its conservative properties. New political systems borrow legiti-macy from the old by nurturing the old ritual forms, redirected to new purposes.

Every culture has its own store of powerful symbols, and it is generally in the interest of new political forces to claim those symbols as their own. Ritual provides one important mechanism for just such symbolic expropriation, the struggle for which can be intense. In the Italian election of 1972, for example, five different parties had the hammer and sickle as their emblem. This was of serious concern to the Italian Communist party, which sought to be recognized as the sole heir of the socialist and communist movements of the past century. The implications of this symbolic confusion were particularly great because parties were represented on the ballot by their emblem only, not by any separate written identification. To address this threat, the Communist party sponsored a series of rites, from publicly parading their flag to decorating their rally platforms with red crepe and hammers-and-sickles, all aimed at making clear the party's identification with the classic sym bolism of communism. Through ritual, then, political forces seek popular legitimacy by identifying with powerful symbols. This may be seen at all political levels, from international movements, through nation-states and political parties, down to local political factions.

In the ancient Kandyan state, in what is now Sri Lanka, a diffuse system of symbols linked the rulers to supernatural forces. The most powerful symbol was the Sacred Tooth Relic, housed in a special temple high on a mountain. More than anything else, this icon legitimated the authority of the political rulers of the ancient state. In recent years, of course, the political system has been entirely changed; the political leaders are elected. Yet, though the ideological basis of authority is new, the rituals involved in legitimating that authority are not. Whenever a new government is sworn in, the first task of the new leaders is to go to the Temple of the Sacred Tooth Relic; the ensuing ritual is broadcast by the mass media to the entire nation.[17]

A new regime can also signal its superiority over its immediate predecessor, as well as establish its own identity and legitimacy, by resurrecting older political symbols. Louis Philippe, who took up the French throne in 1830, sought to express his political enlightenment and mark the difference between himself and his Bourbon predecessors by bringing back the revolutionary tricolored flag as the national symbol and the singing of the "Marseillaise" as the national anthem. Both had been banned by the Bourbon rulers who were restored to the throne following Napoleon's downfall. Just as the Bourbons had sought the delegitimation of the Napoleonic and revolutionary regimes by these measures, Louis Philippe sought to profit from their continuing symbolic power of legitimation. And just as the new Bunyoro king sought legitimacy by expropriating his predecessor's jawbone, so Louis Philippe sought to derive some of his own from what little was left of Napoleon's remains. Indeed, in a solemn ceremony, Napoleon's remote grave was dug up and his bones carried to an imposing crypt in Paris on the banks of the Seine. Heads of state are notorious grave robbers.[18]

The French battle over the symbols of legitimacy continued in the twentieth century when Marshall Pétain attempted to shore up his puppet government's tenuous claim to national authority during the Nazi occupation. Bastille Day celebrations presented Pétain with a political rite he could not ignore. Given the emotional power the day held for many Frenchmen, as well as its revolutionary associations, the rites represented a potential mechanism for whipping up political opposition to the regime. Pétain could either try to expunge the celebrations or to appropriate them for the new regime. In fact, he tried to do both, organizing solemn celebrations in Vichy at the same time as the government forbade popular observance of the rites.

In 1940, 1941, and 1942, Pétain's regime conducted its own Bastille Day ceremonies, dedicated to commemorating the war dead, replete with a parade of troops and a highly publicized celebration of the mass. Meanwhile, De Gaulle, leader of the Resistance forces, led his own Bastille Day observances in London. Back in France, unauthorized rites galvanized the Resistance. Throughout the occupied territories, Resistance members stole through the night to hoist the tricolored flag on top of monuments for the war dead. In Marseille on Bastille Day, 1942, two women were shot to death when an enormous crowd, gathering illegally, waved tricolored flags and sang the "Marseillaise." Pétain's ritual battle for legitimacy became another theater for his political defeat. Try as he might to win them for his own uses, the rites became firmly identified with the Resistance and the anti-Nazi struggle.[19]

Attempts to establish political legitimacy through the continuity of ritual can also be important to political parties undergoing a radical change in direction. The Italian Communist Party (PCI) faced just such a challenge when it dramatically reversed its Leninist policies after the Second World War. Formerly built on the model of the revolutionary cadre party ("every member a militant"), the PCI was transformed into a mass membership organization. At the same time, calls for the dictatorship of the proletariat and an end to "bourgeois" parliamentary democracy were abandoned; participation in the multi-party electoral system was not only championed as a means to power, but as the ideal form of government.

Dramatic discontinuities threaten the integrity of any political organization. In the face of such a threat, potent symbolic means must be used to legitimate both the changes and the power holders responsible for them. Where the changes are made by a new party leadership, this may be done by discrediting some of the old symbols of legitimacy, as the example of the unceremonious evacuation of Stalin's body from Red Square illustrates. Even in such cases, however, great emphasis is given to symbolic continuity: Lenin's corpse remains undisturbed. Where a sharp change in policies takes place with the same leadership at the helm, leaders avoid attacking the old symbolism associated with past policies; rather, they attempt to expropriate those same symbols for their new political purposes. To challenge those symbols is to question the basis of their own authority.

In the case of the Italian Communist party, the list of symbolic and ritual expressions of political continuity is long. I mention just a few of them here. The symbols of the party remain unchanged, from the ever-present red flags and hammer-and-sickle to the obligatory use of *compagno* as a term of address among members. Symbolic expressions of revolutionary aims were almost untouched, despite the abandonment in fact of revolutionary goals and methods. For example, the songs regularly sung at Communist party gatherings remained the same as those sung in the previous era. Indeed, the more revolutionary the song, the greater its emotional impact. One of the favorites is "Bandiera Rossa," whose stirring verses include, "Onward, people, to the insurrection, red flag, red flag; onward, people, to the insurrection, the red flag will triumph; onward, people, united, revolution, revolution . . . "[20]

Many of the most powerful symbols of legitimacy are of religious origin. It should come as no surprise, then, that new political forces eagerly rummage through the preexisting body of religious rituals and symbols to find those that will enrich their own ritual forms. Such is the case today in various parts of the Islamic world, where a wide range of newly emerging political forces employ religious rites to help build their claims to legitimacy.[21]

Political legitimation through the use of religious ritual is not, however, limited to cases where the goals of the political group and the goals of the religion are presented as identical. The power of the ritual transcends its ideological content. The church in Europe certainly learned this lesson over the centuries as it fought losing battles against "pagan" ritual forms. It proved more profitable to expropriate the old ritual to the new organizational ends. Similarly, even when a new political regime is the sworn enemy of the previously dominant religion, it may make more sense to try to expropriate the church-linked ritual than to destroy it. This is not simply a matter of expediency, an admission of the difficulty of suppressing popular ritual forms. It also reflects recognition of the value of those rituals in legitimizing the new system and its leaders.

The Soviet Union provides a good example of this. For centuries, the people of Russia have celebrated New Year's Day as a joyous holiday. In ancient Russia, this was a pagan festival, but when Russia became Christianized in the tenth century, the church transformed the popular celebrations by merging them with Christmas festivities. When the Bolsheviks came to power, in keeping with their atheistic policy, they immediately suppressed celebration of New Year's/Christmas. But the Soviet leaders soon recognized their error. Their suppression of ritual did nothing to solidify the new regime; it only created popular resentment. To remedy the situation, Soviet authorities changed their policy and called on the state itself to sponsor the ritual. They sought to remove as much of the specifically Christian content as they could, while leaving the pagan content largely untouched. A resurgence of paganism was not a threat; renewed popular allegiance to the church was. The traditional figures of Grandfather Frost and the Snow Maiden were reintroduced, and collectives sponsored public celebrations complete with tree lighting. Indeed, Lenin himself took part in a number of these rites. Today, the Soviet leaders continue to do what they can to identify themselves with the celebration, and power holders from the Kremlin down to factory and farm managers use the occasion to report on the past year and announce plans for the next.[22]

Fetishes and Taboo

In hierarchical political systems that lack rites of popular selection of rulers, the use of potent icons of legitimacy are commonly found. In such cases the ruler does not simply take over the legitimating icons by virtue of his office; rather it is his possession of the icons that gives him his legitimacy and his office. Such was the case in the Ankole kingdom in East Africa, where a person became king by taking possession of the royal drum. Should a foreign king succeed in capturing the drum, the people claimed, he would automatically become the new king of Ankole.[23]

Similar beliefs are found in East Asia. Accession ceremonies of the emperors in China involved the transfer of the imperial regalia, which were thought both to protect their possessor and to assure the safety of the empire. These ribbons and seals and other icons of rule came to be so important that later in the Han dynasty people did not regard the emperor as the true Son of Heaven unless he physically possessed them.[24] Similarly, in the Japanese accession ceremonies the passing on of the

Three Sacred Treasures is the key to the succession process and transfers the right to rule to the new emperor.[25]

Whether or not the ruler acquires objects infused with sacred power, he himself becomes a source of sacrality. Given this power, people cannot approach him without special consequences; his aura is a power that can bless or maim. In the ancient Hindu kingdoms, great attention was lavished on the body of the king, for it represented the whole of the country and his physical condition reflected the condition of the country and its people. Accordingly, a person who was able to catch a glimpse of the king in all his splendor—bathed, in good health, and adorned with the royal regalia—shared in this power, which brought good fortune. The beneficent aura of power need not be connected to any specific body of religious dogma. Similar popular reactions were found when Italians encountered Mussolini, and the honor of shaking the hand of the U.S. president is fought over daily as anonymous citizens battle through crowds for a bit of of presidential mana.[26]

The sacrality that invests the ruler also has its darker side, though, for it burns with a force that can do harm to mere mortals. The ruler of the Moundang of Chad exudes just such power, and his normal bodily functions entail dangerous risks for his people. No one may glance at him while he eats, for fear of disturbing this sacred force, and whatever passes from his body presents the greatest peril. Hence the king cannot relieve himself unless a slave is in a position to collect the royal excreta.[27]

The classic form of these royal taboos and, indeed, the term taboo itself come from Hawaii, where royalty were defined by their possession of a dangerous sacred force. This presented problems for conjugal relations, since a mortal could perish if brought into too close contact with the royal power. In Hawaii this led to its logical, though incestuous, conclusion, with brother-sister marriage in the royal family. In Hawaii, too, the ruler's power infected the food he touched, so that others dared not eat leftovers from royal meals, and, like the far-off Moundang, special attendants disposed of the contents of royal spittoons and chamber pots. Execution was the penalty for letting these containers drop. So, too, in seventeenth-century Japan, the ground where the emperor's shadow fell became "infused with power dangerous to lesser beings." Commoners could not look into the face of the emperor; in fact, in the presence of the emperor they had to prostrate themselves. After the emperor finished each meal, his dishes were smashed to prevent the death of later diners who might make inadvertent use of them.[28]

At the same time as the emperor's dishes were being reduced to rubble in Japan, similar practices appeared in Europe. When the king of

Spain rode a horse, for example, no one else was permitted to mount it again. And how far is it from all this to the White House ceremonies where the president uses a dozen pens to sign his name, giving each to a different supporter, a plastic icon infused with the infectious sacrality of rule.[29]

Mystification

That power relations in a society are enveloped in a web of symbolic mystification is but another way of saying that hierarchy requires cultural definition. As Geertz puts it, "A world wholly demystified is a world wholly depoliticized."[30] Two kinds of mystification are especially common. The first involves the belief that the power holder somehow deserves to have power over others. This is most developed in monarchies, with their ideology of the divine right of the king, but it can be found in all hierarchical societies. The second common form of mystification, typical of societies espousing democratic principles, supports the notion that people are all equal. Here, either the power of the few is denied altogether, or alternatively, it is viewed as an expression of the wishes of the many. The more that inequality develops in a society having an ideology of egalitarianism, the more that one should expect to find such mystification.[31] Through such mystification—symbolic representation of the political order in a way that systematically differs from the actual power relations found in the society—inequalities are legitimated and particular views of the political order are nourished.

Mystification is a product of the social construction of reality. It is only through such constructions that we can visualize our political universe. Crick refers to this as the "social misconstruction of reality" and the "social construction of ignorance," nurtured by power holders in an attempt to prevent people from realizing the subservient role that, in some sense, they choose to perform.[32]

The concept of mystification is closely related to the Marxist notion of *false consciousness*, for both emphasize the benefit derived by power holders from the symbolic misrepresentation of the nature of power in the society. In capitalist countries, this commonly entails attributing an individual's power position to his or her individual virtues—for example, intelligence or hard work—rather than conceiving of inequality as created and perpetuated by the economic system itself.[33]

Although mystification of power relations is one of the important ways that legitimation of power differentials occurs, all such inequalities are not equally mystified. The more thoroughgoing and widely accepted the mystification, the more stable is the political hierarchy, and less coercion is needed to maintain the position of the powerful. Exploited people, however, need not have any illusions about their powerlessness or its bases. As many cases of slavery, and perhaps the contemporary example of South Africa, show, in some societies political inequalities rely heavily on physical coercion. Yet even in these societies, it is in the interests of the power holders to do what they can to mystify power relations.[34]

Perhaps the most important ritual of legitimation found in modern nations is the election. Indeed, it is a ritual that has quickly been taken up by countries around the world, nations with very different official ideologies and diverse institutional structures. When the American government's policy of aiding the rulers of El Salvador came under fire on the grounds that the El Salvador regime was oppressive, protecting the rule of the rich rather than the welfare of the poor majority, what happened? An election was arranged to demonstrate to the world that El Salvador was indeed ruled by the democratic masses. Of course, the switch from a regime that arose from a military coup to one that was elected entailed very little change in the government or in the power relations existing within the society. But the ritual of "free elections" nonetheless provided some legitimation.

Similarly, in the Soviet Union elections are important, even though they have no effect on the locus of power or on public policies. The official government view of the political system as the reflection of the will of the masses is ritually legitimated, and the fact that ninety-nine percent of the population votes is taken to indicate broad support for the political hierarchy and its policies.[35]

In the United States, elections foster the illusion that American government is the result of the free, informed choice of the entire citizenry and that all are equal in deciding questions of public policy. The widespread complaint by political analysts that elections in the United States have become too preoccupied with melodrama and hoopla, with villains and heroes, is misplaced. Of course such rituals are laden with emotional content and heavy with standard symbolism. The often-heard claim that things were different back in the good old days should itself be seen as part of the mystification of our election rituals.[36]

Even where the democratic process appears to be most clearly at work, where elected representatives at the local level are making decisions regarding how the community's public monies should be spent, scholars have unearthed a surprising pattern. The town council that goes through all the motions of deciding on details of the annual budget in fact has little effect on budget decisions, which are made by bureaucrats on the basis of other constraints, such as the terms of programs mandated by higher governmental levels. Hence it should be no surprise that there is commonly a "strong negative correlation between the amount of money involved in an issue and the time devoted to [discussing] it." The budget hearings themselves provide the behavior necessary to support the cherished myth of local self-government.[37]

Rites of this sort are found in all hierarchical political systems, and they often promote political stability by mystifying power relations. Yet, once created, rituals take on a life of their own; they are not entirely under the control of the power holders who seek to benefit from them. For example, in the early 1970s Governor Kenneth Curtis of Maine decided to deal with criticism of state expenditures by appointing a special commission on cost management. Curtis chose James Longley, an insurance salesman who had never held political office, to head the commission only after getting assurances Longley had no interest in using the post for his own political purposes. The final report, like most of its genre, had virtually no practical effect, but Longley subsequently used his ceremonial role as the cornerstone of an independent gubernatorial campaign. Indeed, he surprised all the professional politicians by becoming the only non-party-backed governor in the country.[38] Similarly, many a mayor has created a blue-ribbon committee to take responsibility for decisions that the mayor has already made. Yet, sometimes such committees surprise the mayor by going beyond their ceremonial role to identify and publicize mayoral corruption.

Given the possibility of an unanticipated outcome, such rituals of democratic participation might be expected to arise only where power holders feel confident that they can control the result.[39] Of course, to continue with an earlier example, external political pressures may compel rulers to embrace elections as the only way to demonstrate their legitimacy. This was the case in the Philippine election of 1986. But it would do well to recall that Marcos had sponsored such rites in the past and they had served him well. Had he been more successful in stage-managing the election, his end might not have been so precipitate.

Legitimizing Inequality

The rituals that legitimate authority take different forms depending on the official ideology associated with the political system; rites of divine kings differ from the rites of elected leaders. There are certainly power holders who do not benefit from publicly expressed ritual, but not only do they lack the legitimacy that comes with public office and the ritual that goes with it, they are also dependent on power holders who enjoy such legitimacy and such ritualization.[40]

Public investiture of authority is a symbolic process that requires ritual. As such, it is part of a much more general practice of using ritual to elevate a person's status in a public fashion, whether from youth to adult, single to married, or, in some societies, from middle age to elder. Through ritual the individual is separated from his or her previous status and inducted into the new one.

This social process of attaching and detaching roles from individuals creates tensions, for attainment of privileges by some often means loss of privileges by others. Thus, there must be some way of lending social legitimacy to the process, to save it from appearing entirely arbitrary and capricious.[41] Ritual acts not only to instruct people on which roles are being invested in which people, but also to legitimize this allocation of authority. Bloch, with inspiration from Weber, has put this nicely in arguing that those who "acquire power institutionalize it to make it less vulnerable from the attacks of rivals, they put their power 'in the bank of ritual.'" Bloch continues:

They do this by creating an office of which they are the legitimate holders, but which has reality beyond them. This is done by gradual ritualization of the power-holder's communication with the rest of the world and especially his inferiors. As this ritualization process proceeds communication loses the appearance of a creation on the part of the speaker and appears like repeats of set roles specified by the office which appears to hold him. Reality is thus reversed and the creation of the power-holder appears to create him.[42]

Yet once the rituals become established, they take on a life of their own in the same way that culture itself has an existence that transcends the changing collection of individuals who participate in it. The ritual legitimizes the power and institutionalizes it, but at the same time the role of power holder itself becomes transferable, no longer the property of any particular individual.

One of the most striking features of ritual, in fact, is its ability to accommodate conflicting symbols while reducing the perception of incongruity.[43] Thus in many societies, symbols of egalitarianism are combined with symbols of power and authority through rites involving elected officials. The grammatical rules of ritual symbolism are of a different sort than those of natural language, still less do they follow the rules of logic.

Mexican cargo system rites illustrate this ritual mixing of symbols of equality and hierarchy in a very different kind of social system. Among the Zinacantan Indians an egalitarian ideology prevails, enforced by the belief that people who grow wealthy must be witches and are to be dealt with accordingly. The cargo system is a ritual complex in which men can progress over the course of their lives up a hierarchy of offices in the communal ritual cycle. In order to occupy the higher rungs of this ladder, and thus acquire prestige, a man must be relatively wealthy, for the expenses connected with the ritual responsibilities are considerable. He must pay for a variety of community feasts and celebrations. Through these rites, the man is able to transform wealth into publicly recognized status, in spite of the otherwise tenacious adherence of the villagers to an egalitarian ideology.[44]

The King's Divine Powers

Where the gap between rulers and ruled is greatest, rites of rulers are most highly developed. The logical outcome of the sacralization of power is the divinization of the ruler, who reigns not by force, still less by illusion, but by supernatural powers vested in him. Such an ideology cannot take hold without a powerful ritual through which the ruler's supernatural power is made visible to the population.

"The earliest known religion," wrote Hocart, "is a belief in the divinity of kings."[45] Perhaps it would be better to say that there never were any kings without supernatural legitimation, for through most of human prehistory people had religious beliefs and rituals, though no chiefs, let alone monarchs. In societies around the world that have had kings, much of the ritual legitimating their rule was explained as reflecting their special supernatural position: the king links the people to the heavens.

The example of the royalty of ancient Hawaii and the intense sacral power emanating from the elite demonstrate this point. Their power was renewed through rites that commoners dared not perform; only the powers of the royalty afforded sufficient protection to approach the holiest shrines of the gods. Indeed, only the king could enter the god house; by conducting rites of sacrifice on behalf of the people, the king both expressed and reinforced his right to rule. Symbolic adornment further announced this ritual identification of royalty and the gods. The symbols of the gods and of the nobles were one and the same. Just as people had to prostrate themselves before the image of the divinities, they had to prostrate themselves before the passing nobles. Graven images of gods were clothed with special feather cloaks and helmets, spectacularly bright in a rainbow of colors. So too did the nobles dress, with the size of their cloak an indication of the amount of their power. The multi-colored splendor of the noble mirrored the divine splendor.[46]

On the other side of the world, Egyptian rulers legitimated their powers by their divine nature. Pharaohs were gods, not men. The king's right to rule was regularly re-legitimated by the performance of rituals, for he was theoretically the officiant of every temple of Egypt. Whether physically present at the rites or not, he was a part of them.[47]

Similarly, the people of ancient Persia worshipped their king. If he was not present at a state banquet, a special table was set for his spirit, which was served food and drink. When the king went out, an altar with a fire burning on it was carried in front of him in order to herald his special powers. This use of the sacred fire of kings was later taken up by Roman emperors. And in ancient Greece, according to Homer and Virgil, rulers were continually busy with sacred ceremonies. All this may seem of scant political interest today. Yet, though the idiom in which they are expressed differs, the ceremonial schedule of many modern leaders is little different from those of old. President and prime minister rush from one ceremonial occasion to another, thereby not only expressing the charisma of their office, but also enforcing their authority.[48]

The kings of Europe were believed to be divinely ordained, and consequently political battles of succession involved struggles over the rituals of royal legitimation. Henry IV of England was able to bolster his precarious claim to the throne thanks to the propitiously timed rediscovery of a vial of oil, said to have been given by the Virgin to St. Thomas of Canterbury. With this oil, Henry was hastily annointed king.[49]

The most dramatic example of the use of ritual to replenish the king's legitimacy in western Europe was the rite of the wonder cure. As a means of displaying their sacrality, the kings of England and France, from the Middle Ages through the eighteenth century, sponsored a rite of healing. By laying their hand on the sick, they restored them to health. In its classic form this was expressed in the 'touch' for scrofula. The scene was impressive, with hundreds, sometimes thousands, of unfortunate sufferers gathering, awaiting the king's appearance. Afflicted by a variety of ailments—primarily of tubercular origin—these impatient crowds were not a pleasant sight. With inflamed lymph nodes, and suppurations about their necks and faces, they awaited the royal cure, a fetid odor emanating from their sores.

By the seventeenth century these rites had become spectacular affairs in both France and England. Louis XIII and Louis XIV both regularly held curing ceremonies on major holidays. On Easter Day of 1613, 1,070 French sufferers were touched by the royal hand, and on Trinity Sunday of 1701, 2,400 subjects received the monarch's touch. Nor were the English to be outdone. In just four years' time, from 1660 to 1664, Charles II laid his hand on twenty-three thousand sufferers, and, though his medicinal pace subsided somewhat in the years that followed, by the end of his quarter-century as monarch he had laid his hand on one hundred thousand sick subjects.[50]

Again, however, this was not simply a way of reinforcing the political status quo; royal contestants also used the rites to advance their disputed claims of legitimacy and to undermine those of their adversaries. In the bitter fifteenth-century contest for the English throne between Henry VI and Edward IV, Edward succeeded in capturing the crown, but partisans of Henry pointed to their champion's continued touch for scrofula as belying Edward's credentials. Each side struggled to discredit the use of the royal rite by the other. Later, the usurper Henry VII solidified his legitimacy not only by further elaborating these rites of touching for scrofula, but also through the related rite of the 'hallowing' of cramp rings. By ceremoniously touching rings of gold and silver, Henry endowed them with powers protecting the wearer from epilepsy, thus dramatically seizing power.[51]

Rites of Rebellion

The legitimacy of rulers is expressed and renewed through rites of popular obeisance, from the long lines of pilgrims awaiting the royal touch in seventeenth-century France to the Moscow May Day paraders who pass by the central podium pledging loyalty and submission to their leaders.[52] But in some parts of the world alongside such rites are others that, at first sight, are baffling: rituals that are used to revile the leader rather than exalt him. In the classic case, among the Swazi of southern Africa, the people rise up each year on a special day and hurl insults at their king. The king, in turn, divests himself of the symbols of his office and sits naked on the dirt floor, scorned by his subjects.

The controversy over these rituals, largely based on ethnographic observations of a few African societies, occupies a major place in the history of structural functionalism. If society is viewed as composed of harmoniously integrated parts, these rites of rebellion seem anomalous. The king should be ritually elevated, not vilified, for if rites of exaltation are thought to bolster the ruler's legitimacy, rites of rebellion should undermine it.

In the classic anthropological solution to this conundrum, Max Gluckman argued that, in spite of their apparent delegitimating intent, such rites serve to reinforce existing power inequalities. Through such ritual, people are able to ventilate their natural resentments of occupying inferior places in society and, in so doing, allow the system to continue.[53]

As a corollary of his argument, Gluckman claimed that rituals of rebellion would occur only within an "unchallenged social order."[54] It is the safety valve of the steady state. Curiously, in a recent study, Christel Lane argues that rituals of rebellion are entirely alien to the Soviet Union; she holds such rites cannot exist there because the "existing social order is sacred."[55] This view stands in diametric opposition to Gluckman's, for Gluckman rightfully recognizes that all power tends to be sacralized. If rites of rebellion cannot occur where the political system is sacred, where can they occur? Yet both these formulations of the problem leave something to be desired, for they employ an overly mechanistic view of ritual.

Ritual does not act in such a simple and unambiguous way. Power is surrounded by ritual, but power holders cannot entirely control ritual. Traces of rebellion against authority everywhere creep into the ritual that envelops the mighty. Not only is it possible for rites of rebellion to occur in societies which are threatened by rebellion; such rituals should be expected to be everywhere connected with rebellion. To give a European example, the rites of rebellion that regularly recurred in France and other Catholic countries during Carnival did act as a safety valve, releasing pent-up hostilities and reinforcing the legitimacy of the elite. But these energies, and the potency of the rites themselves, could explode into actual revolt. To say that rituals of political disparagement only constitute rites of rebellion when they reinforce the status quo is to render the argument tautological.[56]

Closely related to rites of rebellion are rites of reversal. James Frazer wrote of one such ritual in *The Golden Bough*, when he described an ancient Roman festival in which, for just the one day all year, the "slave might rail at his master, intoxicate himself like his betters, sit down at table with them . . . Masters actually changed places with their slaves and waited on them at table."[57] Not far from Rome, many hundreds of years later, a strikingly similar ritual occurred. At the annual festa sponsored by a local Communist Party section in Bologna, I was munching on some tortellini, surrounded by throngs of working-class celebrants. Our waiter, suitably attired for the occasion, was a national senator who himself had once been a resident of that proletarian neighborhood. He scurried from kitchen to table, laden with trays filled with wine and pasta, as if his future depended on the quality of his service. He was waiter for the day.[58]

Although this ritualized degradation of the power holder may appear to undermine his authority, in fact it has the opposite effect. The Communist senator employs ritual as a convincing and efficient way to subscribe to the party ideology of egalitarianism. Rather than suffering a decline in status and legitimacy by such a performance, his status increases and his legitimacy as a political leader is affirmed. People are assured of the fundamental goodness of the leader, and their fears of uncontrolled power are allayed.[59]

These rites of reversal are but the extreme form of a much more common kind of ritualization that surrounds power holders in formally democratic societies. To the extent that power becomes aloof in such societies, the power holder is mistrusted. Just as there are rituals of exaltation, there are rites of equality, and both are important to the fortunes of the political leader. Through rites of egalitarian interaction the leader can symbolically express his adherence to the democratic ideal at the same time that his powers belie it.

4

The Virtues of Ambiguity

The president lay dead, assassinated in his limousine as the procession was making its way through the streets of Dallas. When the first chaotic reports swept through the nation, people were stunned, yet driven to action. Even across the sea, when news of the murder arrived, swarms of people took subways or buses, taxis or cars, to American embassies to pay their respects. More than a thousand gathered at the embassy in London just minutes after the news reached them that Friday night, November 22, 1963. In West Berlin, Mayor Willy Brandt called on his fellow citizens to place lighted candles on their darkened windowsills, and the city lit up in somber remembrance. Eight abreast, over ten thousand Poles lined up at the embassy in Warsaw, awaiting their chance to sign a hastily procured condolence book.

These expressions of sorrow were modest compared to the massive ritual outpouring of emotion that was building in the United States. People throughout the country felt an overwhelming impulse to lower American flags—on military bases, outside schools, in front of state and town buildings, and on the lawns of private homes. For many, who had only heard the first confused reports about the president's condition, the sight of the lowered flags produced overwhelming grief.

Lyndon Johnson felt compelled to ritualize his transition to the presidency without delay. Although in legal terms he automatically became president upon Kennedy's death, this was not enough. For Americans to think of him as their president, he felt, they must see him go through the inauguration rites. Aboard the plane that would take them back to

Washington, Johnson entreated Jacqueline
Kennedy, who had just watched her
husband die, to stand by his side for the
ceremony. The symbolism of continuity, and
of JFK's posthumous legitimation of the new
president, required her presence. The fact
that her suit still bore her husband's blood,
and her face the muted expression of pain
and grief, only made the rite more poignant.

Meanwhile, at the White House aides
raced to rearrange the East Room as the
widow wanted it for the casket: just as it had
been a century before when Lincoln was
assassinated. They found a photograph of
Lincoln's body lying in the East Room, and
workmen began frantically taking down
aluminum storm windows and putting up
black window curtains. Others scurried to
find just the right kind of yellow
candlesticks, while antique oil lamps were
procured to light up the White House
driveway.

Soon politicians from around the
country began arriving to pay their respects.
For a high-ranking politician not to
participate in these rites meant political
suicide. As several of Kennedy's most bitter
adversaries paraded in public grief by his
coffin, the dead president's aides walked out
of the room in disgust.

On Sunday, the day before the state
funeral, Kennedy's body was taken in
procession from the White House to the
rotunda of the Capitol, where tens of
thousands of people would line up to file
past it. With virtually all of the adults in the
country watching on television or listening
to radio accounts, a black-draped caisson,
pulled by six gray horses, drew up to the
White House to receive the casket. It was
the same caisson that had carried President
Roosevelt's body less than two decades

earlier. At the front of the cortege marched a uniformed honor guard of District of Columbia police, followed by the chiefs of the army, navy, air force, marines, and coast guard. Behind them a phalanx of drummers, their drums draped in black bunting, beat their muffled instruments at a slow, melancholy cadence. A company of navy men, the service in which Kennedy had become a wartime PT-boat hero, strode with the nation's flag. A minister, priest, and rabbi marched with them.

The caisson followed, with a color guard evenly drawn from the various branches of the nation's military. The one novelty was the presence of Green Berets, an addition Jacqueline Kennedy had requested to acknowledge her husband's special commitment to the anti-guerilla force. Behind this group marched a lone sailor, holding the presidential flag aloft. Finally, moving slowly, came a black-draped, riderless horse, the symbol of the fallen leader. With a black-handled sword in a silver scabbard hanging from the saddle, and shiny black boots with silver spurs lodged, pointed backwards, in the stirrups, the horse preceded the limousines carrying the Kennedy family, the new president, and the new First Lady.

At their destination on the steps of the Capitol, the mourners awaited the sounding of military honors. With the navy band playing "Hail to the Chief" at a painfully sad, slow beat, twenty-one rifles fired in unison every five seconds. As the throngs covering Capitol Hill looked on, the military escort lifted the casket from the caisson and slowly bore it up the same steps where, less than three years before, John Kennedy had given his memorable inaugural address.

On Monday, the funeral procession

began with marching soldiers and the
Kennedy family escorting the caisson back
from Capitol Hill to the White House. There,
the full cortege began, with the widow
leading the assembled mourners on foot to
the church. With over a million people
lining the streets in somber silence, a
panoply of world leaders marched by.
Behind the formless mass of foreign leaders
marched the members of the Cabinet,
divided into two even ranks, and, with an
almost martial air, the dead president's
closest aides.

As the procession made its way to the
steps of St. Matthew's, it was met by
Richard Cardinal Cushing, the archbishop of
Boston, who, after sprinkling holy water
about, led the procession into the church. At
this moment, just after noon, Americans
throughout the country stopped their other
activities to join in this rite of national
solidarity. Times Square was silent, as cab
drivers stopped their cars and got out to
stand with bowed heads. Trains stopped in
the middle of fields in the countryside,
buses drew to the side of the road, and
subway cars came to a halt in their
underground tubes. In all fifty state capitals
commemorations were being held, while
millions packed into simultaneous church
and synagogue memorial services. The
Panama Canal was closed, American ships
at sea launched wreaths into the ocean, and,
at that moment, on seven thousand U.S.
military bases around the world, artillery
sounded twenty-one-gun salutes.

Back at St. Matthew's, the cardinal,
resplendent in his scarlet robes, brought the
mass to a close. Outside the church, the
band struck up "Hail to the Chief" for
Kennedy for the last time. As the band

played, three-year-old John Kennedy, Jr., joined soldiers and policemen in a final salute, an image that would produce almost unbearable sorrow for millions of onlookers throughout the nation.

The procession then made its way to Arlington military cemetery through streets that one observer described as "aisles in a theater of solemn grief." At the burial site, fifty air force and navy planes—one for each state—boomed low overhead. They flew in inverted-V formations, with the point of the final V missing: the leader was gone. Trailing the military formation came the president's personal jet, Air Force One, dipping its wings over the cemetery mourners in a final salute.[1]

One of the major issues in modern social theory is the extent to which societies are held together by a feeling of solidarity among their members. Do people everywhere tend to feel a oneness with those around them and, if so, how is this feeling of solidarity produced and maintained? To this societal-level question can be added a more general query: how do the various kinds of political groupings—from states to political parties, from elites to revolutionary movements—create solidarity to further their ends?

Durkheim formulated what has become the most influential theory of social cohesion, emphasizing the key role played by ritual in producing and maintaining solidarity. His theory provides a powerful argument for the significance of ritual in the political process, but it has its limitations in dealing with political change. Here I make use of the valuable core of Durkheim's theory of solidarity and modify it to deal with the dynamic role of ritual in politics.

People are totally helpless if left by themselves, Durkheim argued. At the mercy of their fellows for their existence, they need to comfort themselves by continually reaffirming the strength and goodness of society. This need for social communion can only be met through some common action: "It is by uttering the same cry, pronouncing the same word, or performing the same gesture in regard to some object that they become and feel themselves to be in unison."[2] People can communicate their inner mental states only through the use of such symbols, and the way that they can best express their solidarity is by participating as a group in symbolic action.[3]

The rites of social communion not only express innate strivings for social solidarity, but also do much to build and renew them. Through participation in such rituals, people's dependence on their social group is continually brought to their mind. Just as importantly, it is through these rites that the boundaries of the social group, the group of people to whom the individual feels allegiance, are defined.[4] Ritual activity is not simply one possible way of creating group solidarity; it is a necessary way. Only by periodically assembling together and jointly participating in such symbolic action can the collective ideas and sentiments be propagated.[5] As Durkheim writes:

There can be no society which does not feel the need of upholding and reaffirming at regular intervals the collective sentiments and the collective ideas which make its unity and its personality. Now this moral remaking cannot be achieved except by the means of reunions, assemblies and meetings where the individuals, being closely united to one another, reaffirm in common their common sentiments; hence come ceremonies which do not differ from regular religious ceremonies, either in their object, the results which they produce, or the processes employed to attain these results.[6]

Social solidarity is thus seen as a requirement of society, and ritual an indispensable element in the creation of that solidarity.

In the inter-war period, Radcliffe-Brown was the preeminent anthropological proponent of this view. He argued that orderly social life can exist only if certain sentiments, those that regulate people's interaction, are shared by all members of a society. In his view, rituals are the means by which these sentiments are communicated and reinforced.[7] Fortes and Evans-Pritchard, in their influential 1940 volume on African political systems, similarly echoed Durkheim's claim that rituals do more than simply reflect the existing social system. People also endow the social system "with mystical values which evoke acceptance of the social order . . . The social system is, as it were, removed to a mystical plane, where it figures as a system of sacred values beyond criticism or revision."[8]

The problem with seeing ritual as reflecting the social order and reinforcing social harmony by elevating society to the mystical plane is that in many societies social life is riven with conflicts. Sacralizing the conflicts would appear to do little to bring about social harmony. Victor Turner deals with this point while following Durkheim's approach in studying the Ndembu, a West African people. Turner observes that Ndembu society is filled with instability and strife. New villages are continually being formed and old ones disbanded, while the different parts of the marriage and kinship systems articulate poorly with one another. In such a context, Turner argues, the value of ritual in promoting social solidarity is all the greater. Ritual does not express all aspects of the society, but only those that all Ndembu have in common. Rituals bring all the people together, sanctifying their unity and thus counteracting the divisive tendencies that plague their daily social life. The greater the divisiveness in society, the greater the need for compensatory ritual to hold the society together.[9]

The genius of Durkheim's theory of ritual is that it articulates a psychologically grounded theory of individual needs with a sociologically grounded theory of societal requirements. This is a bit paradoxical in that Durkheim crusaded against psychological reductionism in explaining social "facts" and he avoided detailing his psychological assumptions as such. But there is no denying the fact that individuals are very much present in his theory, and not simply as empty vessels that have been filled with societal norms.[10]

The intriguing aspect of Durkheim's view of ritual, as Nancy Munn has noted, is the importance it assigns to ritual in acting as the switchpoint between "the external moral constraints and groupings of the sociopolitical order and the internal feelings and imaginative concepts of the individual actor." Ritual dramatizes and energizes collective representations that mediate between society and the individual.[11] Munn thus dubs ritual a "societal control system" that links "the individual to a community of significant others through the symbolic mobilization of shared life meanings."[12]

The notion that rites are valuable in producing politically powerful solidarity did not arise in France with Durkheim. Aside from Durkheim's more distant forebears, a number of nineteenth-century French intellectuals publicly lamented the lack of nationalist enthusiasm and called for the creation of new rites to produce greater national communion. Most prominent among these intellectuals was the historian Michelet, whose work was immensely popular in the middle years of the century. In one book he mused, with barely concealed ecstasy, on the effect that properly organized national festivals would have on children. Surrounded by flags, the night lit up, soldiers with shining bayonets marching by, each father would tell his awe-struck child: "Look: there is France, there is *la*

Patrie! All this, it's like a single man. One soul and one heart. All would die for a single one, and each must also live and die for all."[13]

On the other side of the Atlantic, in the same period, Robert Winthrop gave a speech in Philadelphia at the dedication of a memorial to Benjamin Franklin. His premises were remarkably similar to those of Michelet. Winthrop lamented as "one of the neglected elements of our national life," the lack of sufficiently powerful national celebrations. He bemoaned the fact there was "no annual occasion when the hearts of the people thrill with an identical emotion, absorbing in patriotic instinct and mutual reminiscence all personal interests and local prejudice." What was needed, he argued, was "a day for reciprocal gratulation, our own— a time when the oath of fealty could be renewed at the same altar . . ." Indeed, his concern for the lack of integrative ritual was well placed. The year was 1856, and the nation was about to be torn apart by civil war.[14]

Michelet and Winthrop recognized what Durkheim would later argue more systematically: nation-states are no different from hunting and gathering societies in their need for rituals to support social solidarity. Seeking to find the simplest form of social organization so that he could more easily make out the basic principles underlying society, Durkheim turned his attention to the Australian aborigines.[15] He was especially intrigued by the rites surrounding Australian totems which, he thought, symbolized important social divisions. By engaging in these rites together, people defined the membership of their social group while reinforcing sentiments of mutual responsibility.[16]

Just as these Australians observed certain taboos together and thereby reinforced their bonds of unity, members of all societies, including modern nations, participate jointly in ritual to nourish their image of common identity and mutual obligation. Modern nations, like totemic clans, present themselves to people through symbolic representations of the collectivity. Such symbols include The Fatherland and The Chosen People, as well as many other forms. Rituals bring people together, identifying a common allegiance through these symbols and making them feel as one. At the same time, "negative" rituals—witch-hunts, impeachment trials, mass protests against perceived foreign enemies—reaffirm the national purpose and forge national solidarity through reaction.[17]

About fifty years ago, Max Lerner called the United States Constitution the American totem. His words recall Durkheim:

To understand the fetishism of the Constitution one would require the detachment of an anthropologist. Every tribe needs its totem and its fetish, and the Constitution is ours. Every tribe clings to something which it believes to possess supernatural powers, as an instrument for controlling unknown forces in a hostile universe. This is true of civilized nations as well. Men need always something on which to fix their emotions, whether positively in the form of adoration or deification, or negatively in the form of a tabu. Like every people, the American people have wanted some anchorage, some link with the invariant.[18]

The symbolic value of the Constitution as a unifying national force is clearly more meaningful to people than its content. National surveys regularly find large proportions of Americans disagreeing with clauses from the Constitution when they are not informed of their source, even though knowingly to question the validity of the Constitution is virtual heresy in the United States.[19]

According to Durkheim, people have an inevitable tendency to worship their society through rites devoted to its symbolic representation. This premise gave rise to the claim that Americans take part in a full-blown civil religion, a worship of the American state. The proponents of the civil religion thesis are, in effect, trying to save Durkheim's thesis from the contradictions faced in multireligious societies. Since Durkheim's classic study of ritual concentrated on a society having just one religion, religious worship could be equated with worship of the entire society. In polyreligious societies, however, such religious rituals may be societally divisive, as, for example, the Northern Irish case makes clear. Thus, where more than one religion is found, worship of the state gives people a way to express their unity. The very lack of a single common religion creates a "symbolic vacuum," as Michael Novak argues, "which the state itself inexorably fills."[20]

A number of years before the sociologist Robert Bellah kicked off the debate over American civil religion, the anthropologist Lloyd Warner, who had begun his career studying Australian aborigines, outlined a Durkheimian interpretation of American civic rituals in his study of Newburyport, Massachusetts.[21] The American ceremonial calendar consists of a cycle of holidays, he argued, "more sacred than secular," which "allow Americans to express common sentiments about themselves and share their feelings with others on set days pre-established by the society for this very purpose." He compared this calendar directly to that of the Australian aborigines and concluded that in the United States, too, "this calendar functions to draw all people together to emphasize their differences; and to contribute to their thinking, feeling, and acting alike."[22]

Warner illustrated this Durkheimian thesis by examining the celebration of Memorial Day in Newburyport. By focusing on the symbolism of death, he argued, Memorial Day acquires special force, converting the emotion generated by anxiety over death to common sentiments and action uniting people with fellow community members. Social divisions that are important in everyday life become unimportant at times when people perform such powerful symbolic action. The martyrs who are worshipped on Memorial Day "become powerful sacred symbols which organize, direct, and constantly revive the collective ideals of the community and the nation."[23]

If Americans have their civil religion, organized around flags, parades, and holy texts, the British have their rites of royalty, which continue to generate mass enthusiasm. Much of the scholarly response to these outpourings of popular effervescence is based on the same Durkheimian argument used to distinguish American civil religion. In the words of Shils and Young, for example, the 1953 British coronation "provided at one time and for practically the entire society such an intensive contact with the sacred that we believe we are justified in interpreting it . . . as a great act of national communion."[24] A number of years later, when Charles was invested Prince of Wales, similar scenes were reenacted and similar interpretations offered: "Most ordinary Englishmen were caught up in the spirit of the event to an extraordinary degree and communicated their enthusiasm to each other. The feelings about the Queen and Prince Charles, which the Investiture evoked, managed to fuse personal with public concerns in a symbolic fashion that Durkheim would have understood."[25] And at Prince Andrew's wedding in 1986, echoes of Durkheim could be heard from the journalists as well: "The day's pageantry blended patriotism and display, romance and nostalgia into a moment of national communion that can only be described as British."[26]

It would be hard to find a more convincing demonstration of the role of ritual in producing social solidarity than these British royal rites. But two questions arise: How representative are political rites like these, and is it true, as many Durkheimians assume, that such rites succeed by creating and maintaining a common belief system?

In fact, these royal rites represent just one kind of political use of ritual, one that acts to reinforce the status quo. Moreover, far from always creating solidarity by reinforcing shared values, one of the crucial functions of ritual is to produce solidarity in the absence of any commonality of beliefs. The traditional Durkheimian view of ritual largely ignores social conflict. It gives no attention to the role of ritual in bringing about political change, since ritual is seen as reinforcing a preexisting social system. What I intend to do in the remainder of this chapter is to salvage Durkheim's basic insight into the role of ritual in fostering social solidarity by showing how solidarity is produced without producing consensus, and by considering the use of ritual to produce solidarity in situations of conflict.

Solidarity Without Consensus

Just what is the relationship between ritual and belief? From a traditional Christian perspective, beliefs are primary, with rituals merely giving public expression to these preexisting beliefs. Durkheim, following Robertson Smith's pioneering work on the religion of the ancient Semites, argued that the reverse was more nearly the case. Looking at ancient religions, Robertson Smith concluded that it was ritual that was obligatory, not the explanation given to ritual. Indeed, "while the practice was rigorously fixed, the meaning attached to it was extremely vague . . . the same rite was explained by different people in different ways."[27] Edmund Leach subsequently amended this view, arguing that myth (or belief) and ritual are but two sides of the same phenomenon, two ways of making symbolic statements about the social order. He concluded, "myth regarded as a statement in words 'says' the same thing as ritual regarded as a statement in action."[28]

But rites are not simply stylized statements of belief. Participation in ritual is politically important even where participants interpret the rites differently. As the philosopher Ernst Cassirer pointed out, the person participating in ritual "lives a life of emotion, not of thoughts." Cassirer sees ritual as a deeper and more important part of religious life than belief, quoting Doutte, who says: "While creeds change, rite persists as the fossils of those extinct molluscs which serve to date geological epochs for us."[29] Indeed, what any theory of ritual and belief must explain is why rituals are so much more resistant to change than beliefs. Durkheim suggests an answer to this puzzle. Ritual is a means by which we express our social dependence; what is important in ritual is our common participation and emotional involvement, not the specific rationalizations by which we account for the rites.

What does this mean for understanding the role and importance of ritual in politics? It implies that ritual can serve political organizations by producing bonds of solidarity without requiring uniformity of belief. This is of tremendous political value, since what often underlies people's political allegiances is their social identification with a group rather than their sharing of beliefs with other members. Or, as Walt Whitman wrote, "I and mine do not convince by arguments: We convince by our presence."[30] Indeed, what is often so striking about ritual is the way it can carry people along in spite of apparent conflict between such action and their previously held beliefs. Beliefs are privately held and in some sense unknowable, while rituals provide public statements of acceptance of a group's position. As Rappaport argues, it is the "visible, explicit, public act of acceptance, and not the invisible, ambiguous, private sentiment that is socially and morally binding."[31] Socially and politically speaking, we are what we do, not what we think.

All this has been said most eloquently by James Fernandez, who, in his study of the Fang cult of the Bwiti of West Africa, distinguishes between social consensus and cultural consensus. By social consensus, he means general agreement about the appropriateness of certain actions in particular circumstances. By cultural consensus, he means agreement among the people on the meaning of that action. He argues that it is social consensus that holds the cult together rather than cultural consensus, and he concludes:

The prospect of men both acting together socially and thinking together culturally in entire mutuality cannot fail to inspire, but it cannot cause us to forget the degree to which men value acting together and distrust thinking together about the meaning of that action. It cannot cause us to forget that the gut-feeling or moral community created by coordinated interaction such as ritual may be actually threatened by an attempt to achieve moral community on the cultural level where the symbolic dimensions of interaction must be made explicit.[32]

Accepting this position does not mean abandoning Durkheim, but rather developing Durkheim's insights in a particular direction. After all, the emphasis on participating in ritual in common rather than believing in common reflects Durkheim's own emphasis on the primacy of ritual in promoting social solidarity. However, a recognition of the stability of differences in beliefs alongside joint participation in ritual leads to a more complex view of society and a fuller appreciation of the political importance of ritual.

Indeed, one should be wary about attributing too much significance to a person's set of political beliefs, since these are neither consistent nor are they all equally developed and strongly held. Consistency comes through common action, not only because the different participants have different beliefs, but also because each of the participants has a formless morass of conflicting beliefs. There is a misleading tendency to think of a person's "beliefs" as if they were so many equivalent objects residing in his or her mind,[33] and so well-formed, salient, harmonious, and meaningful opinions are assigned to individuals whose thoughts on the subject are ill-defined, logically incompatible, or of no necessary importance to them. The strength of political organizations comes less from any homogeneity of their members' beliefs than from the continuing expressions of allegiance through ritual.

Thus, ritual can promote social solidarity without implying that people share the same values, or even the same interpretation of the ritual. At the same time, it is necessary to face another criticism raised against the neo-Durkheimians, that far from promoting social solidarity in the first place, rituals often foster social divisiveness. The sociologist Steven Lukes, the most eloquent exponent of this attack, points to the Orangeman parade, which celebrates Protestant control of Northern Ireland, to illustrate this thesis. He argues that by strengthening certain social groups—in this case Northern Ireland's Protestant population—ritual may further polarize the society rather than unify it.[34]

This does point to an obvious limitation in Durkheim's thesis when it is applied to large-scale societies, but Durkheim's basic insight remains sound. The case of the Orangemen's parade is, indeed, a dramatic example of ritual serving social solidarity. But, in this instance, ritual bolsters the solidarity of one of the internal political antagonists, thereby undermining the solidarity of the society as a whole. Ritual proves valuable to many political groups and movements in just this way. All this leaves ritual with a more important political role than it would have if it only served to cement whole societies. Since it can bind together all sorts of political groups, it plays a key part in the political struggle of competing power seekers, factions, and subsocieties, and it is a valuable tool in building nationalism, societal chauvinism, and the conditions for war.

The Virtues of Ambiguity

It is the very ambiguity of the symbols employed in ritual action that makes ritual useful in fostering solidarity without consensus. Symbols can have a strong emotional impact on people, rallying them around the organizational flag, in spite of the fact that each participant interprets the symbols differently. This is not simply a matter of the same symbol having varying shades of meaning to different people; the identical symbol may have entirely separate meanings altogether. This is true of such symbols as the American Constitution and the Second World War or the hand signs for peace and victory. Not only do the symbols mean different things to different people, but the same symbol often has diverse and conflicting meanings for the same individual. Human thought processes do not require resolution of such conflict, nor any necessary consistency in symbolic use.[35]

Indeed, the joining together of opposites is one of the most striking features of political rhetoric. Even when carried to what appear to be embarrassing extremes—as when President Reagan named a new nuclear weapon "Peacekeeper"—such merging of opposites can be politically potent. Of course, such obfuscation does not always succeed in concealing glaring disparities between symbols and action. But it is one of the most powerful tools politicians have for placing otherwise unpopular political actions under a symbolic rubric around which people can rally. The value of this symbolic ambiguity to the machinations of the politically powerful, Goldschlager argues, goes beyond simply deluding the public. Propagation of ambiguous symbols creates an atmosphere of strangeness, danger, and fear. Since the political leader is able to juggle these symbols with apparent confidence, people recognize in him a person who is powerful enough to play with danger. It is to such a person that one's fate can be entrusted.[36]

Extending the meaning of a symbol from one referent to another is a common method politicians use to profit from ambiguity. Ritual offers a powerful means for the dramatic presentation of this new extension, a means particularly suited to make the new meaning compelling. This is often seen in the manipulation of symbols and accompanying rituals connected with traumatic national experiences of the past, especially wars, which lend themselves particularly well to a universal form of political symbolism, one that pits the enemy against the savior.

In the United States, rituals involving the American Revolution are used in this way, but such symbolism and ritual are especially strong on countries that have suffered more recently from warfare on their soil. The Soviet Union provides an apt case, for the devastation wrought by the Second World War had an especially traumatic effect on the Russian people. The Soviet government has created a series of holidays that feature symbolic representations of the Second World War, and these identify the strong feelings of solidarity aroused by that experience with solidarity for the current Soviet government.[37]

Postwar Italy offers a similar example. There, the suffering caused by the war, combined with national guilt about the Fascist regime that shared responsibility for the war, produced intense emotions. The symbolism of *la Resistenza*, the guerilla movement against the Fascists and Nazis in northern Italy in the last years of the Second World War, consequently offered an emotionally satisfying basis for building a new national solidarity. This symbolism is especially appealing in identifying the Italians with the anti-Nazi forces rather than as allies in the Nazi cause. The various Italian parties continue to struggle over the use of this symbolism, each attempting to identify itself with the complex of Resistance symbols. Party sections—whether Communist, Socialist, or Christian Democratic—are named after martyrs of the Resistance; flowers are regularly left at shrines commemorating these martyrs; songs of the Resistance are sung at political rallies; and various holidays connected with the Resistenza (for example, the dates of local battles, the date of allied victory) elicit furious competition among the parties for public ritual displays of identification with the Resistance. Not only does each party scurry to make this ritual connection for itself; each also tries to discredit the claims put forth in similar ritual ways by the other parties. The ritual battles of the Resistenza continue to rage decades after the last shot was fired.

Although political leaders may attempt to use the very ambiguity of ritual to produce political solidarity, they face a variety of obstacles. There is always the danger that ambiguity gives way to open conflict about the meaning of the rites. In such cases, rather than producing political unity, the rites can become just another battleground.

The attempts by a variety of French parliamentary leaders in the 1890s to create a national festival in honor of Joan of Arc provide a nice illustration of this. Bemoaning the continued deep division between "Catholic France" and "atheist France," between the partisans of the old order and the champions of the Revolution, a number of parliamentarians proposed instituting a national holiday commemorating Joan of Arc. Whereas the only real national holiday to that point, Bastille Day, had long been boycotted by the Church and the conservatives as glorifying immorality, the new holiday could bring together all of France and help provide a sorely lacking national solidarity.

This strategy was based on Joan of Arc's popularity across a wide range of the French population, itself a reflection of her symbolic ambiguity. Deified as the crusader for national independence, she was portrayed by the republicans and the left as the expression of the power of the people, a fighter against privilege and a precursor of the Revolution itself. For the right, buttressed by the 1894 Vatican decision that Joan should be venerated, she represented the liberator of the nation's territory who made possible the authority of the French royal house, as well as an example of the impossibility of separating French patriotism from French religious devotion.

Rather than bringing the two Frances together by offering them a common symbol of national communion, however, the celebrations soon degenerated into a bitter, and sometimes violent, battle of symbols. Indicative were the rites sponsored by a group of anti-clerics at the new Joan of Arc statue that were held shortly after the ceremonies sponsored by the

Church. The free-thinkers paraded by the memorial, carrying aloft a large wreath bearing the inscription: "Abandoned by the royalty and by the priests, To Joan of Arc, victim of the Clergy." Incensed by this scene, a group of students from the local theological faculty confronted the celebrants and a brawl ensued. So much for the building of national solidarity![38]

If they are to be successful, social movements must create their own esprit de corps, which Blumer defines as the "organizing of feelings on behalf of the movement." People must have a feeling of belonging together and participating in a common effort if their commitment to the movement is to be strong.

But how is esprit de corps created? The answer, according to Blumer, is, in good part, through "participation in formal ceremonial behavior." This includes mass meetings, rallies, large demonstrations, and commemorative ceremonies. Their value lies in providing people with a sense of social support, while the "psychology that is involved here is the psychology of being on parade." This all brings to mind Frederick Lewis Allen's comment about the allure of Ku Klux Klan membership, providing "a chance to dress up the village bigot and let him be a Knight of the Invisible Empire."[39] Through such ritual activities, people gain a sense of self-importance, while the "paraphernalia of ritual" that symbolizes the movement fosters "feelings of common identity and sympathy." By paraphernalia, Blumer means such symbolic vehicles as slogans, songs, cheers, expressive gestures, and uniforms. Because these symbols "acquire a sentimental significance symbolizing the common feelings about the movement, their use serves as a constant reliving and re-inforcement of these mutual feelings."[40]

A person's identification with an organization is only partly produced by the sharing of beliefs with other organizational members, for belief is a fragile, and not entirely necessary, bond. In this context, ritual provides a mechanism for people to express their allegiance to an organization or to a movement without requiring a common belief. Research on the psychology of commitment makes clear that ritual, by inducing people to take public action that identifies them with a political group, serves to build and reinforce the attachment the person has to the group.[41]

The potency of ritual in nourishing emotions of solidarity has been emphasized in Victor Turner's writings on the creation of *communitas*. According to Turner, social life contains within it an inherent conflict. On the one hand, societal norms determine what roles exist in society, placing some individuals above others in the social hierarchy. On the other hand, people recognize that they share a common humanity, a "generalized social bond." The very fact that people spend most of their lives in a hierarchically ordered society generates pent-up tensions that require periodic release. People must somehow express their unity with others, and this takes place through rituals. By employing ritual to bracket off normal time and the alienating relations connected with normal life, people are able to release enormous psychological energy. Such ritual activity evokes "experiences of unprecedented potency," flooding participants with affect.[42]

The emotional potency of ritual helps build political solidarity in many different contexts. With the rise to dominance of nation-states, for example, came the diffusion of the ritual of singing a national song, or anthem, on specified public occasions. From their creation in France and the United States in the late eighteenth century to their establishment in the new nations of Africa in the twentieth, such songs are remarkably similar in content and sentiment. Often calling for God's blessing on the state, they effusively praise the nation and call for undying loyalty. What is instructive about these songs is not their content per se, but rather their use of martial music together with graphic symbolism to create a highly charged emotional atmosphere of national solidarity. Though the American intellectual, for example, may try to examine this cauldron of emotionalism dispassionately, few of his neighbors can hear the chords of the national anthem in a crowded auditorium, with the masses of people singing along, without feeling the stirrings of emotion. Nor is the nonconformist, who refuses to stand up for the rite, likely to receive a dispassionate reaction from those around him. The ritual plays on the emotions rather than the intellect, though the emotions thus aroused have an impact on beliefs as well.[43]

I have already argued that nations can be perceived only through symbolic means. The rites of nationalism foster a certain view of the political world, including the notion that the individual's nation is the most righteous and its governmental arrangements the best. But at the same time, they foster a feeling of national solidarity. Boundaries are symbolically marked and all those falling within these boundaries are made to feel their unity.

Brazil offers an interesting example of how symbolic presentations foster national unity. Like many countries, Brazil celebrates an Independence Day, and, also as in many other countries, this celebration involves a military parade. Under Brazil's recent military government, these festivities were organized by the armed forces themselves and reflected the social order propagated by the authorities. This had three basic divisions: the soldiers, who did the marching; the public, which stood to the side;

and the military leaders, who towered above the proceedings. Various potent national symbols were manipulated in the ritual—from the flag to the coat of arms of the republic—and the visual effect of large numbers of identically dressed and armed men marching in unison further worked to produce an emotional impact on the audience. In short, while the parade mirrored important hierarchical distinctions in Brazilian society, it also, by bringing together masses of people and presenting them with potent symbols of their social identity, nourished a sense of nationalism and a sense of the rulers' legitimacy.[44]

Contrast this with another mass public display in Brazil, one that appears to have no bearing on the political realm: soccer. By symbolically identifying the team with the nation, soccer is a significant force in boosting national solidarity. Indeed, Snyder has gone so far as to claim that soccer is the single most important factor in uniting the people of Brazil: "Illiterate peasants in the hinterlands, who owned transistor radios, became one with the city slickers in fanatical support for the national team." The image of the nation and its government is blended with the symbolism of the national team, and international matches become rituals of national unity. The potency of this ritual was not lost on the military regime of the 1970s. The junta quickly adopted the stirring soccer tune of "Forward Brazil!" as its own, playing it regularly at presidential receptions and other official occasions. Moreover, slogans that had arisen at the national soccer matches—such as "No one will hold Brazil back any longer!" and "Brazil, count on me!"—were expropriated for use by the regime to build support for their actions.

Emotionally charged mass rituals are also used to build solidarity around more limited political units than the nation. The effectiveness of such rites is certainly well known to political party leaders in the United States. Candidates for nomination and for election employ rallies not to communicate substantive messages to their audiences but to create an emotional atmosphere that will stir their followers to go out and proselytize on their behalf. Those great American rituals, the quadrennial Democratic and Republican nominating conventions, serve an important purpose even in those frequent cases where there is no doubt who the presidential nominee will be. Dahl, indeed, has compared these ceremonies to "the traditional tribal rites prescribed for warriors before battle."[46] It is an apt analogy.

Rituals can also be vital means of keeping alive certain principles of political division that cross-cut other, seemingly more important political groupings. A colorful example of just how this works is found in the central Italian city of Siena, where twice a year an ancient pageant pits different neighborhoods (*contrade*) against each other in various competitions, culminating in a horse race through the center of town. For the people of Siena, the *palio* is one of the emotional and communal highlights of the year, with each group of neighbors banding together and expressing their unity in opposition to the other neighborhoods. Indeed, it is the ritual of the palio that has sustained contrada unity and inter-contrada competition through the past centuries. What is found in Siena, then, is the solidarity that comes from common participation in ritual, but it is not the solidarity of an entire society, nor even of the entire community, but a solidarity that pits ritually marked neighborhoods of the same city against one another.

How can one make any sense of such seemingly anachronistic rites? The key to explanation lies in the fact that the contrade are not class-homogeneous units. In what is otherwise a class-conscious society, these local units cross-cut the basic social divisions. Italy's political elite, in Siena and elsewhere, has long sought to discourage the formation of solidary groups based on working-class or peasant membership. Indeed, this is one reason why the elite long gave such strong support to the vertically organized Church. The less such people were organized, the less of a threat they posed.

The Medici princes who conquered Siena were aware of this, and they sought forms of popular enthusiasm that would provide an alternative to groupings that strengthened the solidarity of the powerless. With interclass membership, the contrade, in Silverman's words, "became a strong counterforce against class-based horizontal alliances." To reinforce this cross-class basis of solidarity, and this contrada-centered view of social identity, the later city elite continued to patronize the palio. The palio ritual thus served as a regular means of expressing and nourishing social solidarity, but, far from expressing and reinforcing groupings of people living in common social circumstances, the contrade rites obscure these distinctions.[4/]

Solidarity and Belief

People need to construct a social identity for themselves and they need to express a sense of communion with others. Ritual provides an important means of accomplishing these aims. Yet, this does not mean that any particular social grouping is ritualized, still less that ritual only fosters solidarity around the society or the nation as a whole. Rituals also build solidarity within the various conflicting segments of a society and thereby foster social strife. Indeed, not only are rites used by revolutionary groups to build solidarity aimed at overthrowing the government, they are also used by groups who reject the prevailing definition of the nation or the society altogether, as in the Basque and Palestinian cases.

The common reading of Durkheim, that he identified solidarity with value consensus in his interpretation of ritual, misses the strength of his argument. His genius lies in having recognized that ritual builds solidarity without requiring the sharing of beliefs. Solidarity is produced by people acting together, not by people thinking together.

5

The Ritual Construction of Political Reality

It was a day Ronald Reagan had been dreading, even though it was a rite he felt bound to endure. Walking beside Chancellor Kohl amidst the German military graves of the Bitburg cemetery, he looked stiff and uncomfortable, in awkward contrast to his usual ease. While Kohl brushed aside tears, Reagan looked straight ahead, careful not to glance down at the graves lest he spy the SS symbols sprinkled across the cemetery lawn. In spite of the West German's desire to clasp hands over the graves of the war dead, the President's arms remained resolutely at his side. Earlier in the day, at a hastily arranged visit to the Bergen-Belsen concentration camp, Reagan had laid a wreath inscribed "From the people of the United States." At the cemetery, in a ceremony that he was able to limit to just eight minutes, the wreath he presented bore a somewhat different message: "From the President of the United States."[1]

On November 5, 1529, the imperial procession marched into Bologna. Three hundred horsemen opened the procession, followed by a troop of Spanish lords holding their standards high, three hundred armored knights with red plumes brightening their helmets, ten large cannons on chariots, and fourteen companies of German musicians, waving their huge banners and playing fife and tabor. But this was just the beginning. Carrying the imperial standard came two lords on horseback, followed by squadrons carrying ordnance, German cavalry, then one hundred of the emperor's bodyguards and a group of Spanish grandees. Preceding Charles V, who had been crowned king in southern France nine years before, rode the

Grand Marshal carrying the imperial sword. Charles wore a complete suit of armor, a golden eagle permanently perched atop his helmet. He carried a scepter in his hand and his horse shone with a cloth of gold studded with jewels. Four knights strode alongside him, bearing a magnificent canopy over his head. Eight pages waited on him, and two cardinals rode at his side.

As he entered the gate of the walled city, Charles was presented a cross, which he kissed. In a gesture that was of more immediate interest to the crowds lining the way, the imperial heralds flung handfuls of gold and silver to the multitudes—8,000 ducats in all. Awaiting the emperor at the gate were twenty cardinals, who then dismounted from their mules to salute Charles. Amidst lavish decorations depicting classical themes and artwork portraying the great triumphs of the Roman empire, Charles made his way to the towering church of San Petronio at the center of the city, where he finally dismounted and approached Pope Clement VII, who sat on his papal throne. The emperor bowed three times to the pope, who then got up from his throne and gave Charles three kisses on the cheek. Together they walked down to the central piazza where, amidst the cheering crowd, 2,000 blasts trumpeted this historical reconciliation of pope and emperor. Three months later, in ceremonies that were no less spectacular, the pope crowned Charles emperor, ending years of bloody struggle between them.[2]

I have argued that ritual plays an important political role in bringing about solidarity where consensus is lacking, but this does not mean that it has no effect on political perceptions. Indeed, ritual is an important means of influencing people's ideas about political events, political policies, political systems, and political leaders. Through ritual, people develop their ideas about what are appropriate political institutions, what are appropriate qualities in political leaders, and how well the world around them measures up to these standards. Political understandings are mediated through symbols, and ritual, as a potent form of symbolic representation, is a valuable tool in our construction of political reality.

A flourishing branch of modern psychology, in fact, deals with the question of how people assimilate their perceptions of the outside world into their understandings of how the world works. It is an area of cognitive psychology that offers many intriguing clues for discovering how people's political ideas can be influenced by ritual. I turn to some of these here.

Schematic Thinking

In the heyday of behaviorism, many psychologists disparaged the study of thought processes, arguing that knowledge of what goes on in people's heads is unobtainable and, in any case, not needed to understand behavior. A given stimulus would produce a given response. But in more recent years, cognitive psychologists have shown that behavior cannot be predicted simply on the basis of environmental stimuli; rather, behavior is mediated by cognitive constructs. These constructs are similar to what many anthropologists mean by culture, an integrated body of symbols that structure experience. But what most interests the cognitive psychologists is not the learned nature of these constructs, but the constraints that the nature of the human mind places on the thinking process. As Bandura puts it: "Cognitive factors partly determine which external events will be observed, how they will be perceived, whether they leave any lasting effects, what valence and efficacy they have, and how the information they convey will be organized for future use."[3]

One of the major theoretical ideas in contemporary cognitive psychology is concerned with the way knowledge is organized in the individual's brain. The basic premise is that we do not go out into the world with a clean cognitive slate, ready to interpret what we see in whatever way the experience itself suggests. Rather, the information we take in through our senses is "processed" through "preexisting systems of schematized and abstracted knowledge."[4] These organized knowledge structures are termed schemas.[5]

Since we cannot perceive everything that we come upon in the world, our perception must be selective. What we do perceive out of the multitude of possibilities is not simply a matter of chance. Rather, our perceptions are the product of the schemas we have, which make certain kinds of information worth noting at the same time that they suggest a means of interpreting that information. As Neisser pointed out, "information can be picked up only if there is a developing format ready to accept it. Information that does not fit such a format goes unused."[6] These schemas define certain expectations about events and experiences and suggest appropriate responses to them.

Social schemas are the abstract symbolic systems that structure our cognition of the *social* world. As with all schemas, these are important because they permit tremendous cognitive economy. We are, in effect, "cognitive misers," who try to get the most out of our limited mental abilities. By providing us with a means of selecting what stimuli to attend to, and then by fitting this information into a predefined system of symbolic understandings, social schemas provide cognitive efficiency at the same time that they lend stability to the symbolically constructed world in which we live. Schemas "direct attention to relevant information, guide its interpretation and evaluation, provide inferences when information is missing or ambiguous, and facilitate its retention."[7]

Like the social world in general, the political world can overwhelm us with its complexity and ambiguity. Most people ignore the great majority of available political information, and they skip lightly over the ambiguity and contradiction in the little information they take in.[8]

There is thus a strong conservative bias built into our perceptions and our thought processes. Since we interpret what we encounter in daily life in terms of preestablished schemas that tell us what to expect, we tend to ignore information that conflicts with our schema, just as we seize on any information that appears to confirm it.[9] We all make use of a variety of schemas, however, and this gives us some cognitive flexibility, for by switching from one to another we can interpret the same realm of experience in different ways.[10]

Our likeliness to employ one schema over another depends partly on its availability, or to use the technical term, on *construct accessibility*. The more frequently a construct, or schema, is employed, the more "available" it becomes for dealing with future experience.[11] A schema's accessibility is not only based on how frequently it has been used in the past by an individual, but also by its *salience* in memory. Salience, in turn, depends on both the *prominence* and *distinctiveness* of the schema. A schema is prominent to the extent that it has striking or intense features; it is distinctive insofar as its features are unusual.[12]

When people try to make sense of their experience, a number of cognitive rules come into play. Tversky and Kahneman refer to these principles as *heuristics* for making judgments under conditions of uncertainty. One of these heuristics, termed *representativeness*, is especially relevant here.[13]

Representativeness refers to the extent of similarity between the observed phenomenon and the constructs or categories the person has for interpreting them. We interpret the world by dividing up our perceptions into categories: people may be policemen, say, or soldiers, or firemen. We assign an object or a person to an appropriate category as a result of judgments we make about which category the principal features of the person or object resemble.[14] The individual is limited, however, by the conceptual categories he or she has and is led by these to focus on certain aspects of phenomena and not others. The person who employs an inappropriate schema can pay a high price. In battle, the soldier who divides people up by the color of their hair rather than the color of their uniform may not live to make another schematic mistake.

Through such categorization of experience, we assign meaning to events in the world around us (indeed, we come to define just what constitutes an event in the first place). As the example of the confused soldier illustrates, our mode of categorization is much more than a matter of passive speculation. The schema we select influences our subsequent behavior, what we regard as the appropriate response to what we see going on in the world. By placing the individuals we meet into categories of people who are presumed to share important characteristics, we avoid having to attend to all possible features of each individual we encounter. This, in turn, encourages us to deal with people as members of certain categories. Social interaction, then, is heavily conditioned by the symbols of social identity that people employ, for these symbols are used for social categorization. In the extreme case, where people wear uniforms that symbolically trumpet one principle of categorization as particularly appropriate, they are especially likely to be dealt with as members of the well-defined category and have only certain features of their identity attended to, or even assumed, and the rest ignored.[15] Once internalized, schemas exert a powerful influence on our perceptions and judgments. So strong is the power of schemas we hold that our perceptions are likely to be bent in the direction that makes them conform best with the schema.[16]

Yet, this cognitive approach does recognize the possibility of change. The potential for cognitive change derives from two factors. First, there is frequently more than one schema available to the individual for interpreting an experience, and thus the choice of which schema to apply affects how that experience is interpreted. The struggle to elicit political support thus involves the struggle to establish one schema as the appropriate one for interpreting experience. Second, just as people must acquire schemas in the first place, old schemas are sometimes revised or even rejected, while new schemas are embraced.[17] Such change is especially likely when a sharp disjunction exists between our perceptions and the categories provided by our schemas. Change is also more likely when the action we take in response to our interpretation of events leads to unanticipated and unwelcome results. In such cases, we may judge our action to be inappropriate and so place our schema in question. The processes by which such changes occur are as yet little understood.[18]

Other Cognitive Characteristics

In addition to the cognitive features loosely associated with the schema concept, some other cognitive elements are worth mentioning in considering the role of ritual in establishing political beliefs. Although cognition is sometimes contrasted with emotion, it is well known that emotion and cognition are closely intertwined. For example, the more emotionally aroused people become, the more narrowly is their attention focused and the fewer are the categories they use to interpret their experience. One implication of this is that the more emotionally excited people become—whether with anger, grief, or exaltation—the less finely tuned are the distinctions they make in categorizing other people. Carried to an extreme, the emotionally-charged individual may operate with an overriding cognitive division of people into just two categories: "with me" and "against me."[19]

Also of obvious relevance to the problem of politics and ritual is the fact that people pay much more attention to vivid, concrete information than to more colorless, abstract information. This was put in pithy, if callous, terms by Joseph Stalin. The death of a single Russian soldier, he observed, is a tragedy, while the fact that millions of soldiers die is simply a statistic. People pay more attention to concrete cases than to abstract data. Not only are they apt to remember such information, but they are also more likely to base their later judgments and behavior on it. "Information may be described as vivid," explain Nisbett and Ross, "that is, as likely to attract and hold our attention and to excite the imagination to the extent that it is (a) emotionally interesting, (b) concrete and imagery-provoking, and (c) proximate in a sensory, temporal, or spatial way."[20] The correspondence of these criteria to the features of ritual is more than a little striking. In this context, it is not surprising that a mass demonstration has greater political impact than a speech.

We are also more likely to notice an object, a person, or an activity when it is distinctive within its environment.[21] One individual in soldier's uniform in a platoon of soldiers is much less likely to be noticed and remembered than that same individual standing amidst the uniformed soldiers but dressed only in a bathing suit. The same might be said for the ritual officiant dressed in a cleric's robes, or the king garbed in royal robes with a crown on his head.

Our perception of objects or people is also influenced by the order in which we learn their different features. This is referred to as the *primacy effect*. We employ our earliest observations about the characteristics of an object (or person or situation) to make generalizations about the nature of that object. This entails placing the object in a broader category and filling in the blanks in our knowledge by assigning it a series of characteristics in harmony with that categorization. As new information about the object becomes known (we learn that the person previously considered a reactionary has always voted Democratic), we may revise our view to accommodate that knowledge, but due to the conservative nature of our cognitive processes, our view is "revised insufficiently in response to discrepancies in the later-presented information."[22] This theory not only helps account for the lasting importance of childhood rites—such as saluting the flag and attending Independence Day festivities—in shaping adult perceptions and views, but it also argues for the great power of those who are in a position to provide others with the earliest information on a topic.

The form in which a message is received also has an effect on how the receiver interprets it. For example, statements made in generic terms have a much stronger impact than statements made with various qualifications. The hypothetical example of two Radio Albania broadcasts is instructive. The first asserts that "Some imperialists have occasionally used a few inhuman weapons." The second version contains the pithier message: "Imperialists use inhuman weapons." The first has little cognitive and emotional impact, while the latter packs a much greater wallop, even though its message is highly ambiguous.[23] The power of ritual communication lies just in its lack of caveats, in the very ambiguity of its symbols.

Anthropological Perspectives on Ritual and Cognition

Recent developments in cognitive psychology have had some impact on anthropological studies of ritual, but most of the essential ideas outlined here have also been expressed in other disciplines.[24] The core concept of schema, for example, was formulated many decades ago. The philosopher Alfred Schutz argued that the interpretation of lived experience consists of the "referral of the unknown to the known, of that which is apprehended in the glance of attention to the schemes of experience."[25] Experiences do not *have* meaning, according to Schutz; rather, we give meaning to our experience through reflection.

That observations are shaped by preexisting interpretive schemas and that perception itself depends on these schemas has long been argued by anthropologists as well. Two decades ago, Rodney Needham told the story of a blind man who is operated on and is able to see for the first time. Recovering from the operation, he "is afflicted by a painful chaos of forms and colours, a gaudy confusion of visual impressions none of which seems to bear any comprehensible relationship to the others." How could he make sense of this onslaught on his senses, if not by developing a means of categorization that would allow him to see patterns, to select certain observations and neglect others?[26]

Some anthropologists view culture itself as nothing other than the system people have for categorizing the natural and social world. Of special relevance here are the ritual studies conducted by Mary Douglas, who used the concept of schema in 1966, citing as her source for this use a 1932 work. She argues that, by employing schemas to make the world appear more predictable, we make ambiguous perceptions conform to our schematic pattern and so reject discordant observations. A conservative bias is built into our thinking; observations that might threaten our guiding schemas are ignored or distorted so that the schemas are protected from disconfirmation. Social reality is too complex and ambiguous for the human organism to handle, hence the innate drive to render it simpler and unambiguous, to create order where there is only chaos.[27]

Nor has this psychological approach to cognition been limited to anthropologists and philosophers; a number of political scientists have recognized the powerful political implications of these schemes of simplification. Murray Edelman expresses this best in his comments on political myths:

Myths and metaphors permit men to live in a world in which the causes are simple and neat and the remedies are apparent. In place of a complicated empirical world, men hold to a relatively few, simple, archetypal myths, of which the conspiratorial enemy and the omnicompetent hero-savior are the central ones. In consequence, people feel assured by guidance, certainty, and trust rather than paralyzed by threat, bewilderment, and unwanted personal responsibility for making judgments.[28]

The Ritual Representation of Political Reality

As one important kind of symbolic activity, ritual structures our experience; it guides our perceptions and channels our interpretation of those perceptions.[29] Through ritual, as through culture more generally, we not only make sense of the world around us, but we also are led to believe that the order we see is not of our own (cultural) making, but rather an order that belongs to the external world itself.

Rituals seem rather peculiar devices to accomplish this mission, for they seem practically to call attention to their artificial, made-up nature, and, by extension, to the fact that all culture is invented rather than discovered.[30] But, paradoxically, what is persuasive about ritual is the way it discourages critical thinking. As a form of formalized communication, it presents us with a well-defined course of action. In Bloch's words, "What is being said is the right thing because by the acceptance of the formalisation of language it has become the only thing."[31]

Some of these features of cognition help explain just what it is about ritual that makes it an important means for structuring our political perceptions and leading us to interpret our experiences in certain ways. For one thing, ritual highlights a limited series of vivid images, while excluding much else from the perceptual field. Only certain characteristics of those involved in the rites are brought to attention, and these are often focused on with great intensity. At the same time, the symbols employed suggest a particular interpretation of what is being viewed.[32]

In a simple, though sanguinary, example, the Mexican royalists, after they had finally put down the popular uprising led by Hidalgo in the early nineteenth century, were eager to communicate a certain view of the rebels and of the fate of others who might be tempted to join them. What could be simpler, or more to the point, than the solution they found? After shooting the leaders of the revolt, they hacked the heads from the corpses of Hidalgo and three of his revolutionary colleagues. These they took to the town of Guanajuato, which the rebels had stormed not a year before. There, they put each rotting skull in a separate metal cage and placed one cage at each of the corners of the town granary. Apparently feeling the message had continuing efficacy, they left the heads to decay on the granary for the next decade. Though there are no surviving reports on the effect these incarcerated crania had on the townspeople, it is easy to believe that the message was powerful.[33]

A slightly less grisly and more recent example is provided by the ritual battles waged during the capture of the U.S. embassy in Iran. A group of Iranians descended upon the embassy in 1978, occupying it and holding the Americans there hostage. What meaning should be assigned to these events? Indeed, first, amidst the revolutionary upheaval in Iran, the meaning to be attributed was unclear to both Americans and most Iranians. Over the following days, and then months, a process of symbolic manipulation took place, in which ritual forms occupied a prominent place. It was through these rites that the Iranian and American publics assigned clear meanings to what had occurred, and thus were able to relate the actions of otherwise unknowable individuals to their own lives.

Though perhaps unaware of the primacy effect, the captors lost no time in staging mass rites to spread the interpretation that they wanted placed on their action. Through a variety of symbols of American villainy, which simultaneously linked the United States to the image of the wicked Shah and identified the captors with the work of Allah and the Iranian revolution, the kidnapping was portrayed as an act of national liberation on behalf of all the Iranian people and, more broadly, for the benefit of all the oppressed peoples of the world.

Back in the United States another ritual complex arose, spreading from the White House to Knights of Columbus posts in countless communities. President Carter did all he could to dramatize the events. Lights on the White House Christmas tree were to remain dim until the hostages were freed; life could not go on as usual; the president could not leave the White House to campaign for the Democratic nomination. The nation was under siege. If the Iranian revolutionaries had blown up the embassy, killing all the Americans there—an approach later used by Lebanese in dealing with the American military presence—there would have been no national crisis, and little opportunity for ritual elaboration. But the holding of these people captive allowed a national crisis to be symbolically mounted. Flags throughout the nation were lowered to half-staff, where they remained as constant reminders of the embattled state of the nation until the captives returned, many months later.[34]

As these examples make clear, the emotional climate that ritual can create is itself a powerful molder of beliefs and perceptions. Clifford Geertz put the matter succinctly:

It is in some sort of ceremonial form . . . that the moods and motivations which sacred symbols induce in men and the general conceptions of the order of existence which they formulate for men meet and reinforce one another. In a ritual, the world as lived and the world as imagined, fused under the agency of a single set of symbolic forms, turn out to be the same world. . . . [35]

Ritual not only structures our perceptions and suggests certain interpretations of our experience, but it does so in a setting that makes these perceptions and interpretations particularly salient and compelling.[36]

Although Durkheim recognized that rituals inculcate particular political paradigms, he only considered rituals that unify all of society, rituals that offer a conservative and consensual interpretation of the polit-

ical order. But, rituals are not simply a blind product of communal existence; rather, they serve certain political interests and undermine others.
They must be analyzed in political terms to determine how they arise,
how they are maintained and altered, and who benefits from them.[37]

Far from simply reflecting existing power relations, rituals are often
important in doing just the opposite, that is, in fostering beliefs about the
political universe that systematically misrepresent what is going on. As
Da Matta put it, "rituals hide and reveal; they can both delude or clarify."[38] What is important about the effects of ritual on cognition is as
much what the rites lead us to ignore as what they lead us to see. Political
rituals erase as much history from our memories as they inscribe on
them.[39] Far from simply projecting the political order onto the symbolic
plane, ritual propagates a particular view of the political order.[40]

The notion that ritual leads to particular interpretations of political
relations is certainly nothing new to the world of diplomacy, where extreme care goes into the proper planning of ritual occasions so that the
desired view of political relations is fostered. Indeed, messages sent
through such rites have regularly led to altercations and even bloodshed.
This phenomenon dates back well before the first nation-states arose to a
time when rival chiefs vied for ritual positions of honor. But a better-
documented encounter is found in the case of the British ambassador to
China.

From their earliest contacts with the Chinese court, British envoys
faced difficulties with the rituals surrounding the emperor. In the emperor's presence, according to Chinese tradition, all must kowtow, that
is, completely prostrate themselves, in a supreme display of inferiority.
When, in the early nineteenth century, Lord Amherst was sent by Britain
to speak with the emperor, he was tormented with indecision and concern. To kowtow to the emperor would be an act incompatible with the
"national dignity" of Britain, in effect, a national disgrace. A fierce argument with the emperor's representative ensued, with Lord Amherst trying to persuade the court to allow him to bow by bending his knee rather
than completely prostrating himself on the ground. A compromise was
finally reached by which, for this occasion only, Lord Amherst was ex-
cused from kowtowing as long as he bowed nine times before the imperial table and, when received by the emperor, knelt on one knee nine times
in succession.

Yet this was not the end of it. Enraged by this British affront to his
position, the emperor insisted that the envoy kowtow to him, refusing to
accept any of the British presents unless this were first done. Lord
Amherst, fearing national humiliation, responded that he would kowtow

to the emperor only if a Tartar of a rank equal to his did the same before a portrait of the British monarch, or if the emperor issued a decree stating that from that time forward any Chinese ambassador to the British court would kowtow before His British Majesty. When this request was summarily refused, Lord Amherst announced his intention of returning to Britain immediately and, indeed, he left forthwith. He might bow, but he would not scrape![41]

As this example suggests, the use of ritual to convey a particular interpretation of political relations can be quite conscious. Yet, as this case also makes clear, participants' recognition of the artificiality of the ritual in no way undermines the emotional energy invested in it.

Japan provides a more recent, but no less dramatic, example of this conscious use of ritual to channel political perceptions by using emotion-laden symbolism. In downtown Tokyo, Yukio Mishima, Japan's preeminent novelist, carried out the time-honored ritual of suicide. Long a crusader for a return to the old virtues and the old regime, Mishima sought the restoration of imperial rule and the rebuilding of the military. On November 25, 1970, Mishima and a group of followers invaded Tokyo's military headquarters. Taking a general hostage, they demanded to address the troops. Twelve hundred soldiers were hastily assembled in the courtyard below, while Mishima, with hopes of provoking immediate rebellion, called on the troops to adopt the "spirit of the *samurai*" and restore imperial Japan. Bringing his insurrectionary pitch to its stirring crescendo, Mishima thundered "Let us die together!" Yet, rather than sparking any mutinous spirit among the soldiers, he was met by their laughter. Furious at the soldiers' derisive response, Mishima cried out three times "Long live the Emperor!", and returned inside where he prepared himself for the suicidal rites. Following the ritual script, he plunged a sword into his stomach to disembowel himself; his chief lieutenant (after several ineffectual tries) completed the ceremony, slicing off Mishima's head.

In spite of its quixotic and self-conscious character, Mishima's ritual suicide had a significant impact in Japan. Because the rites combined such rich historical symbolism with a dramatic display of political devotion, the act provoked widespread reflection on the problems afflicting the current political system. Mishima's ceremonial death became a symbol in the Japanese search for a renewed nationalism following the debacle of World War II.[42]

Although few political rituals are as dramatic as this, the element of drama is often a central part of what makes the ritual effective. The vividness of the symbolism makes the ritual more memorable and its effect longer-lasting, while the emotional excitement produced in the ritual focuses attention on these symbols and discourages more critical inquiry into what is being asserted.

Both the power of ritual to communicate relations between countries, and the use of ritual drama by a leader to send a powerful message to his own people are illustrated by the case of the king of Swaziland. In 1968, after decades of British colonial rule, Swaziland was to become an independent state. The ceremonies through which this independence would be marked took on tremendous importance to the Swaziland elite, who would use the rites to define a new political status quo. One of the most important elements involved continuing relations with Britain, and hence the presence of a suitable representative of Britain at the rites. It was thus with considerable pleasure that the king and his aides learned that the Duke of Kent, Queen Elizabeth's cousin, would represent Britain. A photograph of the duke was prominently displayed in all the official programs prepared for the ceremonies. Shortly before Independence Day, however, the duke's mother died, and other ritual duties made his visit impossible. The Swazi leaders still held out hope that a suitable replacement would be found, but were sadly disappointed to learn that in place of the duke, Sir Francis Loyd, the outgoing British envoy to Swaziland, would represent Her Majesty. It was too late to remove the duke's picture from the program. The ritual message the Swazi leaders wanted sent—the importance Britain attributed to its relations with the newly independent state—was undermined.

In spite of the rebuff, the ceremonies went on as planned in a large open stadium where thousands of Swazi could attend. Subhuza, King of Swaziland, entered the stadium in a huge new black Cadillac limousine, wearing full, traditional regal garb, replete with high-plumed headgear. After circling the stadium he mounted the dais, as the band played the new national anthem. Upon the subsequent arrival of Sir Francis, the band struck up "God Save the Queen." Swaziland might no longer be a British colony, but the importance of the country's continuing ties with Britain were ritually trumpeted.

The ceremonies followed European example until, beneath the seated diplomatic dignitaries, the voices of thousands of Swazi warriors began to rise with the rhythmic warrior song of old. The king and prime minister left their seats, joining the swaying regiments below as the ceremonial dancing began. The crowd let loose with piercing whistles of approval, as the two leaders danced along. The dance moved to its crescendo when the warriors—the king in the middle—crouched beneath their shields and then, in unison, jumped forward, raising their shields high over their heads. It was a stirring moment. The king and prime minister returned to their seats, leaving soon thereafter in their stretch Cadillacs to attend the diplomatic reception.[43]

There are many ways the king could have communicated to his people what the nature of the new state would be, as well as the nature of his role as king in such a state. He could have issued proclamations, or made sure that instruction on the new system be provided at schools and at political meetings. But it is unlikely that any of these could compare with the rituals at Independence Day for getting his message across. The emotions generated at the ceremonies, together with the mix of symbolism portraying the new blend of European and traditional principles of rule, produced a powerful cognitive effect.

It is much more difficult to appreciate the role played by ritual in shaping our own political perceptions because we are so caught up in the symbols and symbolic actions that surround us that we lack perspective. In this regard, Edelman points to the ritual dramas regularly performed at Geneva, Vienna, or wherever American and Soviet leaders engage in highly publicized arms negotiations. With such powerful dramatizations of the leaders' desire for disarmament and peace, Edelman asks, who can doubt the good intentions of the national leadership?[44] What matters most to the public is not the physical result—who has ever seen a nuclear weapon—but the symbolic process.

Indeed, American political leaders participate in an endless series of public spectacles. In these carefully crafted dramatic presentations, powerful symbols are manipulated to create a trusting mood and to engender particular political beliefs both about the participants and about the political system itself. The president is undoubtedly the country's premier ritual actor and symbol manipulator. Standing in a national shrine—such as the White House—next to the dual icons of the flag and the presidential seal, his entry trumpeted by the rousing chords of "Hail to the Chief," the president is in a potent position to influence individuals' perceptions of people they have never seen, of places they will never visit. Like other ritualists, the president manipulates symbols and rites. Yet, he does not totally control them, since they have a history of connotations and emotions for the people who look on. Ritual is precious to politicians because of its emotional power and because of its history of associations, but that same power can rouse discontent. If used unskillfully, rituals can provoke perceptions that are dangerous for the very power holders who sponsor them. Ronald Reagan painfully learned this lesson on his visit to Bitburg.

Properly staged rites are just as important to the political lives of congressmen, governors, and big-city mayors, whose fortunes can rise or fall depending on their success in staging ritual events. In a political ethnography appropriately called *Tribe on the Hill*, anthropologist Jack Weatherford turned his attention to the culture of the United States Senate. Relations between senators and the American public, he concluded, are dominated by ritual encounters and displays.

One of the most dramatic, and most effective, of these public rituals involves the congressional committee hearings that periodically dominate public attention. In these carefully staged events, with television cameras in place, the congressmen are able to pit themselves in ritual combat against the forces of evil. A senator can try to look virtuous at the expense of an opponent in a debate on the Senate floor, but this can be a risky proposition if he faces articulate opponents. By contrast, the senator risks nothing by setting himself against a Mafia mobster, foreign spy, or drug czar in the hearing room. These rituals encourage the belief that the congressman is working on behalf of his constituents, protecting them from the forces of darkness, while they also shore up confidence in the political system itself. The fact that they may have no practical impact in repressing organized crime, international espionage, or drug trade is of interest only to the scholar, not to the politician or the public.

These rites, however, can sometimes be valuable in changing certain political beliefs, as was evident in the congressional hearings on President Nixon's misconduct. Through these rites, a hodge-podge of disparate actions were welded together into a dramatic unity, a unitary symbol: Watergate. This presentation had a powerful effect in creating the public view that the president should be impeached, a view previously—with many of the same facts available—identified with the lunatic fringe in American politics.[45] The popularity of the public congressional hearings in 1987 that dealt with the shipment of arms to Iran and illegal payments to the Nicaraguan guerillas showed the continuing appeal of these ritualized battles with the forces of political darkness.

These examples illustrate the ubiquitous political rituals through which public enemies are identified, denounced, or cast out from the community. Bergesen offers an intriguing perspective on these political witch-hunts, seeing them as "ritual mechanisms that transform individuals, groups, organizations or cultural artifacts from things of this world into actors within a mythical universe." Arguing from a Durkheimian perspective, he suggests that such "rituals are the social 'hooks' that keep sacred transcendent forces present in the lives or ordinary people and relevant for everyday institutional transactions." In other words, through such rites people come to interpret their everyday experiences in terms much larger than themselves or than anything they could directly experience. Rituals help define these terms of "us" and "them," hero and fiend. In light of this ritual transformation of everyday life into a battle of larger forces of order and disorder, Bergesen argues, "It is no wonder . . . that witch hunts appear irrational, terrifying and *unreal*. In some sense, they are truly unreal and irrational, for their logic derives from the symbolic significance of the ritual encounters between mythical beings and forces and not from the actualities of human conduct."[46]

Highly dramatic political rites are not a monopoly of the elite, although the people with the most power are also most often in the best position to sponsor such ritual. Attempts to change public policy are also made through ritual drama, and skillful manipulation of symbols in such presentations can affect the beliefs of broad portions of the population.

In the United States, both the civil rights movement of the 1960s and the anti-Vietnam war movement of the late 1960s and early 1970s show just how central such dramatizations are to groups seeking to change popular political perceptions. To fit into the appropriate mythic mold, though, such dramatizations require both a villain and rich symbols of villainy. This is just what the 1963 Alabama civil rights demonstrations succeeded in arranging. Marching through the streets of Birmingham or Selma alone would not have gotten the activists far in changing perceptions throughout the nation. It was Sheriff Bull Connors, with his police dogs and fire hoses, who made the symbolic battle of good and evil convincing.[47]

In the case of all successful—even moderately successful—popular movements for changing political perceptions, initial attempts to employ symbols for dramatic purposes are followed by more highly structured rites. The symbolic presentations become increasingly uniform throughout the country. Ritualization entails the repetitive use of emotionally charged symbols in symbolically significant locations at symbolically appropriate times. New symbols need not be introduced in rites in order to get people to change their political beliefs. The American flag can be as valuable to the civil rights marchers as to the Ku Klux Klan in defining what is good for the community. The trick is to introduce dramatic variations on these powerful symbols, to change their meaning by changing their context.[48]

The Rites of Bitburg

Symbols have a history of cognitive and emotional associations. Their power comes in part from this history: the childhood memories they arouse, feelings of past solidarity, the way they have been used to define one's own identity and one's understanding of the world. Meanings cannot be declared by fiat, although new shades of meaning are continually being created and old ones lost through the incessant attempts by political leaders to manipulate the symbols.

Ronald Reagan's phenomenal popularity in the United States was in no small part the result of his skills in reworking symbols and staging rites to guide perceptions of both the external world and of his own heroic role in it. It should not be surprising, then, that the most withering criticism he faced in his first five years in office regarded his planned participation in a ceremony, a rite to be held at Bitburg in the spring of 1985. He had overseen numerous controversial political and military actions, from the firing of thousands of striking air traffic controllers to the stationing of American troops in chaotic Lebanon, yet none of this produced the furor that met his planned cemetery rite.

The decision to stage this rite can be traced to two ceremonies observed in 1984. In the first, leaders of the World War II Allied powers celebrated the anniversary of the Normandy landing. German Chancellor Kohl expressed his consternation at being excluded and was, by way of consolation, invited by French President Mitterand to celebrate a memorial ceremony at a Verdun cemetery where victims of the First World War were buried. Kohl and Mitterand solemnly embraced amidst the sea of crosses.

But the Verdun ceremony was not what Kohl needed. In fact, no one was concerned about the memories of the First World War, and thus there was no need for ceremonial reconciliation. What the Germans were uneasy about was being identified with Nazism and all its evils. Mitterand had ritually absolved the Germans from the wrong war. What was needed was a rite of absolution for the Second World War, one that would take place on German soil and have powerful symbolic content. The place was the Bitburg German cemetery; the sacral aura would be furnished by Ronald Reagan.

The value to Kohl of the rites lay in dispelling the discomfiting hold the Nazi symbolic legacy had on his countrymen. In doing so it would bolster his own stature and that of his party. The very staging of the rites demonstrated Kohl's power, all the more so when Reagan, by coming, showed he valued his commitments to the German chancellor above the passionate pleas of American congressmen and the American people. Reagan, for his part, was repaying Kohl in this ritual currency for a variety of both symbolic and material expressions of support that Kohl's government had given Reagan in the past. The most notable of these involved stationing a new battery of nuclear missiles on German soil. More generally, such rites would help nourish a political alliance that kept large numbers of American troops in Germany.

If Mitterand had tried to substitute the symbolism of the First World War for that of the Second, Reagan's mission was to transform the symbolism of the Second into that of the First, to take a still festering historical sore and, in Habermas's words, "bestow on the present the aura of a past that had a settled look."[49] Reagan began these attempts to rewrite the past even before he left for Germany. Defending his planned visit to honor the German war dead, Reagan told an American audience that the dead German soldiers were "victims of Nazism also, even though they were fighting in the German uniform, drafted into service to carry out the hateful wishes of the Nazis. They were victims, just as surely as the victims in the concentration camps."[50] The evils perpetrated by Nazi Germany, in other words, were the responsibility of a tiny group of leaders who forced the German population to do their wicked bidding. Although this was the message Reagan hoped his cemetery ceremonies would send, he ran afoul of the symbolic construction his listeners had already placed on the events of the past.

For many Germans, by contrast, the rites were a satisfying vindication of their view that Germans had been unfair victims of malicious propaganda, that the Second World War was but another in a long line of European conflicts for which no one people could be singled out for blame. And even in the United States, where a chorus of protest sang out, the rite had a significant cognitive effect on millions of people. The fact that their president could join the head of the German government in such a rite in a German war cemetery would bolster the intended view of German innocence, of Germans as victims, rather than perpetrators, of Nazism.

In the end, though, the symbolism of Nazism proved too powerful for Reagan. Years after they had killed their last Allied soldier, decades after they had herded their last victim into nearby concentration camps, these dead German soldiers continued to inflict pain. And just as Reagan struggled to redefine the symbolism associated with his ritual appearance, his antagonists sought to discredit the rite through their own manipulation of powerful symbols. This took various forms. Perhaps most notable was the "discovery" that among the thousands of graves were thirty-eight bearing the mark of the Nazi SS, the *Schutzstaffel*, Hitler's infamous secret police. So powerful was the stigma associated with the symbol of the SS that Reagan's own staff grew alarmed about his participation in the rites, while the presidential aides who had helped select the site were showered with scorn. The Nazi army was one thing—indeed, it was not a Nazi army but a *German* army—the SS quite another in the symbolic construction of the German past. Just what the one or the other had actually done many decades before, few but the historians knew, but the symbolic distinction remained potent.[51]

Reagan's ceremonial plans spawned special outrage in the wake of his earlier announcement that he would not visit a Nazi concentration camp memorial during the trip. Yet, when the president subsequently added a visit to the Bergen-Belsen concentration camp, many of these same critics protested. As a *Jerusalem Post* writer cried out, "Do not drag our dead into your reconciliation with Kohl's Germany. Do not mention our victims in the same breath with those who lie at Bitburg."[52] By holding the two ceremonies on the same day, the concentration camp victims and their killers would be placed on equal symbolic footing.

The ceremonies went ahead, but Reagan did what he could to douse the sacred flames he had helped kindle. From refusing to join hands with Kohl at the cemetery, to his last-minute pilgrimage to Bergen-Belsen, he was able to tailor the rites to reduce his political costs. Kohl, for his part, made sure that the lesson of the rites was not lost in the face of Reagan's backsliding. The "visit to the graves in Bitburg," he declared, is "a widely visible and widely felt gesture of reconciliation between our peoples, the people of the United States of American and us Germans, reconciliation which does not dismiss the past but enables us to overcome it by acting together."[53] The past exists through its symbolization in the present. Overcoming the past means changing the symbols of the present, and this is just what the rites at Bitburg were intended to do.

In its editorial the day before the cemetery visit, the *Chicago Tribune* lamented that we "live in a time when symbolism has replaced rational debate as the medium of political exchange."[54] The medium of political exchange has always been symbolism; it is an exchange that not only redistributes political rewards, but that also builds our political understandings. If symbols and rituals are used to build political reality, it is because, as humans, we can do it no other way.[55]

Political Belief

By repetitively employing a limited pool of powerful symbols, often associated with emotional fervor, rituals are an important molder of political beliefs.[56] Political reality is defined for us in the first place through ritual, and our beliefs are subsequently reaffirmed through regular collective expression.

But what does all this say about our rational faculties, our ability to think logically and independently, to examine a problem critically and come to a rational conclusion based on an examination of the evidence? Unfortunately, it suggests that this view of our essentially rational nature is hard to defend. As Edelman observed, our most cherished and deeply rooted political beliefs are rarely if ever subjected to debate or critical examination. It is just because they are so deeply held that any sincere debating of their validity is so threatening, for to do so is to recognize implicitly that they may be erroneous.[57]

Years ago, from his cell in a Fascist prison, Antonio Gramsci made a similar point in explaining why it is so difficult to change people's political beliefs. Among the masses, he argued, "philosophy can only be experienced as a faith."[58] People do not construct their basic political conceptions by critically analyzing competing political ideas. Rather, people acquire these ideas through the society they live in, and these ideas are largely determined by those who exercise control (hegemony) over the society. Indeed, Gramsci held that a world in which a person's political beliefs depend on rational argument is inconceivable, for in such a world individuals would have to change their beliefs whenever they encountered a better educated and more articulate antagonist.

Gramsci was certainly not claiming that it is impossible to change people's beliefs, only that it is naive to imagine that such change can be brought about simply through logical persuasion. For an individual to change his or her beliefs without subjecting them to rational debate, a conducive social context is needed. Ritual provides just such a context. For example, when political elites form new international alliances, there is commonly considerable ritualization—much public hand-shaking and mutual parading of symbols. The nation or group that had previously been mistrusted, or even loathed, is placed in a new symbolic nexus, viewed now as benevolent rather than threatening.[59] Reagan and Kohl were still engaged in this process decades after the end of the Second World War, while the periodic rites of Arab unity aim to shore up popular perception of alliances that have very little other basis.

Ritual can foster common action without necessitating common belief. People's behavior may in many circumstances be better explained as the reaction to situational pressures rather than as the manifestation of a deep-seated belief. Indeed, a number of psychologists have warned against assuming that people's attitudes determine their behavior, in spite of the fact that this notion seems intuitively correct.[60]

According to Snyder and Swann, people are especially likely to act on the basis of situational pressures rather than out of underlying beliefs in social settings that:

(a) are novel, unfamiliar, and contain sources of social comparison . . . (b) make individuals uncertain of or confused about their inner states . . . (c) suggest that one's attitudes are socially undesirable . . . or deviant . . . and (d) sensitize one to the perspective of others and motivate concern with social evaluation and conformity with reference-group norms. . . . [61]

But I would take this a step further by suggesting that the beliefs themselves are not so stable. In social settings of this sort, people may change their beliefs as well as their actions. Public political rituals meet many of these criteria. They are occasions on which people are brought closely together with others and in which failure to conform to the behavior of others can make one a pariah.

The powerful emotions that rituals can induce lend further force to this drive toward conformity. Bagehot, in 1912, observed the uncharacteristic servility of that imperious English statesman, Lord Chatham, when the peer went to consult the king. During these conferences with King George III, Lord Chatham remained kneeling at the king's bedside. "Now no man," Bagehot observed, "can argue on his knees. The same superstitious feeling which keeps him in that physical attitude will keep him in a corresponding mental attitude."[62]

The primacy of the ritual in determining behavior is expressed in a rather different way in the Islamic world. What is important to be a good Moslem, the Prophet Muhammad reportedly advised, is to pray five times each day; what goes on in the worshiper's mind, he said, is between him and Allah.[63] Participating in the common prayers with fellow worshipers is a firmer basis of religious allegiance than private belief. Yet, at the same time, people who participate in ritual tend to develop beliefs that rationalize their behavior and support their allegiance.

Cognitive Dissonance

In examining the role rituals play in influencing political beliefs, I have already suggested the tensions which are produced when people hold beliefs that are mutually inconsistent or when a person's beliefs differ from those of socially significant others. These are both situations in which an individual is especially likely to change beliefs. Such change, however, is not a foregone conclusion: people go through life holding logically inconsistent views, and they are also likely to hold some views that differ from those of their neighbors.

The now venerable theory of cognitive dissonance, first fully developed in the late 1950s by Leon Festinger, sheds some light on this problem. By dissonance, Festinger simply refers to inconsistency among cognitions; conversely, consonance refers to the mutual consistency of beliefs. The theory holds that when people find themselves holding dissonant beliefs, they experience psychological discomfort. This, in turn, motivates people to reduce the dissonance. Not only do people try to reduce dissonance when it appears, they also actively avoid situations and information that are likely to increase dissonance.[64]

One common kind of cognitive dissonance occurs when our perception of events in the world conflicts with our beliefs about those phenomena. In such cases, Festinger argued, "the reality which impinges on a person will exert pressures in the direction of bringing the appropriate cognitive elements into correspondence with that reality."[65] The greater the amount of dissonance an individual experiences, the stronger is the pressure to reduce it. Cognitive dissonance is especially powerful in situations where our beliefs conflict with those of socially important others, and where no simple empirical referent can be used to demonstrate the validity of one's own beliefs. Where strongly held views are shared with others, though those beliefs seem to conflict with what is observed in the outside world, little cognitive dissonance is experienced.

The Nazi salute offers a good case for applying this approach to political ritual. The salute symbolized allegiance to the Nazi regime in general and to Hitler in particular. One of its purposes was to provide a systematic means to spot disloyalty, while simultaneously serving to reinforce the allegiance of the masses. Bruno Bettelheim recognized the political and psychological potency of the rite:

To Hitler's followers, giving the salute was an expression of self assertion, of power. Each time a loyal subject performed it, his sense of well-being shot up. For an opponent of the regime it worked exactly opposite. Every time he had to greet somebody in public he had an experience that shook and weakened his integration. More specifically, if the situation forced him to salute, he immediately felt a traitor to his deepest convictions. So he had to pretend to himself that it did not count. Or to put it another way: he could not change his action—he *had* to give the Hitler salute. Since one's integration rests on acting in accord with one's beliefs, the only easy way to retain his integration was to change his beliefs.[66]

The power the rulers exercised through this Nazi ritual, as Bettelheim pointed out, came not only from the fact that it reached "the minutest and most private life activities of the individual but more, that it [split] the inner person if he resist[ed]."[67]

Emotion and Cognition

To celebrate the tenth anniversary of the death of Lassalle, the socialist workers in Breslau, then part of Germany, dedicated a new red flag. In addition to the inscription, "May 23 1863, Ferdinand Lassalle," the front of the flag bore the mottoes "Liberty, Equality, Fraternity," and "Unity is Strength." On the back was the legend: "The social-democratic workers in Breslau 1873." The power that this socialist icon held over those who identified with its symbolism is told by its checkered itinerary of the ensuing decades. When Bismarck's anti-socialist laws threatened the flag, it was smuggled into Switzerland. Later, during the Nazi regime, it was buried in a garden, then hidden in a plumber's cellar. When Red Army officers, moving into Breslau at the end of World War II, heard of its existence, they went to salute it, but its guardian refused to give it up to them. Later, when Breslau was annexed to Poland, the flag was smuggled out to West Germany, where it was given to the Social-Democratic Party, which was presumed to be the legitimate heir of all it represented. Over several decades, people had risked imprisonment and worse to guard the flag.[68]

If political rites encourage certain interpretations of the world, they do so in no small part because of the powerful emotions that they trigger. Our perceptions and interpretations are strongly influenced by our emotional states, but the process works very much in the reverse direction as well. Our fears are aroused, terror incited, joy created through rites that channel our political perceptions. Before concluding this look at how ritual affects people's political beliefs and perceptions, I should like, briefly, to consider the role played by emotion.

The "ultimate force of symbols," writes Ioan Lewis, "depends at least as much on their power to stir the emotions" as on their cognitive content.[69] But these psychological processes should not be split into two separate forces. Indeed, what makes the emotional side of ritual so interesting and so politically important is frequently its connection to particular cognitive messages. Rituals do not simply excite, they also instruct. But the potency of that instruction depends heavily on the power of ritual to place the individual in a receptive frame of mind. Sensory devices of all kinds are used to affect the person's emotional state, from rhythmic chanting to stylized dancing and marching, from powerful singing to the doleful tolling of bells. The most effective rituals have an emotionally compelling quality to them: they involve not just part of the personality but the whole personality.[70] In the intensity of ritual, people focus their attention on a limited range of symbols. The greater their emotional involvement the more the rest of the universe is obliterated, and the more the symbols embodied in the rites become authoritative.[71]

What is the source of the emotion found in ritual? A clue is provided by Durkheim, who attributes the emotional intensity of rites to the fact that they express the powerful dependence people feel toward their society. But in addition to regularly scheduled rites, rituals are also typically found when individuals confront transition points in their lives. The strong emotions associated with ritual here reflect the inner conflicts, uncertainties and fears that afflict people in such circumstances.

In funerary ritual, for example, the emotional state of the mourner is affected by confronting death and by the changes in his life implied by that death. People use ritual to cope with these strong emotions, a practice from which many political systems have profited by inserting their own symbolism. From burials at Arlington military cemetery in the United States, to party- or state-organized funerals in certain communist countries, there is a ceaseless quest to politicize these emotionally potent rites.

Political forces also create new rituals to produce emotional states that can be used to influence people's perceptions of the political world. This is found in all contemporary societies. In the Soviet Union, for example, earlier idealistic views of people as rational actors—and hence of ritual as a form of superstition to be jettisoned—gave way to intricate plans to use the emotional impact of ritual to structure political beliefs.[72]

Just how the emotions generated by ritual infuse and affect its cognitive message remains an intriguing question. Victor Turner provides one of the best-known anthropological answers to this question in discussing the two poles of ritual, the emotional and the cognitive. In the performance of ritual an exchange takes place between these poles, and the emotions aroused in ritual infuse the cognitive view fostered by the rite, rendering it compelling. Like Durkheim, Turner sees such beliefs largely in consensual terms. This exchange of meanings between the poles of ritual "makes desirable what is socially necessary by establishing a right relationship between involuntary sentiments and the requirements of social structure. People are induced to do what they must do."[73] But the value of his argument regarding the exchange of qualities between the poles of ritual goes beyond this static and homogeneous view of social life.

Observers of crowd behavior have often noted the contagiousness of emotion. This operates in collective rituals as well, where people's emotions are heavily influenced by the emotions displayed by others around them.[74] Collective rituals are seductive, and the emotions previously associated with such collective ritual celebrations continue to be felt when similar rites are performed later, alone, or in more limited company.

Ritual can be seen as a form of rhetoric, the propagation of a message through a complex symbolic performance. Rhetoric follows certain culturally prescribed forms whose built-in logic makes the course of the argument predictable at the same time that it lends credence to the thesis advanced. Kenneth Burke described this as the "attitude of collaborative expectancy" that the formal pattern of rhetoric elicits from its audience. The very form of the presentation leads us to believe in the message put forth. Of special relevance to an understanding of the political uses of ritual is the emotionally compelling structure of we/they imagery. As Burke writes:

Imagine a passage built about a set of oppositions ("*we* do *this*, but *they* on the other hand do *that*; *we* stay *here*, but *they* go *there*; *we* look *up*, but *they* look *down*," etc.). Once you grasp the trend of the form, it invites participation regardless of the subject matter. Formally, you will find yourself swinging along with the succession of antitheses, even though you may not agree with the proposition that is being presented in this form. Thus, you are drawn to the form, not in your capacity as a partisan, but because of some "universal" appeal in it. And this attitude of assent may then be transferred to the matter which happens to be associated with the form.[75]

Successful ritual has just this structure. It creates an emotional state that makes the message uncontestable because it is framed in such a way as to be seen as inherent in the way things are. It presents a picture of the world that is so emotionally compelling that it is beyond debate.

6

Rite Makes Might: Struggling for Power through Ritual

On April 15, 1967, they took over the streets of Manhattan, the largest peace demonstration in decades. A hundred thousand (some said over a quarter million) strong, the festive crowd massed at Central Park, having poured into the city by the busload from cities, suburbs, and campuses near and far. At the front of the march strode Martin Luther King, Benjamin Spock, Harry Belafonte, and a variety of other civil rights and religious leaders, arms linked. For four hours marchers would spew out of the park in a continuous mass, making their way past cheering and jeering bystanders to United Nations Plaza. Amidst the anti-war signs and banners voices rhythmically boomed: "Hell no, we won't go," and "Hey, hey, L.B.J., how many kids did you kill today?"

In demonstrations within the demonstration, various groups preceded the march with their own ceremonies at the park. On one verdant knoll, youths brandished signs proclaiming themselves the United States Committee to Aid the National Liberation Front of South Vietnam. Before them stood a forty-foot tower, made of black cardboard and topped by the blue and red flag of the Vietcong. Nearby, others raised the stars and stripes up a flagstaff high enough so that all could see the flag aflame. An hour before the march began, seventy young men stood on top of a rock in the park and began to kindle little white slips of paper—their draft cards. Hundreds of others came to join them, forming themselves into a circle. The individualized cigarette-lighter immolations gave way to more centralized combustion as new arrivals passed their cards on to a young man who

presided over a fire-spewing coffee can.
Cheers greeted each man who passed his
card along to its flaming end, and chants of
"Resist, resist!" peppered the smoky scene.
Not to be excluded from the ceremonies,
some women took their partners' draft
cards, carefully burning half before
returning the other half to their mates to
complete the job.[1]

Four and a half centuries earlier, near the
banks of the Elbe, another crowd composed
largely of students and young men gathered
in Wittenburg. It was December 1520, three
years after Luther had posted his Ninety-
Five Articles on the church door. The pope
had just issued a formal condemnation of
Luther and his teachings, and in response,
before the assembled university officials,
Luther ceremoniously burned the papal bull
that had condemned him. His student
supporters soon joined him, a hundred of
them mounting an early carnival procession.
They had built a large boat-like float, the sail
of which consisted of a giant papal bull.
Students poured into it; some played music,
while one of them dressed as a charioteer
and another as a trumpeter. The latter
carried another papal bull skewered by his
sword. As the float rolled merrily through
town, others joined in the celebration.
Students tossed firewood into the float as it
passed through the streets, together with
books by Luther's principal clerical
opponents. When the float returned to its
starting point, Luther's supporters piled up
the accumulated bulls and books and set
them afire. Around the conflagration they
celebrated, singing religious and popular

songs. One of the participants, dressed as
the pope, removed his tiara and tossed it
into the flames.[2]

———————————

Far from simply propping up the status quo, ritual provides an important
weapon in political struggle, a weapon used both by contestants for
power within stable political systems and by those who seek to protect or
to overthrow unstable systems. Having already examined what makes
ritual so valuable to the political process, I now turn to the question of
how ritual is used by individual contestants for power and by groups that
seek to change the political system itself.

Since people need to express their social dependence through ritual,
political forces that have control over community rites are in a good
position to have their authority legitimized. Through such rituals, authority is dramatized and thereby glamorized.[3] This dramatization not
only establishes who has authority and who does not; it also defines the
degrees of relative authority among the politically influential. On the Red
Square reviewing stand in Moscow, proximity to the center of the stage is
an important indicator of the latest result of the Soviet leadership's on-
going power struggles. In past centuries, and more recently among nonliterate peoples, there was no way to express such a power hierarchy
except through ritual and related symbolic behavior. In the absence of
writing, it was ritual that defined people's power relations.[4]

But the point of this chapter is to show that these rituals are far more
than means of communicating the result of political struggles that take
place in other arenas. Rituals have their own power and are themselves
an important field of political struggle.

Communication Through Ritual

In the struggle among political competitors, ritual is used both to make
claims to power and to send messages to the public. This is seen at all
levels, from international diplomacy to village politics.

The case of the British ambassador who would not bow, although a
bit exotic, is not at all atypical of the ritual regulation of international
relations. Diplomacy without ritual is inconceivable. Protocol is ever
important, and the right symbols must be manipulated in just the right

way. Tremendous anxiety can attach to the most apparently trivial details. Wars have continued and people have died because of arguments
over the number of sides of the table to be used for negotiations and the
relative positioning of the participants. And, of course, when a foreign
official is to be received, there is always great concern over just what level
of ceremonial is to be performed by the hosts, with potential ill consequences if that reception is too elaborate or not elaborate enough, as the
Soviet ambassador to Iceland discovered at the 1986 summit.

In Renaissance Venice, officials kept a record—the *Libro Cerimoniale*—to record the exact ceremonies performed for each visiting dignitary so that future guests could be received with the precise ritual
elaboration due them. For each visitor a raft of ceremonial decisions had
to be made: how far out into the lagoon must the senators (and how many
senators) go to meet the visiting dignitary; should the doge—the Venetian head of government—rise from his seat or come down from his dais
in the Collegio in order to greet an ambassador; how valuable should the
gold chain be that was the customary gift to foreign representatives; and
what were the Venetian officials to wear at the reception? Why were these
important? Because they defined the status of the Venetian polity vis-à-
vis other polities in a way that could not be done as effectively by any
other means.[5]

The Venetian authorities were not only concerned with the niceties
of rituals aimed at other states; they were even more preoccupied with
their own relative ritual positioning, for this defined their place in the
political hierarchy. It was in the ducal processions that the political rank-
ings were given concrete form. Indeed, as Muir puts it, "in effect, the
ducal procession was the constitution." There was no written document
in which these lines of authority were specified, and through the rites the
various patrician families competed to assert their place over others. In
the procession, "position was everything."[6]

Although the Venetian processions or Soviet reviewing stands had a
built-in fluidity in defining power relations, a similar use of spatial symbolism in imperial China showed much more fixity. Indeed, they were
engraved in stone. The staggering scale of Chinese emperors' tombs is
well known, but the practice of accompanying burials is less so. Emperors, particularly in T'ang times, rewarded their key political supporters—including their ministers and generals—with the promise of burial
at the imperial mausoleum. This not only helped solidify their followers'
continued political support, but also guaranteed subsequent support
from their followers' descendants, whose own political fortunes were
greatly enhanced by the honor of having their ancestor buried by the

emperor's side. The relative standing of members of the imperial elite was thus posthumously defined by the size, shape, and siting of their graves.[7]

Perhaps nowhere was the political struggle over ritual geography so well developed as in France, where members of the aristocracy, clergy, and Parlement battled for centuries over their ritual placement. In 1484, the Parlement of Paris enhanced its authority by successfully asserting its rightful place in royal processions to be just before the king, the place of honor.[8] The following centuries, though, found members of Parlement embroiled in an endless series of ritual skirmishes in which they tried to defend and expand their authority against the king's encroachment. Typical of such ritual tensions was the order by Louis XIII in 1632, which required the presidents of Parlement to rise when the royal seals-keeper entered the chamber for a special session of Parlement led by the king. Upon hearing of this, the Parlement leaders were enraged, arguing that the dignity of Parlement was being undermined, that they had never stood for this royal official. When the seals-keeper subsequently arrived in Parlement, he was angered to find that the presidents had circumvented the rite by arranging to be already standing, conversing with each other, at his entry. The same scene was repeated each of the next two years, and hostile barbs were exchanged with the seals-keeper upon his entry.[9] Through such ritual relations the king and Parlement battled over their political turf.

The more the king became the sole source of authority, the more a person's status depended on being closely identified with him. In such a setting, the royal rites were potent weapons. Nobles, clerics, and officials struggled mightily to win symbolic expressions of favor in court rites. Because ritual traditions defined the hierarchy of powers, the ruler was able to bring about changes in status simply by departing from precedent. It mattered not at all that the rites were transparent inventions; power holders could not afford to take them lightly.

This extravagant ritualization could take on a life of its own, just because to change precedent meant to change rank. The results were occasionally ludicrous. The *levée* (rising from bed) of the French king and queen formed part of this system of ritually denoting rank. When the seventeenth-century king, Louis XIV, got out of bed it was no simple matter: dozens of aristocrats and others were involved in a complex choreography of power. Still in the eighteenth century, Marie-Antoinette underwent such a rite each morning. The queen's maid of honor had the right to give her her chemise, while the lady-in-waiting then helped her get into her petticoat and dress. If, however, a royal princess happened to be present, she had the honor of putting the chemise on the queen. One

day, after Marie-Antoinette had been entirely undressed by her attendants, the maid of honor was about to give her her chemise when in
walked the Duchess of Orléans. Attentive to the duchess's higher rank,
the maid of honor handed the chemise back to the chambermaid, so that
she could then pass it to the duchess. No sooner had the duchess acquired the chemise than the higher-ranking Countess of Provence made
her entry. Though the queen still stood entirely naked before the noble
crowd, the duchess had no choice but to pass the chemise back to the
chambermaid, so that it could then be given to the countess. Fortunately
for the queen, the countess was able to get the chemise to her before any
higher-ranking noblewoman arrived.[10]

Ritual in the Battle for Public Support

Although today these examples may seem quaint, the battle for position
through ritual is still very much present. Of tremendous importance to
the politician is the public image he presents, and there is no more powerful context for image construction than the political rite. If, in certain
small-scale societies, leaders perform public rites only after carefully decorating their bodies with the appropriate dye, tying their hair in the
proper fashion, and wearing just the right outfit, so too do American
politicians paint their skin, sport just the right coiffure, and meticulously
select the right clothing for their ceremonial appearances.[11]

But the symbols employed in the American politicians' attempts to
communicate something about themselves to the public go well beyond
bodily adornment. Not only does the politician struggle to position himself at the center of political ceremonies, but he also seeks to surround
himself with appropriate symbols to lend his performance the aura of
legitimacy. The important thing is public performance, not substantive
action.

The United States Congress abounds in examples of this. When the
nuclear reactor at Three Mile Island broke down, generating widespread
anxiety, dozens of congressional committees and subcommittees competed with each other to hold the first public hearings on the crisis.
Members of each sought to profit from public concern over the disaster by
displaying their own concern and offering their own rhetorical assurance
that something would be done about the threat.[12] Most of these committees would have little or nothing to do with the situation at Three Mile
Island or with changing the nuclear regulatory system. What changes
would take place would come about quietly, deep in the bureaucracy,
rather than out in the public eye.

The manipulation of symbolism is perhaps even more evident in the ceremony surrounding the delivering of speeches on the floor of the House of Representatives. The representative stands at the center of this national shrine, his speech filled with potent symbols and dripping with concern for his constituents, while the whole performance is videotaped for the voters back home. What is not shown is that often the only others present in the hall are the few congressmen awaiting their turns to enact similar performances.[13]

The greatest political sociodrama and the most elaborate competitive use of ritual in American politics come each four years with the campaign for the presidency. The metaphor of a journey guides the entire enterprise: campaign as pilgrimage.[14] The population is supposed to get to "know" the candidate through his highly ritualized appearances, while the candidate uses the rites to present a certain image of himself and to contrast this with the image he creates of his competitors. In this effort, the use of symbols both to define certain ideals and to ignite the emotions is crucial, as Novak suggests:

Winning the loyalty of hundreds of thousands of volunteers, workers, and doorbell-ringers is beyond the competence of the candidate as mere manager or executive. It is a task for the candidate as symbol-maker. The presidential candidate must evoke a huge symbolic response, issue significant symbolic rewards. People must feel that what they are doing is good, worthy, and important.[15]

After all, the stuff of campaigns is not programmatic platforms, but American flags, limousines, kissing babies, eating knishes and pizza, wearing a yarmulke, appearing at construction sites with hardhat in place, and strolling arm-in-arm through the cornfields with the (preferably overall-clad) farmer.

Through these sociodramas, politicians try to establish a public image of themselves as bastions of morality and tireless servants of the public good. One of the curious features of American politics can be seen in this light, namely, the emphasis given to ritual appearances of the candidate's spouse. In other nations, especially where candidates are seen as representatives of a party and where private life is distinguished from the public arena, such rites are laughable, if not simply inconceivable. But in the United States, where the ideology of individualism and the mystification of ideology lead voters to judge candidates by their perceived personal charms, the family must be ritually presented in the campaign. Botching this family symbolism, as Gary Hart discovered in his abortive presidential campaign of 1987, can be politically fatal. From the rite of announcing one's candidacy to the rites prescribed for declaring victory or defeat on election night, the candidate without spouse at his or her side is as exposed as Marie-Antoinette, both victims of political rites.[16]

The 1986 arms control meeting between President Reagan and Secretary-General Gorbachev in Iceland provides a curious example of this ritual battle of the spouses. In contrast to the very visible ritual role that First Ladies have long played in the United States, wives of Soviet leaders have always stayed in the background. Since the Stalin era, the Soviet leader's power has been based on his position in the party apparatus, and not on personal traits that link him directly to the people. Yet one of Gorbachev's main goals has been to change the image of the Soviet leaders and thereby win more support abroad, particularly in the West. Few rites were more appropriate to this attempt to humanize the Soviet leadership before world opinion than those incorporating the Secretary-General's wife. Reagan was involved in his own symbolic struggle, attempting to define the meeting as a non-summit, a preliminary 'business-like' round of preparations for a later summit meeting. Accordingly, it was decided that Nancy Reagan should not attend, in order to avoid having to schedule a round of rites that would recall the recent Geneva summit meeting. When the Soviets announced that the Secretary General would bring his wife to Iceland, the Reagan administration was caught off guard. By enacting the series of wifely rites of people-to-people visits, the Soviets furthered their efforts to display their own humanity, to dramatize their own desire for a world at peace.

The ritual battle for legitimacy not only pits national leader against leader, or politician against politician, but also political party against political party. Such ritualization is especially crucial to parties that have been previously stigmatized, as the case of Israel's conservative Likud party coalition illustrates.

In the first two decades of the nation's existence, the forces behind what became the Likud movement were political pariahs, disparaged as former terrorists and reactionaries. Israel's central legitimizing symbols, sanctified in the rites of the state, sprang from the idealistic, socialist Zionism identified with Theodore Herzl, Chaim Weizmann and David Ben-Gurion. When Likud finally won control of the government in 1977, Menachim Begin, Likud's historical leader and the new prime minister, sought a way to solidify his coalition's strength by bolstering its popular legitimacy.

Emblematic of these attempts were the elaborate state rites held at Likud's urging in 1980 to celebrate the one hundredth birthday of

Vladimir Jabotinsky, the ideological father of Likud and Begin's mentor. Likud ensured that the rites would be more elaborate than those sponsored by the Labor party on the anniversary of Ben-Gurion's death. Indeed, the rites held on the sacred site atop Mount Herzl mixed the symbolism of the state with the symbolism of the Likud movement, the emotionally powerful Jewish prayers of mourning with the anthem of Likud's major youth movement. Presided over by the chief rabbi of the Israeli military, with the participation of the president, the speaker of the Knesset, the prime minister, foreign diplomats, and other dignitaries, the rites "elevated to the universal mythical plan of one of the greats of the nation a previously partisan figure, who had been considered by many— including leading intellectuals and key figures in the media—to have been a pariah in the Zionist movement."[17] It was a precious political victory for Begin and a blow to Labor's former monopoly of the symbols of national legitimacy.

Descent and Caste Ritual

Throughout much of the world, political relations traditionally have been structured by an ideology of common descent. People were given their place in society on the basis of who they were descended from, and if they wished to improve their social position, they needed to work together to improve the position of the entire descent group to which they belonged.[18]

Membership in a particular descent or kinship group is customarily marked through common ritual observances—such as worship at a common ancestral shrine or observance of certain taboos—and the struggle for influence among such groups is often waged through ritual. In the millennia before the predominance of centralized states, these were the typical forms of political life among agricultural and pastoral peoples. It is not necessary, however, to delve into the archaeological record to see what role ritual has played in the political struggle among local descent-based factions. Modern cases of conflict in both North Africa and South Asia provide adequate examples.

In the Tunisian village described by Abu-Zahra, two factions, the Zawya and the Ramada, dominate political life. Membership in the Zawya group, which has long had the upper hand in the village, is based entirely on descent from an Islamic saint, Sidi Mateur. Along with this saintly descent, the Zawya claim to have inherited a privileged status and certain ritual powers that make them the custodians of community ritual life. All ritual occasions in the village, then, relate to Sidi Mateur. Among them is a series of rites especially devoted to the memory of the saint, attended by his devotees from many other villages. Because the saint is important to all villagers, even non-Zawya villagers routinely visit the Zawya shrine, singing hymns praising Sidi Mateur, when they celebrate their weddings and circumcision ceremonies. The privileged status of the Zawya group is also evident during mourning, for only Zawya mourners have the privilege of going to the saint's shrine to receive condolences.

In contrast, the opposing Ramada faction is not an exclusive descent group; anyone living in the village's Ramada quarter may join. Ramada members are in a weaker position than their Zawya rivals because they have no traditional role in community ritual life, nor do they have rituals that bring them together through common ancestor worship or responsibility for village ritual welfare.

Had it not been for the impact of outside influences, this ritually-reinforced Zawya dominance could have lasted for a long time. But, in recent years, a number of Ramada men have received a formal education and acquired some wealth, in spite of the local disadvantages they faced. Once they acquired some resources, they sought to reverse their inferior position by undermining the ritual and political domination of the Zawya. Consequently, the Ramada began to downplay the importance of Sidi Mateur and to deny that the people of the Zawya group are of "noble" descent. To futher undercut their rivals' claims, they started comparing Sidi Mateur unfavorably to other saints, who they argue are more important, and they began to disparage the Zawya ritual performances as insufficiently dignified.

At the same time, these politically ambitious Ramada men began developing their own ritual to compete with the Zawya in the battle for local dominance. To celebrate a circumcision or marriage ceremony, they hire belly dancers and musicians from Tunis in order to display their wealth and make their ceremonies more festive than those of their competitors. On such occasions they also slaughter animals and, in a show of magnanimity, invite all villagers, as well as prominent men from neighboring villages, to their lavish, ceremonial dinners. Here they imitate the former Zawya custom of slaughtering many animals on festive occasions and hosting a village feast, a custom that current Zawya economic circumstances no longer permit. In short, the economic changes that gave some Ramada men the opportunity to gain wealth have led to a challenge to the old political order of the village. This order was upheld by a ritual complex, and it has been through ritual attack that the Ramada men have begun to redefine the local hierarchy to their benefit.[19]

Ritual, then, is not simply a means by which a politically dominant group perpetuates its privileged position. The fact that ritual can be so important in establishing and maintaining local political influence also means that the struggle by competing groups to improve their position or to overthrow the powers-that-be will take place in part through ritual.

The South Asian caste system provides a revealing example of this use of ritual in the political struggle of subjugated groups. The caste system is especially instructive because so many have seen it as demonstrating the conservative role of ritual. In this view, the rites of caste fossilize hierarchical relations, supporting an unchanging political order of dominance and subordination among local descent-based groups. Yet, even though there is no question that the caste system shows the power of ritual to support a political elite, it also demonstrates just how ritual can be and is used by lower-ranking groups to improve their position.

In order to stake out a claim for higher status, members of lower-ranking castes practice what Srinivas terms *Sanskritization*, that is, they change their ritual customs to resemble more closely those associated with the higher-ranking castes. Claims to higher group status, and hence greater influence in local community decisions, must be made through the ritual symbolism of the caste system. Asserting such claims does not mean, however, that they will necessarily be accepted by other community members. It can take decades for such attempts to succeed and for the group's higher status to be recognized; in many cases the attempts to bolster the group's status are simply rebuffed.

Given the massive changes brought about in the years of British colonialism, it is not surprising that intense ritual struggle led to periodic riots and to governmental involvement in ritual regulation. Typical is the case of the Nadars in southern India.

Over the past two centuries, the Nadars have been able to rise from a position of political, economic, and ritual inferiority to one of considerable status and power. To engineer this change, they had to fight a constant battle over the rituals that were used to keep them in their lowly place. A variety of rites fixed the status of the group. A Nadar could not come too close to someone of higher caste: thirty-six paces must separate the Nadar from a Brahman, while the Nadar could come no closer than twelve paces from a Nair. Nadars were forbidden from carrying umbrellas or wearing shoes; they could not live in houses more than one story tall and they were not allowed to milk cows. Nadar women could not carry pots of water on their hips, as this was a mark of women of the higher castes. But the symbol that most relentlessly exposed their subservience was their dress: neither Nadar men nor women could cover their bodies above the waist or below the knees.

By the beginning of the nineteenth century, the British had opened up opportunities that permitted the Nadar to improve their economic position. Yet, the rites of caste inferiority meant that they were still treated as beneath the other groups of the community and could exert little influence over community affairs. Nadar attempts to improve their social and political position began to focus on the master symbol of their inferiority, their women's bare breasts.

With the support of the missionaries, who viewed Nadar toplessness as a sign of paganism, the Nadar lobbied the colonial government for relief. In response, during the second decade of the nineteenth century, local British authorities issued an order granting permission for the Nadar women who had converted to Christianity "to cover their bosoms." The order, however, forbade them from wearing the upper cloth associated with women of the higher castes.[20]

The Nadar were not willing to abide by this restriction, because it left them in their inferior state, and they increasingly began to wear the upper cloth as well. The result was a series of riots during the ensuing decades, in which higher-caste crowds surrounded Nadar women, beat them, and tore the offending upper cloth from their breasts, often stripping off the rest of their clothes for good measure.

The Nadars ultimately succeeded in carving out a higher position for themselves in the southern Indian hierarchy, but it was only after many years of fierce struggle. That the rites of hierarchy played a major role in this struggle is clear both from the intensity of the reaction to their attempts to change these rituals, and from the continued willingness of the Nadar themselves to risk violence and physical injury in order to assert their new symbolic self-definition.[21]

Similar cases abound throughout India. In the western Bengali village studied by Davis, for example, the Bagdis, the village's second largest caste, began to challenge the Sadgops, who were the principal landowners. The Bagdis had been able to improve their economic situation by acquiring village land and attracting Bagdi caste members from elsewhere to move into the village. But in order to translate this economic role into political and social influence, they turned to ritual.

The Bagdis asserted their claim to be a caste of the higher-ranking Kshatriya varna in various ways. They adopted middle names characteristic of higher status and began to employ the ritual services of a washerman, a barber, and a Brahman priest. The still-dominant Sadgops, fighting to keep their political control, staunchly resisted these claims. Lamenting that money could now buy anything, they lost no opportunity to denigrate the Bagdis' new ritual baggage.

The grudging acceptance of the Bagdi claims to higher caste status—though not to a status as high as that of the Sadgops—was triggered by the impact of national political forces. National legislation required villages to elect governing councils, *panchayats*, through universal suffrage. Though no one contested the fact that a Sadgop would be elected council head, there were two faction leaders within the Sadgop caste battling for the post. Since the Sadgops were split between the contenders, the Bagdis held the balance of electoral power.

It happened that at this time, Khudi, a prominent Bagdi, was making plans for his daughter's wedding. In the past, citing reasons of caste purity, Sadgops had always refused to attend such Bagdi weddings, and they would not eat food served by the ritually impure Bagdis. Khudi, seeking recognition of the higher status that his caste was claiming, offered the political support of the Bagdis to the Sadgop faction leader who would attend the wedding. When one of the faction leaders accepted the invitation, the other felt compelled to do so as well.

This decision was not made lightly, for the Sadgops recognized the political importance of assuring their continued ritual superiority. Hence, the local Sadgops called a caste meeting and decided that they would attend the wedding only if the food were prepared by a Brahman cook and if the Bagdi caste made a contribution to the village fund for the privilege of having Sadgops present. This was agreed to by Khudi and the Bagdis. Thus, for the first time the Sadgops attended a Bagdi wedding, raising the status of the Bagdis while using the ritual to assert their own continued caste superiority.

In each of these cases, changes in the larger political economic system gave a lower-ranking caste the opportunity to improve its economic status. They took advantage of these economic improvements and the altered national political circumstances to use ritual to assert their right to higher status in the community and to more power over community affairs. Such ritual assertions of higher status face the hostility of those who benefit from the caste's continued low status. The power of the higher-ranking groups depends on their ability to salvage their own position of ritual superiority. The resulting struggle—combining economic and ritual elements—determines just what the new constellation of power relations will be.[22]

The Battle over Rites of Passage

In the West, where the struggle for power has often involved competition with established churches, rites of passage commonly provide the battleground for political combat. Even where other institutional bases of church influence have been undermined, transition rites continue to bind people to the church, providing them with a national or international allegiance outside state control. Where state elites see such allegiances as threats, they seek to substitute the state for the church as sponsor of these rites. Similarly, where the church is heavily identified with the state, insurgent political movements may try to devise their own alternative rites of passage to deny this source of support to the rulers.

An assumption underlies this thesis: namely, that people generally feel some need to have rites performed at certain transition points in their own lives and the lives of others near to them. There is much evidence for this, given the ubiquity of funeral rites, the near universal existence of marriage rites, and the frequency with which a variety of other rites of passage—such as baptism and attainment of adulthood—are found in otherwise dissimilar societies. One of the notable features of these rites is that they generally call for the services of an outsider, a specialist. People are not ritually self-sufficient.[23]

The popularity of church rites of passage in Eastern Europe is well known and is one of the major bonds tying the general population to the church. As such, it represents a threat to the communist leadership, even though the churches in these countries are typically careful not to challenge state authorities directly. Although East European governments have established state alternatives to church rites of passage, the churches have continued to use these rites as a means of retaining popular influence. In Yugoslavia, for example, it is typically only Communist party activists who choose non-church weddings, while in many parts of the country church baptism is universal.[24] In the various Eastern European republics incorporated into the Soviet Union, as well as in the Asian regions of the U.S.S.R. that never were Russian Orthodox, continued reliance on religious rites of passage serves as a badge of pre-Soviet national identity. The rites help create and maintain a political identity that conflicts with the official ideology of Soviet citizenship.[25]

Soviet officials have long been concerned about this pattern, and the government has mounted a series of campaigns to wean people from church-sponsored rites by offering them rites of passage sponsored by the state itself. Although these attempts have met with only limited success, the Soviet government continues to devote considerable resources to the construction of an alternative ritual system.

The state offers elaborate ceremonies aimed at replacing baptismal and funeral rites.[26] Reversing the government's earlier position that there was no need for "irrational" ceremonialism in socialist society, a chain of

Palaces of Festive Events now provide the atmosphere deemed appropriate for such rites. Female officiants, dressed in long gowns and standing before an altarlike table, preside over the rites. At their side stands a white bust of Lenin, with an eternal flame burning nearby. Celebrants are encouraged to use the flame to light their own torches, giving their rite a bit of extra flare. Appropriate music, either from an organ or, for full effect, from an entire choir, helps create the proper mood.

In place of baptism parents bring their children to the Festive Palace to celebrate the Ceremonial Registration of the Newborn. There, in lieu of a cross, the child receives a "name star," which symbolizes the October Revolution. The robed officiant places this star around the child's neck. The officiant addresses the parents, exclaiming: "Let this star light the path of your son as the Star of October lights the path for the whole world."

Although churches have continued to compete successfully with the Soviet state in rites of baptism and, especially, funerals, the government has had more success in replacing the church in celebrating weddings. Here, too, traditional symbols are carefully blended with those of the Soviet state. At one ceremony, for example, as the officiant stood at the altar beside the huge white bust of Lenin, she charged the newlyweds: "You have given your hand to each other at a happy time, under the peaceful sky of the motherland and of the Soviet people, led by the party of Lenin along the bright path to the Communist future."[27]

Italy has the world's largest nonruling Communist party, and Communist efforts to win popular allegiance away from the church and the church-allied Christian Democratic party produce fierce battles over rites of passage. The struggle was especially lacerating in the first years following the fall of Fascism, as the church bitterly fought the Communists' attempts to establish an alternative system of rites of passage. Indeed, those who chose to be married in city hall rather than in their parish church risked public condemnation and even excommunication at the hands of church officials.[28] When the Communist party (PCI) attempted to wean the children away from catechism and First Communion with an alternative series of rites of coming of age, they were attacked mercilessly by the church. In recent years, the hysteria has subsided, but the struggle over rites of passage, and for popular influence through those rites, continues.

Even in the most heavily Communist areas of the country, where only a small minority of the population attends Sunday mass, almost everyone enters and leaves the world through church rites of passage. This is of no little importance to the continuing power of the church, for it is largely through this ritual monopoly that people come to depend on the church. Moreover, by sending their children to catechism so that they can celebrate their First Communion, anticlerical parents insure that their children will recognize the social centrality of the church.

Consider the case of Albora, a heavily Communist working-class quarter in Bologna, capital of Italy's so-called red belt.[29] Of the nine thousand residents, eighteen-hundred belong to the PCI, while just thirty-nine are members of the rival Christian Democratic party. In this area, the church provides the primary organizational alternative to the Communist party. The Christian Democratic party, in spite of its dominant role at the national level, is viewed locally as an appendage to the church.

At both national and local levels, the church continues to see the Communist party as its principal rival for popular influence, and Communist and Catholic loyalties are considered to be incompatible. By contrast, the official PCI position sees no conflict between being a party member and being a loyal churchgoer. Yet, in spite of this longstanding PCI attempt to appeal to the church faithful, there are few more potent symbols of Communist allegiance than refusing church rites of passage. In Albora, few adult men attend mass, and only a small percentage of women attend regularly. Though more attend special Christmas and Easter masses, the only regular contact that the majority of people in the community have with the church is through celebration of rites of passage.[30] Without church control of these rites, the church, priests, and lay church leaders would be isolated. And, only by turning away from church sponsorship of the rites of passage does the individual make the final break from the church and thus undermine the church's popular influence.

Yet, Communist attempts to wrest control over rites of passage from the church have met with only limited success. Though experimentation with Communist baptism has a long history in Italy, going back to the socialist movement of the nineteenth century, there is currently no Communist alternative to baptism, and very few people forgo church baptism of their children. People do have a choice of wedding ceremonies. In Bologna, as elsewhere, a couple can celebrate their wedding in a church or in city hall, where a city official presides. This choice often leads to considerable family tensions, and many tales are told of mothers, aunts, or grandmothers insisting on a church wedding over the objections of the young couple.

The Communist activist may emphasize the political significance of the civil rites by asking a Communist municipal official to perform the ceremony and a party activist or official to give the charge to the couple. In such cases the traditional clerical pleas that the couple establish a good Christian family are replaced with a charge to build a good socialist family. After a quarter century of often bitter church-PCI struggle, as late as 1970 only seven percent of Bologna weddings took place outside a church. But the church's holding power finally began to decline in more recent years, and by 1977 the proportion of civil weddings had skyrocketed to twenty-eight percent in Bologna, a chilling statistic for the church.[31]

In contrast to wedding rites, funeral ritual is not simply a matter of choosing between church and civil sponsorship, for a wide variety of options are available in Bologna. These range from a full church funeral, with confession, Last Rites, and religious burial, to the Communist funeral, in which the symbolism of the party replaces that of the church. Few people forgo church involvement entirely in their funeral rites, though signs of tension are evident here, too. Typical was the case of a non-activist Communist woman who died in Albora in 1972. Her son, also a PCI member, met with the parish priest to arrange the details for the religious procession that would take the coffin from the home to the church, where a funeral mass was to be celebrated. Although the local party leaders marched at the back of the priest-led procession, they would not enter the church, but waited outside in the street until the mass was over.

To accommodate Communist funerals, the city hearse, which caters to all tastes, has a removable silver cross on its roof. Although the form of the Communist funeral rite is much the same as the church's, the church's symbols, like the hearse's cross, have been replaced. Comrades carry bright red flags, bearing the name of the deceased's party section as well as those of neighboring sections. At the end of the procession, a color guard of these flags is formed, and the hearse passes through. A local party official delivers the eulogy which, rather than extolling the deceased's Christian virtues, pays tribute to his or her dedication to the Communist cause. In a last political hurrah, the comrade shows his loyalty to the Party struggle as his body is lowered into its grave.

Indeed, the practice of turning a funeral to political advantage has a long history in Italy. Mark Antony's use of Julius Caesar's funeral led to large-scale riots, driving Brutus's faction in terror from the city.[32] Even in the twentieth century, deathbed and funeral rites have been made to serve different political masters. Under Mussolini, rites of allegiance to the regime were carefully monitored, and especially enthusiastic or notable rites of obeisance were publicly noted and rewarded. In the 1930s, the press proudly reported on the loyalty shown by the swelling number of people who insisted on being buried in their Fascist black shirts. Italians also learned of cases like that of the impoverished, thirty-year-old mother of three small children, struggling for her last breath in her hospital bed in 1934. Finding herself surrounded, as it happened, not only by her family, but also by the hospital inspector, she steeled herself for a final political effort. Painfully, she lifted her arm up before her in Fascist salute, crying "Viva il Duce! Viva l'Italia!" In that melancholy moment, she was moved less by Fascist fervor than by the hope that this dying act of ritual allegiance would prompt the Fascists to provide for her young children. Her rite was the unwritten testament of the poor.[33]

An Italian peasant may have had similar benefits in mind when, at around the same time, he had a will drawn up in which he directed his family to dress him in the Fascist black shirt for his funeral. He would go to the grave a Fascist. Whether the mere fact of drawing up such a will won him any political favors, no one knows. But, as it happens, the man survived the Fascist era and, with the change of political winds, joined the Communist party at the end of the war. Considering all that was going on in Italian society in these years, one can understand how he might have forgotten altogether about the provision he had written into his will. When he died, an old man and a proud member of the Communist party, his relatives, to their horror, discovered his legally binding wish to be buried in a black shirt. No doubt with his posthumous blessing, they refused to honor his funeral instructions.[34]

Mass Ritual and the Struggle for Power

In the struggle for power, mass rallies are one of the most effective means to demonstrate popular support. Such demonstrations are effective both in dramatically exhibiting a group's political strength and in fostering certain images regarding the nature of the group and its goals. In addition to their value in communicating directly to the public and to the opposition forces, such mass rites also have powerful effects on the participants, increasing their identification with the group and reinforcing their opposition to the foes that are symbolically represented in the demonstration. Such mass demonstrations gain their force through the careful manipulation of symbols, combined with the emotional impact of having so many people together for a common cause.

Given the political value of these rites, it should not be surprising that opponents often try to undercut their effect through direct confrontation. This is a common enough sight in the United States, where, for example, antiwar demonstrators in the late 1960s were frequently greeted by prowar counter-demonstrators, each waving their sacred symbols (often the same symbols, such as the American flag). Opponents try to offset the impact of their competitor's rites, to diminish their image of strength, and to undermine the symbolic message being sent to the general public.

Government-sponsored rites, similarly, provide a symbolically powerful setting for rites of opposition. When one thousand German soldiers swore allegiance to the West German state at a ceremony commemorating the twenty-fifth anniversary of NATO, seven thousand demonstrators staged a vigorous and violent protest.[35] Similarly, when a ceremonial reception was held by the president of the United States for the queen of England in 1983, a wide variety of protestors—ranging from Americans protesting the president's economic policies to Irishmen protesting Britain's role in Northern Ireland—staged a mass demonstration.[36] This is not only a matter of taking advantage of an occasion that will receive mass media coverage, but also an attempt to diminish the symbolic potency of one side through the symbolic action of another. Irishmen can demonstrate in the United States whenever they want, but to hold a demonstration alongside the rites of British royalty makes a much more powerful and symbolically direct political statement.

The setting of these mass rites is, indeed, crucial to their impact. As Berger notes, mass demonstrations are not generally held at politically strategic locations, such as railway stations, barracks, radio stations, or airports, but rather at symbolic centers. "A mass demonstration," he writes, "can be interpreted as the symbolic capturing of a city or capital." Hence, demonstrators in Washington favor the Lincoln and Washington monuments, not the headquarters of the military or the FBI.[37] Even though the demonstrators do not have the power to take over the city or the nation, they transform the streets into "a temporary stage on which they dramatise the power they still lack."[38]

When a person espousing antigovernment sentiments in a bar or a sports stadium is beaten up by enraged patriots, the event has little impact. Yet if the same person is assaulted for expressing those same views at a mass demonstration, the matter takes on serious political repercussions, generally benefiting the opposition force and undermining government strength. The struggle between political forces is exceedingly abstract and distant from the everyday experience of most people. One of the primary ways it can be made palpable is through the symbolic dramatizations of conflict that such mass demonstrations make possible. Individuals can then identify abstract political principles with actual people, and they can identify political positions with tangible symbols.

The sight of people who are peacefully parading these symbols being physically assaulted by police can have a powerful emotional effect on onlookers.

In 1905, for example, crowds gathered in St. Petersburg to present a petition to the tsar. They were shot down by the tsarist forces, and this helped precipitate popular revolt.[39] In January 1972, the Northern Ireland Civil Rights Association held a nonviolent, though illegal, protest march in Derry. When British paratroopers responded by killing thirteen of the unarmed demonstrators, a tremendous political reaction shook all of Ireland. "Bloody Sunday," as the event came to be called, was a major catalyst for the replacement of the Protestant-dominated Northern Irish government by direct British rule.[40]

Government officials are well aware of the power of these mass rites and the danger of playing into their opponents' hands. When United States and German officials were arranging President Reagan's visit to Bitburg cemetery and the Bergen-Belsen concentration camp, they learned that Jewish protesters were planning to come to the camp dressed in the striped uniforms of concentration camp inmates. The authorities would not, under any circumstances, allow their own ritual presentation at the camp to be undermined by this counter-rite, but they dreaded the thought that the demonstrators would resist police attempts to keep them out. The prospect of television and newspaper images of officers in German uniforms assaulting or carting off Jews in concentration camp rags caused dread as the date for the rites approached.[41] As it happened, the German authorities were able to keep the demonstrators well away from the official ceremonies and from the sea of cameras, much to the consternation of the protesters.

In staging protest demonstrations, opposition groups must take care to present the right constellation of symbols. Use of the wrong symbols can sabotage the impact of the rite. Organizers of antiwar demonstrations in the United States during the Vietnam War, for example, were constantly in conflict with groups who wanted to display symbols that the organizers thought would tarnish the symbolic effect of the rite. North Vietnamese flags were banished and the burning of American flags often suppressed by the protest organizers themselves.

I began this chapter with a view of one such demonstration, the burning of draft cards in Central Park. This rite illustrates both how protest rituals begin and what purposes they serve. As the other introductory example makes clear, the symbolism of burning an object that represents the enemy has an ancient history. The same symbolism was employed by Catholic priests in the Inquisition, by Luther in the Reformation, by American revolutionaries seeking independence, by Nazis condemning books written by Jews and socialists, and by Third World demonstrators the world over protesting American imperialism. But the symbolism of incineration is so powerful and so universal that it is not compromised by past associations with discredited causes. It is repeatedly reborn, in new form, through rites of protest.

The draft-card burning was more than simply a way for a person to dramatize his political position. The rite also provided a means of unifying opponents of government policy throughout the United States in the absence of any strong organizational structure. For example, a few months after the New York antiwar demonstration, "Resistance Day" was held. On the same day—the symbolic importance of simultaneity being great—people gathered in cities throughout the United States to enact the same draft card rites. In each city, following a rally in which the cards were collected from the participants, a procession marched to Selective Service headquarters, where the cards were returned to the officials. In some cities, cards were also burned, as in Boston, where seventy-six protesters stepped up to the altar of the Arlington Street Unitarian Church and used the holy tapers to light their cards. Another 214 young men handed their cards to the three clergymen who stood there as representatives of the three major faiths.[42]

The draft-card rites became standardized, with the dates for their celebration fixed well in advance. Other rites of protest, though, are more spontaneous. The year after the Central Park march, the 1968 Democratic convention was held. There, in Chicago, the carefully choreographed rites of party solidarity and party virtue were seriously undermined by the counter-rites of antiwar protesters marching outside the hall. But one moment within the hall was equally moving if less dramatic. After hours of debate, the antiwar plank proposed for the party platform was defeated in a roll-call vote; when the result was announced, with that symbolic victory denied them, antiwar delegates slipped on black armbands and, with great emotion, sang "We Shall Overcome."[43]

In the face of defeat, rites such as this have kept up the morale of many a protest group, while legitimating their own cause and, by implication, delegitimating that of their antagonists. Such rites are also important in attaching participants to a longer tradition of protest, lending the legitimacy obtained by the earlier protest movements to the newer movement. Most of those delegates singing "We Shall Overcome" no doubt recalled—if only subconsciously—an earlier rite, one that was celebrated five years earlier beneath the Lincoln Monument in Washington, D.C. There, thousands of civil rights demonstrators also sang

"We Shall Overcome," swaying to the tune, just before Martin Luther King launched into his own speech, "I have a dream . . . ".[44] By expropriating this symbol in their own rite, in a different political context, the protesters both built their own self-image and communicated a particular interpretation of their actions to others.

Under the proper conditions, and with skillful manipulation of symbols, mass protest rites can have tremendous political consequences. Such was the case of the 1973 student demonstrations that ultimately led to the downfall of the Thai government. For decades, four principal symbols had been employed to legitimize the government: the nation, religion (Buddhism), the monarch, and the constitution. Not only did every government in the preceding fifty years claim its legitimacy by identifying with these symbols, but all significant changes in governmental leadership or organization involved an appeal to them.

The demonstrations helped topple the government by successfully identifying the protesters with these sacred symbols. The students sang songs of national loyalty and carried the national flag. Pictures of the king and queen were frequently displayed, and a large statue of the Buddha was placed in a prominent position at the center of the demonstration. The students succeeded, through their manipulation of these symbols, in creating a public impression of themselves as the true defenders of the most sacred principles of Thai political order, while undermining the government's attempts to identify the protesters with various stigmatized symbols (such as "communist subversives").[45]

Mass rites sponsored by nongovernmental groups can have reactionary as well as revolutionary goals. One effect of these rites is to keep conflict alive by periodically reenergizing sectarian allegiances. Northern Ireland has a long history of just such rites, with the Protestant Orangemen parading through the streets with their sacred symbols, reminding the Catholic population of Protestant domination and renewing bonds of Protestant chauvinism through these emotion-laden activities.

The bitter arguments between Orangemen leaders and government officials in the summer of 1985 are symptomatic of this use of ritual. As in previous years, the Protestants were preparing annual rites to commemorate King William of Orange's victory in the 1690 Battle of the Boyne, which established British control in Ireland. But British authorities, citing a regulation that banned parades likely to catalyze violence, forbade the Orangemen from marching through a heavily Roman Catholic neighborhood in Ulster. In previous years, when the parade had moved through Catholic streets, homes had been destroyed and people had been shot. Many Catholics left the city rather than face the marchers who, in bowler hats and orange sashes, would wave the British flag, paint the sidewalks red, white, and blue, and burn effigies of the traitor Bundy. Citing a one-hundred-fifty-year tradition of taking that route, the Orangemen murmured threats of violence if the order to avoid the Catholic district remained, but with British troops in place, the marchers were ultimately forced to alter their route.[46] Yet, the rites of Protestant celebration would remain politically potent, regardless of whether any shots were fired or any homes sacked. The Protestant-Catholic struggle in Northern Ireland, like so many other political battles, continues to be waged as much through ritual as through any other means.

7

Conflict and Crisis

Notorious among anthropologists as one of the world's most bellicose societies, the Yanomamo Indians of Venezuela and Brazil struggle to survive in a world of continual conflict. Raids between villages are frequent. Festering wounds from battle are a common cause of death among men, and women live in fear of being abducted. In order to protect themselves, the Yanomamo are ever in search of intervillage alliances.

In order to cultivate an alliance, a Yanomamo village holds a feast, inviting the members of one or two selected villages to it. A village that accepts such an invitation is obliged to reciprocate eventually with its own feast. Guests must spend several days at the host village participating in a series of rites. Meanwhile, ties of solidarity are created, binding the villages in political alliance.

But feast invitations do not put an end to the mutual suspicions and hostilities that mark so much of Yanomamo political life. The very fact that the host village is compelled to feed the large number of guests—the men, women, and children of the invited villages all come—over the several days of the feast, can itself lead to conflict. Hosts charge guests with gluttony and food theft, while guests respond by ridiculing their hosts for their niggardliness.

Last-minute preparations for the feast involve the hosts in a storm of activity. The women paint themselves with red pigment and then plaster their bodies with feathers. The men, after bringing in huge amounts of food to give their guests, prepare for the event by blowing a hallucinogenic drug through a long tube into each other's noses. The visitors soon enter, two at a time, their bodies painted and their hair decorated with white feathers. They dance around the village clearing to the approving shrieks of their hosts. Each dancer comes into the village clearing screaming, pivots around, and dances in place before lurching forward a few paces and repeating the performance. He carries weapons which he aims periodically at his hosts, a wild expression on his face. All the male guests then gather together, each rooted to his chosen spot, his spear pointed to the sky; they puff out their chests in a final flourish of bravado.

Though these feasts are designed to seal alliances, the ever-present tensions commonly lead to fighting between hosts and guests. The anthropologist Napoleon Chagnon, who spent years among the Yanomamo, describes the course of just such a ritual escalation of violence. After a day trading insulting comments as well as food and gifts, the guests, shrieking and hooting, returned from their camp to the host village after nightfall, armed with axes, clubs, and bows and arrows. Circling the settlement, they brandished their weapons threateningly before gathering in the village clearing. There they were surrounded by the hosts, the milling throngs embroiled in frenetic vituperation.

Two clusters of animated, menacing men separated, each containing opposing groups of hosts and guests. As if on cue, one man from each cluster stepped forward to begin the ritual combat. With legs spread wide apart and chest thrust out, the first combatant dared the other to strike him. Using his arm to measure the distance to his challenger's chest, the opponent carefully prepared his blow, winding up to get all his force into it. His fist struck the man's chest, staggering him. A huge welt immediately rose from the challenger's chest, as he shook his head in a desperate attempt to maintain his balance. If he fell, he would be defeated, and the men of his opponent's side would break out in wild hooting. But the challenger was waiting his turn; for each blow his opponent struck, he was entitled to strike one of his own.

After three hours of this chaotic mutual punishment, tempers flared to the point where one group challenged the other to move on to side slapping. The side-slapping procedure was much the same, but here each combatant presented his side, rather than his chest, for his opponent's blow, considerately stretching his arm behind his back to give his opponent a better target. The opponent tried to strike the challenger's side between the rib cage and hip with as much force as possible. When, just a few minutes into this new phase, one side's champion fainted, his comrades became enraged. The visitors began swinging their axes wildly at the hosts, who responded by getting out their bows and pointedly smearing poison on their arrows. The hostilities seemed about to get out of control, when the leader of the guests turned his back and led his group back out of the village. The political goals of the feast had not been realized, but a potential bloodbath had been averted.[1]

Are People Like Birds? The Ritualization of Conflict

In the traditional functionalist view, rites that appear to contest political power are commonly interpreted as actually maintaining the system's harmony. In this perspective, such rites are seen as safety valves which allow political opposition to be dissipated in harmless ways, leaving the system and its leaders intact.

One of the scientific bases for this view of ritual comes from the work of ethologists, who make much of the stylized displays—often termed rituals—certain animals use in situations of conflict. Indeed, Huxley argues that "the great majority of animals' behaviour-patterns have been subjected to the process of ritualization."[2] The use of ritual as a means of keeping conflict within tolerable limits has been noted at least as much by ethologists as by ethnologists. Like the anthropologists, they define ritual as standardized, repetitive symbolic action. Unlike students of human behavior, however, ethologists view symbols as part of the genetic "hard-wiring" of the organism rather than as a product of cultural learning.

The basic point, though, applies to humans as well as to other animals: given the inevitability of intraspecies competition over resources, it is important to species survival—particularly in higher species—that there be some mechanism for preventing conflict from regularly ending in violence. This mechanism, the complex of behavior employed by many animals to avoid physical aggression in conflict situations, is what ethologists refer to as ritualization.

Konrad Lorenz, author of some of the best-known accounts of animal rites, argues that those species that evolved ritual means for controlling intraspecies conflict were at a competitive advantage over those that had no such control mechanism.[3] Like our fellow species, humans must have been under similar evolutionary pressure to develop ritualized means of avoiding conflict. Indeed, in writing of the use of ritualization to ensure unambiguous communication, Lorenz applies this model to human behavior:

All the means of ensuring unambiguity of communication are employed exactly as in phylogenetic ritualization. Mimic exaggeration, redundant repetition and typical intensity are clearly marked in most human ceremonies. In particular, 'measured' speed, frequency and amplitude are symptoms that mark human ceremonial behaviour. The deans walk into the aula of the university with measured step; the catholic priest's chanting during mass is strictly regulated in pitch and rhythm by liturgical rules. The riot of form and colour accompanying human ceremonial, all its pomp and pageantry are developed, in cultural history, in the service of the same functions and along lines astonishingly parallel to those seen in phylogenetic ritualization.[4]

Parallels between human ritual and what ethologists call ritualization in other animals are certainly fascinating, and they merit serious study. Consideration of Lorenz's own case, however, shows the dangers of regarding human ritual as simply an advanced form of nonhumans' stylized displays. What is most notable about human symbols is certainly not their lack of ambiguity, but the fact that they mean different things to different people and may, indeed, have different, sometimes conflicting, meanings for the same person. The meaning of the commencement procession for a professor forced by social pressure to attend, for a graduate's joyful mother, and for a passing streetsweeper are quite different.[5]

Far from simply serving to divert hostile impulses in a harmless direction, human ritual is employed to exhort people to war and violence in situations where they would otherwise have no reason to harm others. Certainly one of the most striking, and yet common, aspects of human warfare is that people must wear the symbolic markings of their side so that all participants know whom to kill and whom to protect. These symbols of bodily adornment are supplemented by a panoply of other symbols and associated rites that serve to demarcate which side the combatants are on and to provide them with a rationale for killing.[6]

The animal model of ritual is thus inadequate to the understanding of the political uses of ritual. There are, however, many circumstances in which rituals do act to channel political tensions in relatively harmless directions. It is necessary, though, to examine each case of political ritual to see what effects it actually has.

I have already mentioned that Brazilians, like many other people around the world, view international soccer contests as a battle between themselves and other nations, and in this way ritually ventilate their national chauvinism and their hostilities toward other nations. This use of national sports teams as a symbolic means of international combat is institutionalized in the quadrennial Olympics, where nations are pitted against one another in struggle. The West Indies provide a similar example. There, cricket matches pitting the West Indian team against the British provide a regular ritual means for the lower-class West Indians to do battle with their historical oppressors. Cricket itself symbolizes upperclass British colonial rule, and by beating the British at their own game, the people can symbolically liberate themselves from their rulers. Yet, often ignored is the fact that a loss to the opposition, here the British team, can bring formerly controlled emotions to the boiling point. The same rite that serves to displace political hostilities can also serve to activate them.[7]

For as long as intergroup hostilities have existed, rituals have been used to express them. These rites assume a wide variety of forms around the world, sometimes limiting physical aggression, but often, simultaneously, keeping tensions alive. The occasions for these rites are themselves varied. Many such rites involve symbolic forms of intergroup combat. These range from mock battles between rival clans and rival age groups within a society to mock skirmishes between rival tribes.[8] Indeed, in many parts of the world, warfare itself is highly ritualized, with a special permanent site for the hostilities, special bodily adornment, special songs and verbal insults, and rules about the actual conduct of combat. In many of these cases, as soon as an individual is seriously wounded, hostilities cease and a round of post-battle ritual begins.[9]

Not all rituals that regulate intergroup tensions involve participation of both groups. Many rites are staged by a single side; such rites identify the enemy, recounting their moral inferiority while glorifying the celebrant's own group. Such rites keep alive political antagonisms without necessarily exacerbating them to the point of physical hostilities. In Renaissance Venice, for example, among the most frequent occasions for public festivals were celebrations of past victories in war. Through these celebrations, Venetians regularly defined their enemies, who were associated with a variety of derogatory symbols, while trumpeting the virtues of their own polity.[10]

It is in cases where rituals directly prompt violence rather than redirect hostilities into symbolic form that the limitations of the animal model of ritualization become most apparent. The Northern Irish example is a classic case, but it is nothing new. From the beginning of the Catholic-Protestant struggle in Europe, ritual has fomented violence. Natalie Davis, for example, describes the regular celebrations of Corpus Christi Day, highlighted by public processions, in sixteenth-century France. Catholics with homes along the parade route celebrated the holiday by hanging lavish decorations from their windows; Protestants' homes, by contrast, remained conspicuously unadorned as the cross- and banner-bearing marchers passed by.

The battle of symbolism, catalyzed by the rite, often led to violence, as happened in Lyon in 1561 when Catholics slaughtered offending Protestants. During their own processions, Protestant marchers were frequently pelted with stones, and so they sometimes carried weapons to protect themselves. At other times, Protestants became so enraged by the dancing, music, and costumes of the Catholic communal rites that they attacked the celebrants. Indeed, far from facilitating peaceful coexistence, Davis argues that these rites served to "dehumanize" the opposition. Encouraging hatred, they became "rites of violence."[11]

Ritual as Political Safety Valve

Although rites do in fact stimulate political conflict and intergroup hostilities, this is not all they do. In fact, ritual can provide an important safety valve for political tensions. Just how this might happen can be seen in the following cases.

I begin with a colorful example. In the Indian village of Kinsman Garhi, a great festival, the Festival of Love, is celebrated once each year. When McKim Marriott, an anthropologist doing fieldwork in the village, first viewed the festival, he saw only chaos. It seemed like a riot. But, as he learned more about village life, Marriott realized that beneath the pandemonium was a systematic reversal of many of the cultural norms that governed everyday social life. Rich, upper-caste men smiled while women flailed away at their shins. The women who showed the greatest gusto in delivering these beatings were the wives of their victim's low-caste hired laborers. A high-caste boy, notorious for bullying lower-caste youths, rode by on a donkey, facing backwards, while six "Brahman men in their fifties, pillars of villagɟ society, limped past in panting flight from the quarterstaff wielded by a massive young Bhangin, sweeper of their latrines."[12] In rites much like these throughout the world, the powerless switch places with the powerful on the designated day; the Dickensian dream becomes a ritual reality.

Anthropologists have customarily viewed these rites of reversal as mechanisms through which the oppressed can release pent-up frustrations and hostilities and, by so doing, preserve the status quo. Eva Hunt furnishes a clear statement of this approach in her Mexican Indian study. Where groups are in conflict, where no mechanism exists for restructuring their relations, and yet where the antagonists must continue to live together, she writes, "ritualism provides a safe outlet for the expression of potential conflict, as well as a restrictive frame in which the potential anomie or entropy is under control." In short, she argues that ritual provides a psychological means to reduce anxiety while preserving the "structural status quo."[13]

But why are oppressed people willing to be placated by ritual actions that do not ultimately improve their lot? It is possible to understand why members of the elite would be eager to engage in such rites, but why would the latrine-sweepers of the world be taken in by them? Murray Edelman, in considering such rites in American politics, argues that the rituals do have value for the many people who otherwise feel impotent before the powers that rule over them. The value of the rites is psychological; they reduce people's anxiety level and give them the healthier impression that they do have some control over their lives.

This argument recalls Malinowski's classic explanation of magical rites among the Trobriand Islanders. For Malinowski, the distinguishing feature of magic is the performance of ritual in situations where a positive outcome is important, but where the people have no objective control over the events. In spite of this powerlessness, they still feel the need to do something, for by doing something they assure themselves that they do have some control over their fate. They thus engage in ritual behavior aimed at demonstrating their ability to influence their world. The unfathomable is made fathomable.[14] With regard to the American case, neo-Malinowskians would argue that it is in people's psychological interest to feel that they have some control over the course of government policy that affects them, even though in fact their influence is negligible.[15]

It is not always so clear just what effect political rites have, even those specifically aimed at changing the political status quo. Do mass protest demonstrations, for example, serve as a ritualized means of ventilating discontent which, like the rites of reversal, permit the system to continue? Lee, for example, characterizes the periodic peace marches organized by pacifistic groups in Northern Ireland as "conscience-soothing exercises in reconciliation. Their ritualistic and band-aid procedures inflict a kind of social anesthesia on those they influence."[16] They do nothing to bring about the desired result but merely have the effect of making the people feel they are doing something politically useful.

In addition to channeling political opposition in directions that do not threaten the system, ritual also helps societies deal with many kinds of interpersonal conflicts that threaten to poison social life and tear the community apart. Indeed, judicial procedures, from the simplest societies to modern nation-states, are highly ritualized. Rites of the law court are not all that different from rites of the royal court. In both cases the image of sacrality, of legitimacy, is fostered through ritual, while aggressive behavior is sharply contained and lines of authority bolstered.

In small-scale societies which are not under direct state control, ritual forms take on special importance in handling disputes, for a bureaucracy of violence (police, army, jails) is totally absent. Among the Ndembu of West Africa, for example, anthropologist Victor Turner found just this pattern: The "profusion of types and frequency of performance of ritual in Ndembu society are, in a way, confessions of failure in the power of secular mechanisms to redress and absorb conflicts that arise in and between local and kinship groups."[17] As Turner sees it, Ndembu local groups are, by their very nature, continuously wracked by dissension.

Conflicts typically surface when a person suffers some misfortune, such as illness or accident, which is immediately blamed on another. Only by sublimating these antagonisms through ritual means for dealing with adversity can the conflict be kept within control. The rites assert people's common interests as Ndembu and enable them to deal with their frazzled emotions and their hostilities in ways that do not endanger the social order.[18] To act in this system-maintaining way, the rites need not actually settle the conflicts, but only, to use Gluckman's words, "lead to temporary truces, and at times conceal the basic conflicts between competitors."[19]

It is in this light that some of the judicial processes that seem most bizarre to modern Western eyes have been explained. By taking the highly charged power of determining guilt in interpersonal disputes away from individuals and assigning it to some extra-human agency, ritual serves a pacifying purpose in many societies. The use of the Constitution as a holy book beyond human meddling is indeed just one manifestation of this mystifying effort to place adjudication beyond human will. Neither the jurors nor the judge are to make any decision of their own regarding right and wrong, but only, according to the image fostered by the judicial rites, to take "facts" and allow the book of laws to determine guilt or innocence.[20]

In many societies, questions of guilt or innocence are handled by a different divinatory device: trial by ordeal. A painful or life-threatening ordeal is meted out to people accused of crimes in order to determine their guilt. The guilt of the accused is thus established not by the individual who had made the accusation, but by the rites. As in Western court rites, the judgment is depersonalized, and punishment is made the responsibility of the entire society rather than a matter of personal vendetta.

In the case of trial by ordeal, the rites often have a painfully dramatic quality. The scalding ordeal of the Tanala of Madagascar, described by Linton earlier this century, provides an apt illustration:

Water was boiled in a large pot and a stone fastened to a cord, like a plumbline. The stone was dropped vertically into the pot, but was not submerged. . . . The suspect's hand was washed and examined to see whether he had any scars on it, also whether it had been rubbed with medicine. After the *Anakandriana* had made the usual invocation, the accused approached the pot and seized the stone from below, plunging his hand into the boiling water. He then plunged his hand into cold water. The hand was bandaged and the accused shut up in a guarded house. The next morning all assembled to see his condition. If there were blisters on the hand he was guilty. If accused of sorcery he was killed on the spot, or, if the king was merciful, he was expelled and all his goods seized.[21]

To the west of Madagascar, among the Baganda of Uganda, serious disputes were settled by poison ordeal. This was used in cases where there was no obvious way of determining who was right. Each of the disputants was given a cup of a drug made by boiling the fruit of the datura plant. Both were seated until the drug could take its effect, at which time the officiant asked them to walk over to him. The disputant who was able to go to the officiant, kneel, and thank him for settling the case, was vindicated. If neither could do so, they were both considered guilty, and if both were able to walk over to him, they were both regarded as innocent. It was not unusual for one of the disputants to die from the aftereffects of the drug; this was viewed as the just punishment of the gods.[22]

Ritual Responses to Political Crises

When societies are unexpectedly torn by political crisis, rituals can provide a key means of coping with the threat to the political order. By their nature, such crises threaten people's confidence that their world is secure. This security, in turn, is based on their symbolic construction of what the world is like, a view that sees the world as predictable. Crises that threaten to discredit this symbolic complex are thus especially unsettling. And, from the point of view of the political system itself, survival means having the mechanisms necessary to withstand periodic crisis. Ritual serves as one of the most important of these means.[23]

Americans who doubt that a sophisticated nation would deal with important political crises in such a symbolic manner might consider the response to the taking of the hostages at the American embassy in Iran in 1979. The crisis itself was not directly thrust on the American people, but rather created through a rich symbolic production, which identified a variety of acts thousands of miles away with large symbols of national identity, as well as with such abstract principles as democracy and terrorism. The hostages were symbolically transformed into the American state itself, and their captors identified with a variety of stigmatic symbols. It was a war of ritual, with the Iranians parading their symbols through the nearby streets of Teheran, creating a larger symbol out of the American embassy itself, while in the United States the general public was swept into this international struggle through its own series of rites, which ranged from protest marches, to the lowering of flags to half-mast, to the preparation of petitions addressed to the captors. When the hostages were finally released, Americans participated in the event through another series of rites: processions, awards ceremonies, and the raising of the flag.

To give a better idea of such ritual responses to political crises, I would like to look at two cases in some detail. Each involves a fundamental threat to the legitimacy of a government, and each ultimately involves the murder of a national leader. The cases are the kidnapping and murder of Aldo Moro by the Italian Red Brigades in 1978, and the shooting of Indira Gandhi by Sikh assassins in 1984.

The Red Brigades

Not since the fall of Fascism and the Nazi occupation had Italians experienced a period as emotionally traumatizing and politically destabilizing as the one that began on March 16, 1978. On that day, the Red Brigades not only kidnapped Aldo Moro, head of the ruling Christian Democratic party, but, through a series of ritual dramas, the *brigatisti* captured the unwavering attention of millions of Italians. Through a process of symbolic transformation, the government itself became the hostage. The government was locked in a war of perceptions, as well as a war of emotions, with the Red Brigades. Even years later, those who dared portray these events differently than the image so painfully constructed by the country's political elite faced vitriolic denunciations and threats from government leaders.[24]

On the morning of March 16, Aldo Moro was being driven from his home to Parliament, accompanied by two carloads of bodyguards. While making their way through the streets of residential Rome, the cars were ambushed, the bodyguards killed, and Moro, unharmed, was ordered at gunpoint into a waiting vehicle. The alarm quickly went out, yet though the massacre and kidnapping had taken place in Rome in broad daylight and involved many conspirators, the massive police chase turned up no one, let alone the missing Christian Democratic president. For the next fifty-four days, the police, aided by the army, mounted a ceaseless search for Moro and his abductors. Security blockades brought traffic throughout the nation to a near standstill, and police and military teams descended on thousands of homes, warehouses, and abandoned buildings. Yet Moro was not to be found.

The political significance of this event is best appreciated in the light of its symbolism. In purely material terms, the immediate result of the event was the murder of six men. However, even though there was some popular concern about these deaths—including instant ritualization surrounding the spot of the murders, which became a shrine—this soon dissipated. What held popular attention was the fate of Moro.

On that March morning, Moro was en route to Parliament to lead a

historic vote for a Christian Democratic government supported by the
Communist party (PCI). Critics on both right and left attacked this new
coalition, leftists charging the PCI with "selling out" its sacred role as
guardian of the working class in order to share the spoils of government.
For the Red Brigades, who had long denounced the PCI as being in
cahoots with the bosses, portraying themselves by contrast as the only
true communists in Italy, the entrance of the PCI into the government had
great symbolic import. From the Red Brigades' perspective, it was the
PCI's firm grip on the Italian working class that was smothering the proletariat's true revolutionary proclivities. With the Communist party's
support of the Christian Democratic government, the PCI was finally
showing its true colors. Moro himself, as chief architect of the Christian
Democratic rapprochement with the Communists, was the preeminent
symbol of both the forces that had ruled Italy since the war and the
Communist-Christian Democratic alliance.

As usual, the Red Brigades had carefully selected their victim and
their timing to deliver an electrifying message. But the Red Brigades' use
of political melodrama did not end there. The kidnapping evolved into a
complex ritual, complete with standardization, repetition, mass participation, and complex symbolism, including revolutionary icons. The
symbolism was largely borrowed from headier days of revolutionary
communism, mixed with some new symbolic touches that gave the group
its distinctive identity. Most notable was the red flag with the *Brigate Rosse*
star in the center, the now obligatory backdrop for publicly distributed
Polaroid photographs of their poorly-shaven hostages.

By employing rituals in such dramatic contexts, the Red Brigades
were able to establish a public identity. A tiny, clandestine group like the
Red Brigades requires great economy of communication. They had no
hope of engaging the general population in an extended dialogue on the
virtues of their political credo. They could only hope to catch the attention
of the public fleetingly through dramatic action. They needed a highly
efficient means of communicating a powerful message. This they could
do through the ritual surrounding all their kidnappings. In addition to
catching people's attention and tying themselves into an important symbolic system, the rituals, as David Moss observes, "provide their per-
formers with a history and publicly inscribe the logic and continuity of a
project and set of beliefs; by tracing out the fact of a past, they indicate the
possibility of a future."[25] The Red Brigades thus transformed the kidnapping from a random, bloody, and pointless exercise into a meaningful
political statement, thus establishing the organization as a regular actor
on the Italian political scene.

As in previous Red Brigades kidnappings, judicial rites occupied a prominent place in Moro's captivity. The symbols of state justice were employed, but with inverted content. When state agents forcibly abduct a person, people interpret the event not as a kidnapping, but as an arrest, not as a crime but an action taken against crime. The significance comes not in the action, but in its interpretation. The Red Brigades sought to turn the state's interpretation of their abduction as murder and kidnapping on its head. Using judicial rites, they portrayed their action as the legitimate detention of a suspected criminal. Building on this symbolic inversion, they labeled the state's arrest of their comrades as political kidnappings by the police. To make their case most effectively, they followed many of the symbolic forms of the state's judiciary system. The hostage was transformed into a defendant facing a "people's tribunal."

Political kidnapping dramas typically follow the classic structure of rites of passage. The victim is first separated from the normal social structure, through capture at gunpoint and removal from normal society. He is then placed in a liminal position, lacking his former roles and deprived of normal stimuli. During this period he suffers both physical and social degradation. In Moro's case, as in others, this involved pleading his captors' cause and begging his friends in government to meet some of the Red Brigades' demands. At this stage, having lost his former social identity and no longer in any normal social context, the hostage becomes dangerous to society: he is no longer himself. When finally released, the victim is reintegrated into society, but has a new social identity, the product of his liminal experience.[26] Unfortunately for Moro, his reintegration into Italian society would only occur over his dead body.

As it turned out, the Red Brigades would have no monopoly on rites of trial in the unfolding Moro drama. Four years after Moro himself was put on trial by the Red Brigades, his captors, penned like animals into specially constructed cages lining the courtroom, would themselves be on trial. But the counter-rites of the Italian political elite began long before this. Right from the beginning, the politicians responded to the news of Moro's kidnapping with a flurry of ritual activity. The elite relied heavily on these rites to channel people's emotions and perceptions in a safe direction.

People mobilized for rites of response from the halls of Parliament to the streets of cities, towns, and villages throughout the country. When news of the kidnapping reached Parliament, the members—out in force for the historic vote on the new government—rose to their feet to pay solemn tribute to the police killed at the site of the kidnapping and to demonstrate their solidarity with Moro. Subsequently, in an unprecedented move, they pushed through a vote of confidence in the new government virtually without debate. In the streets outside, national labor organizations, themselves closely tied to the ruling parties, called for a general strike, and sixteen million people took part in associated demonstrations. These were of great importance in directing the anxiety and rage felt by the Italian public against the Red Brigades rather than against a seemingly incompetent government and its constituent parties. The demonstrations were also of great political value in expressing the solidarity of the Communists and Christian Democrats, since segments of both parties had opposed the national alliance that was voted in Parliament that day.[27]

The Communist party faced the special symbolic challenge of dissociating itself from the Red Brigades, for the Brigate Rosse presented themselves as the heirs of the communist legacy and relied heavily on the symbolism historically associated with communist parties, including the PCI. Thus, the PCI was particularly threatened by the ritual performances of the Red Brigades; their own rites and symbols were being expropriated and used against them. On the one hand, the trustworthy, reformist image that the party had succeeded, with great difficulty, in building in the face of conservative skeptics, was undermined by the Red Brigade flaunting of the sacred communist symbols in the context of murder and kidnapping. On the other hand, the Red Brigades' expropriation of the PCI's historical symbols threatened to undermine the PCI's claim to be the bearers of a proud revolutionary tradition. Through the Red Brigades' ritual presentations, the legitimacy of the PCI's claim to the symbolic legacy of Marx, Lenin, and the anti-Fascist resistance was put in doubt. Behind the symbols of communism, these rites suggested, lurks a party of accommodation, a pillar of bourgeois rule. In this highly charged atmosphere, PCI leaders knew they had to enact their own ritual dramas if they were to retain their public claim to these sacred symbols.

The PCI thus faced the delicate task of revivifying its claims to the revolutionary symbols that defined it in the public eye at the same time as it made clear its solidarity with the Christian Democrats against "terrorism." Throughout the kidnapping and its aftermath, PCI leaders performed a series of rites to demonstrate this solidarity. In one particularly emotional scene, when news of Moro's purported execution reached the Communist headquarters, party head Enrico Berlinguer, along with other PCI officials, walked the brief distance to the Christian Democratic party headquarters to offer their sympathies to Benigno Zaccagnini, Christian Democratic party head, and Giulio Andreotti, prime minister and head of the government.

In this symbolic battle between the Red Brigades and the national leaders of state and parties, the most vivid blow came on May 9, when a Red Brigade phone call led police to a car parked in the middle of Rome, equidistant between the national headquarters of the Christian Democratic and Communist parties, perhaps a hundred meters from each. There, in spite of the unprecedented police and military dragnet that had covered the whole country, and that had particularly concentrated in the capital, lay the body of Aldo Moro, killed that same day. The state's impotence could hardly have been more dramatically demonstrated. One more plaque, one more monument joined the pilgrimage sites that were to be the legacy of the Moro kidnapping. The crowds of citizens who had already begun leaving flowers each day at the kidnapping site could now complete their ritual journey by visiting the place where Moro's journey ended.

Yet, neither Moro's ritual odyssey nor his physical journey were over quite yet. Deaths of political leaders are always heavily ritualized and their funeral rites employed for political purposes. In cases such as Moro's demise, where the very legitimacy of the government and its leaders are thrust in doubt, this ritualization is likely to take on special weight. The Christian Democrats and the Communists desperately needed to use the ritual following Moro's death to define what had happened and to retain the sympathies of a population that might otherwise have reason to doubt their capacity to rule.

The course of ritual following Moro's death began, predictably enough, with a race among the political parties to get the flags at party headquarters throughout the country lowered to half-staff. The confident ritual plans of the political leaders were, however, soon scuttled when, to their horror, they read a statement released by Moro's widow, Eleonora. The martyr's body was the property of his family, not of the state, or so Eleonora Moro claimed:

The family desires that the authorities of state and of the parties fully respect the precise will of Aldo Moro. That means: no public demonstrations or ceremonies or speeches; no national mourning, no state funeral or commemorative medals. The family closes itself in silence and asks for silence. Of the life and death of Aldo Moro, history will be the judge.[28]

Shortly thereafter, the family made it clear that neither Zaccagnini, the avuncular head of the Christian Democratic party, nor any of those holding power were welcome at the house of mourning.

Behind the decision of the Moro family lay their conflict with the Christian Democratic party leadership that had developed during the kidnapping. The family had pleaded for negotiations for Moro's release, but the party leaders had refused, arguing that negotiations would lend legitimacy to the Red Brigades. In one of his last letters from captivity, following his earlier epistolary pleas for negotiations, Aldo Moro insisted that, if he were to be killed, none of the political leaders should profit from his death through commemorative or funerary ritual. It was a sentiment his family fully shared.

Although the Christian Democratic and Communist leaders tried every means of persuading the Moro family to relent and permit a state funeral, the family held firm. But this did not dissuade the politicians, who sought a powerful ritual means to bring the fiasco to a tolerable political end. The leaders required a rite that would dramatically demonstrate the government's solidarity while identifying the political leaders with the potent heroic symbolism that surrounded the martyred Moro. To do without such ritual was unthinkable.[29]

Thus, at the same time that the Moro family was sneaking Aldo Moro's body out of Rome to a country parish for a hasty burial, government leaders were planning a magnificent state funeral, to be beamed into the homes of the Italian population and, through satellite, to audiences around the world. It was a funeral without a body, but what the politicians were so eager to bury that day were not the remains of Aldo Moro, but the political disaster his kidnapping and death had produced.

On May 13, three days after Moro's body had been placed beneath the earth of an obscure rural parish, Pope Paul VI, himself, left the Vatican and entered the beautiful basilica of St. John in Lateran to preside over the memorial ceremony. In the pews of this church, where tradition has it St. Peter himself celebrated mass, sat Italy's political elite. Indeed, the great church was empty except for these state and party officials. Television cameras beamed the picture of Berlinguer, Zaccagnini, and Andreotti sitting together, the ritual portrait of political solidarity, tempered by a common humanity.

The Assassination of Indira Gandhi

Like the Moro case, the bloody conflict that convulsed India in 1984 was fought with ritual by all sides. Yet, unlike the Moro kidnapping, the practical effects of the Indian conflict also involved large-scale violence and the deaths of many thousands of people. The Indian case shows how difficult it is to separate material effects from ritual effects. From the challenge to the government posed by rebels' occupation of the Sikh Golden Temple, and their demands for political autonomy for the Punjab region, to the jostling between rival politicians over urns bearing Indira

Gandhi's ashes, the political battles were waged through ritual at the same time that they were fought with guns, knives, and fists.

Events came to a head in the spring of 1984. A large group of Sikh rebels, seeking popular support from the surrounding Sikh population of the Punjab, had established their base in the Golden Temple, holiest shrine of the Sikh people. This symbolism worked doubly to the rebels' benefit, both closely identifying them with all that was holy to the Sikhs, and making it difficult for the government to come after them without defacing the holy Sikh symbols and thus bolstering the rebel cause. By stationing their arms in the temple, beneath paintings depicting bloody scenes of Sikh martyrdom, the militants could link their own armed action to a tradition of sacred self-defense.[30]

When Indira Gandhi finally ordered Indian troops to clear the militants from the temple, the soldiers were met by a well-armed force, one that carried thirty machine guns. As the generals were at great pains to make known, the troops took heavier losses than militarily necessary in order to avoid firing on the temple's inner sanctum.[31]

If government officials thought these measures would avoid hostile reaction from the Sikh population, they were wrong. The hundreds who died in the temple were martyrs, the troops and the government not just murderers but, worse, desecrators of the holy shrine. Throughout India, Sikhs mounted protest demonstrations, many of which ended in violence. In many cities, Sikhs closed their stores in symbolic protest, while a well-known Sikh historian, Khushwant Singh, publicly returned the Padma Bhushan, one of India's highest honors, to the nation's president in protest. Throughout India, many Sikhs wore black turbans to symbolize their mourning for the Sikh martyrs, while at the main Sikh temple in Delhi three thousand people rallied, burning a straw effigy of Indira Gandhi while shouting chants for an independent Sikh homeland. The rites, far from simply providing a politically harmless release for Sikh outrage, reinforced what had previously been considered an extremist wing of the Sikh autonomy movement.[32]

Government leaders did what they could by way of counter-rites of their own, but to little avail. Shortly after the raid, in response to the building Sikh opposition movement, Indira Gandhi made a well-photographed pilgrimage of her own to the Golden Temple. Once inside, she bowed down to the floor, touching her shrouded head to the ground of the golden inner sanctum, and made an offering of rupees. Continuing the traditional rites, she chewed a mouthful of the porridge that symbolizes the hospitality and refuge offered by the temple. Her every move was beamed by television throughout the country.[33]

Although reluctant to remove the troops occupying the temple, in part because of fear of the Sikh reaction to the damage done to the holy shrine, the government finally relented. The decision to return the temple to the Sikhs followed an ultimatum by Sikhs to the government. If it were not returned to them in thirty days, a "liberation march" consisting of huge numbers of Sikhs would be staged, with the Golden Temple as its destination.[34]

Just a month later, the desecration of the Golden Temple was avenged. Two Sikh members of Indira Gandhi's bodyguard shot and killed her on the lawn in front of her official residence. Hindu anger at the Sikhs, already building in response to Sikh militancy in Punjab and elsewhere, boiled over as, throughout India, enraged Hindu crowds marched on Sikh homes, stores, and temples, burning them down and beating or murdering the Sikhs they found. Indira Gandhi had led India for the better part of two decades; in the wake of the assassination, the country threatened to fall apart.

It was in this sanguinary setting that Gandhi's son, Rajiv, orchestrated a complex series of rites designed to bring stability back to the country, to keep the regime intact, and to build up his own leadership. These centered on the dual legitimating symbols of Hindu funeral rites and of Indira Gandhi herself. Like so many other fallen national leaders, Gandhi's body lay in state for public viewing. But the political instability triggered by her death could not be so easily quieted. When three-hundred thousand angry and tearful mourners tore through the barrier that separated them from the prime minister's official residence, where the body lay, police had to brandish riot sticks and shoot tear gas cannisters to regain control. Later, amidst terrible rioting and the murder of hundreds of Sikhs, political leaders from around the world converged on New Delhi to pay their respects to the Gandhi family and to the government leaders.

The funeral itself involved a four-hour, seven-mile procession through the streets of the city, an Indian version of the ceremony held for John Kennedy over two decades earlier. Gandhi's body, too, was mounted on a gun carriage, while the heads of the three branches of the military served as her chief pallbearers. At their destination, a sandalwood funeral pyre, sat a long line of religious dignitaries representing all of India's religions but one: no Sikh clergyman would attend. Indeed, in the large crowds lining the procession route and massed at the funeral ceremony, no Sikh turbans could be seen. Given the fate of so many Sikhs at the hands of hostile crowds in those days, it is not hard to imagine why they would not appear, even if they had wanted to pay their respects. The government, however, urgently needed to show that Sikhs, too, were part of the system. They were also in desperate need of sending the message out that Sikhs were not to be treated as traitors or assassins. Thus, three Sikh politicians from Gandhi's Congress party were prevailed upon to sit in the line of clergymen, even though they had no claim to priestly status. Similarly, the red and purple turbans of a half-dozen Sikhs were clearly visible in the military honor guard.

Indira Gandhi's body had been draped in the national flag and covered with garlands. Following ancient rites, it was placed on top of a funeral pyre. Her son, Rajiv, took a flaming stick of sandalwood and circumambulated the pyre before setting it afire. The president, Zail Singh, a Sikh, climbed up the steps alongside the pyre to sprinkle handfuls of rice on Indira Gandhi's flaming corpse. The funeral pyre stood just a few hundred feet down the river from the site of Mahatma Gandhi's cremation and nearly the same distance from the pyre of Indira Gandhi's father, Jawaharlal Nehru, the first prime minister of independent India.[35]

But though Indira Gandhi's body was incinerated on the pyre, her legitimating sacrality lived on. In the uncertain political situation following her murder, identification with the martyred leader was the safest means for mainstream politicians to win popular approval. This was especially true for Gandhi's son, Rajiv, who had scant political experience yet who wanted to parlay his dynastic position into the post of democratically selected prime minister. For him, his relation to his mother and grandfather was everything, and he needed to make all he could of this tie. There was no more effective way to do this than through ritual.

No sooner had the flames died down, than Indira Gandhi's ashes were collected and divided into portions, each placed into a copper, silver, or gold urn. Under Rajiv's direction, these urns were each sent out to a different state or territory, thirty-one in all. The population of the entire country was to be tied to the regime through rites surrounding the remains. In many of the localities where the urns were displayed, fights broke out between local politicians struggling to take possession of the sacred urn. That national elections were to be held within two months lent all the more urgency to the politicians' efforts to be ritually identified with the fallen leader. Indeed, opposition politicians complained that the elaborate rites of carrying the urns throughout the country were the opening moves in Rajiv's national election campaign. They would not risk making such complaints public, though; such was the power of the rites.

Rajiv Gandhi himself had not seen the last of the ashes. Dressed in white, and followed by television cameramen, he brought one of the urns to the Nehru family estate in northern India. There, in a rite identical to the one he performed for his grandfather, Nehru, twenty years earlier, he placed the urn under a tree. A few days later, when all the urns had completed their pilgrimage and were returned to the capital, Rajiv combined the old symbolism with the new. Respecting his mother's wishes that her ashes be scattered over the Himalayas, Rajiv, a former airplane pilot, flew above the mountain cave where the Hindu lord Shiva is thought to have lived and scattered her ashes there, officially ending the twelve days of state mourning. Shortly thereafter, Rajiv won a major victory in parliamentary elections.[36]

For those left behind, death—especially if unanticipated—can induce emotional turmoil and uncertainty. So, too, the sudden death of a political leader can lead to a feeling of disorientation and painful uncertainty for a people. In the one case, as in the other, a web of ritual is spun to produce a new equilibrium, to reassure the living while sacralizing the past.

The Politics of Carnival

The rites through which people cope with crises and conflict are not just products of a political elite, whether conservative or revolutionary. On the contrary, one of the most important aspects of such rites is that they provide a means for the powerless to take power, for the people lacking any formal means of political control to have a political influence. Through rites the powerless can overcome their politically debilitating isolation, their lack of bureaucratic organization, and be united to challenge the position of the elite.

The most durable form of this type of ritual in European history involves certain Catholic community rites. Most notable of these are the rites of Carnival, held each year before the beginning of Lent. Rulers and members of the elite have long been aware of the virtue of popular celebrations in which the people could, this one day, ridicule symbols of authority and flaunt the normal restrictions on emotional display. The safety valve effect of rites of rebellion was on their mind long before it was first formulated by anthropologists. In this vein, one sixteenth-century French lawyer wrote, "It is sometimes expedient to allow the people to play the fool and make merry, lest by holding them in with too great a rigour, we put them in despair. . . . These gay sports abolished, the people go instead to taverns, drink up and begin to cackle, their feet dancing under the table, to decipher King, princes . . . the State and Justice and draft scandalous defamatory leaflets."[37] This view, of course, goes back to the Romans and even earlier in Europe, and, no doubt, occurred to political elites wherever hierarchical political systems were found.[38]

Yet even though the elite recognized the potential political value of these community rites, they also saw their dangers. By ridiculing authority, the people were playing with fire. In Renaissance Venice, for example, Carnival season involved an extended series of rites, which began the day after Christmas and ended only with the appearance of Lent. These were festive public occasions, in which the populace filled the alleys and squares, feasting, drinking, and masquerading. They chased bulls, built human pyramids, performed comedies, and detonated fireworks. The Venetian authorities had mixed feelings about all this, for while the rites gave the elite a chance to play a central role in community life, there was always the underlying threat that the celebration could get out of hand. To ensure their control of the rites, the elite sponsored the most expensive and extravagant shows. They even participated in rites of reversal with the commoners, jointly enacting a parody of the normal symbols of hierarchy and governance. Imitations of ducal processions were held, but with the order of the march—the symbolization of hierarchy—reversed.[39]

Not infrequently, such Carnival celebrations went beyond merriment and led to direct confrontations between rulers and ruled, between wealthy and poor. For example, in the town of Romans in France in 1580, a group of artisans dressed in carnival masquerade came upon a group of the rich and threatened to eat them. Apparently not sharing their holiday spirit, and interpreting their ritual threat as insupportable effrontery, the wealthy men set upon the paraders and killed them.[40]

But the poor would have their revenge, and the popular rites served frequently as a means for whipping up insurrectionary feelings and delivering revolutionary messages. In 1647, the oppressed Neapolitan masses rose up in revolt against their aristocratic rulers through use of festival rites. Subsequent challenges to the ill-fated revolt were also dealt with through ritual forms. When, for example, the Caraffa brothers tried to assassinate Masaniello, leader of the revolt, they were not simply killed. Rather, an elaborate rite of popular justice was enacted. Their corpses were dragged through the streets of Naples, pelted by rubbish thrown by the agitated crowd. Subsequently, the bodies were beheaded and the heads placed on pikes, which were paraded through the city to the accompaniment of drums. A crown of "false gold," the symbol of treachery, was placed on one head, while Masaniello himself showed his disrespect for the other by pulling at its mustache. In case there should be any doubt about the message of this degradation rite, placards proclaiming "Traitor to the People" were placed around the remains of these and other victims of the revolt. The same message was delivered in other ways as well. When the rebels displayed the head of one especially unpopular official in a central piazza, it was covered with chunks of melon rind and orange peel. The head had previously adorned the body of an official responsible for the fruit tax.[41]

France has a long and well-documented history of the use of annual community rites, especially those of Mardi Gras, for expressing class conflict and political protest. Only through the rites of Mardi Gras could the common citizen give public vent to his anger at the elite, with targets ranging from the king himself down to the local tax collector. Dramatic presentations, often with political themes, were a frequent part of these celebrations. In a common parody, the king was portrayed as a dupe of evil advisors who connived to tax, pillage, and steal all they could. Specific officials also came in for attack in this symbolic form. In Dijon in 1576, for example, the king's Grand Master of Streams and Forests in Burgundy was ridiculed both for beating his wife and for taking advantage of his position to exploit the forests for his own profit. This political use of the carnival reached such a developed state that the verses of these dramatic productions were sometimes printed, to be given wider circulation.[42]

Such rituals undoubtedly did often vent pent-up political hostilities in a way that dissipated them without threatening the political status quo. But the very fact that the rituals encouraged mockery of the politically powerful made them a prime occasion for launching more direct threats to the political order. In Switzerland in 1513, for example, in the wake of some community festivities, three hundred peasants from neighboring villages decided to march on Berne to punish their oppressors and ended up sacking the city. During the revolt of the Netherlands, Carnival costumes and symbols were used in one revolutionary episode, when rebels, dressed as fools, carried fools' scepters topped with the head of the despised governor Cardinal Granvelle. And in the Côtes du Rhône region of France in 1588, a Mardi Gras carnival was transformed into an uprising that ended in a bloodbath of government repression.[43]

The political use of these annual community festivals remained important in the following centuries as well, again providing a means for the politically disenfranchised to organize and publicly express their views. Solidarity with the democratic socialist movement that was spreading throughout the French countryside in 1849 was given public expression in towns and villages through transformation of community rites. Each year, for example, the coopers in Montpellier held a festival in honor of their patron saint, marching through the streets to the rattle of tambourines and holding their flags high. But in 1849, a new element was added in this public rite, for, in time with the tambourine's beat, they chanted "Down with the Whites, long live the Reds!" as they marched along.[44]

With the development of the rebellious Montagnard movement, the community rites took on more precise political symbolism. Typical was the case of the 1851 Corpus Christi procession in a village near Rennes. The procession was different from previous community celebrations in only one respect: a huge picture of Jesus, portrayed as a revolutionary hero, was borne aloft, the accompanying label proclaiming "Jésus le Montagnard."[45]

Indeed, the symbolism of these protest rites could be painfully explicit in striking at precise local targets. At the Narbonne carnival of 1849, for instance, a group of masked men carried a mannequin dressed up in the uniform of the National Guard. After first decapitating it, the celebrants tossed it into the river. Even more personal was the Mardi Gras celebration two years later in Brou, where a costumed crowd burned an effigy bearing the symbols of the surveyor's trade and carrying two white flags. The conservative mayor was a surveyor and, having no difficulty interpreting the message, he rushed to the scene with local police at his side. Upon their arrival, the crowd took up the chant: "Vive la République! A bas les aristos! A bas les blancs! A bas le maire!"[46]

Processions in this period often involved elaborate symbolic statements of class conflict. Some of these showed the wealthy as herdsmen driving cattle-like workers, while others, by way of utopian inversion, showed The Worker and The Farmer lording it over manacled figures of priests, nobles, and bourgeoisie.[47]

Typical was the Mardi Gras procession of 1851 held in the village of Collioure on the Mediterranean coast. At the front were two women who each represented the goddess of liberty. They were triumphantly carried through the town, followed by a dozen men clad in red. The goddesses each carried a dagger in one hand and the tricolored flag of the French Revolution in the other. The villagers paraded the symbols of revolutionary France in the face of a conservative regime. Throughout France in 1851, harsh political repression of rural radicalism had set in, and all formal political clubs and organizations of the landless peasants were forbidden. The Mardi Gras procession provided a means by which the ordinary political world could be reversed and the will of the people proclaimed.[48]

In this situation, political dissidents made use of all available public ritual forms to express their opposition, even when this meant participating in church-sponsored rites. In this light, it is not so surprising that vociferous anticlerics regularly took part in the choirs of the Maundy Thursday processions of 1850 and 1851 in order to lead them in a political direction.[49]

The authorities, though sometimes helpless, did not simply look on tolerantly while they were being vilified in these rites. Concerned officials had, indeed, tried to prevent such rites many times over the centuries. French Carnival-like processions were banned by François I in 1538 lest they take up Reformation themes hostile to the government.[50] A century later, in 1647, for fear of riots, the archbishop of Naples canceled the customary procession in honor of St. John the Baptist.[51]

Similarly, French authorities in the mid-nineteenth century struck back at the ritual attacks mounted on them. The women of Collioure, the revolutionary goddesses described above, were imprisoned for their ritual impudence, but later returned to a hero's welcome in the village. Local prosecutors regularly reported to national authorities on the occurrence of such events in their communities, and sometimes charges were brought against the demonstrators. Such was the case in a village of Provence in reaction to a procession that took place on Ash Wednesday, 1850. Peasants and artisans marched along the main street of the community, led by someone carrying a rod from which a lantern representing a head was hung. Behind him came a dummy dressed in white. Arriving at one of the village squares, a tribunal was set up and a man carrying an ax decapitated the dummy, whose head, according to the local *procureur*'s report, "was then flung into the midst of the crowd who shared it up, uttering the most odious vociferations." A bottle of red wine was attached to the dummy to simulate gushing blood. The celebrants called the white-clad dummy "blanc," thus making it represent the mayor and, more generally, French officialdom. The beheading of the dummy, needless to say, recalled the revolutionary guillotine, with all its chilling implications.[52]

Even when no political symbolism was directly introduced into the community rites, these celebrations provided an occasion for the powerless masses to gather, an occasion that was otherwise lacking. In the community of Corneilla-la-Rivière in 1850, for example, the parish's traditional celebration of its patron saint's day became an occasion when peasant radicals from throughout the area could congregate. They could profit from this legal gathering of the peasant population to spread their message, while the peasants themselves could demonstrate their solidarity. Following various political harangues by peasant activists, a policeman attempted to remove a red emblem from a participant's shirt. Enraged, the crowd began to jostle the gendarme menacingly, and two hundred agitated peasants went off to stone the justice of the peace, a government appointee.[53]

Carnival celebrations continue today in many parts of Europe as well as in other parts of the Catholic world. Where circumstances are propitious, Carnival rites remain an important means for the politically powerless to organize and to take action. Both of this century's Spanish dictators—Miguel Primo de Rivera and Francisco Franco—recognized the rebellious potential of Carnival rites and, accordingly, banned them.[54]

On the other hand, the debate over their function as a safety valve continues. According to Stanley Brandes, who studied an Andalusian community, the festival is "the symbolic means through which the governing powerholders provide the commoners of their town with a sop." It operates to "reinforce extant social relationships" through their symbolic negation. Brandes goes further, for he does not simply argue that the local elite manipulate the populace through the festival, that they "pull the wool over their eyes." Rather, by displaying in the frenetic festival the social chaos that would exist if there were no social control system, the people "demonstrate to themselves the advantages of predictability in social life and some of the ways in which predictability can be attained."[55] The festivals, in this view, have political significance, but mainly as a way of propping up the hierarchical political order.

Yet even in this cultural context Carnival rites can serve to fan the flames of class conflict rather than simply smother them. Indeed, in the Andalusian community of Fuenmayor, anthropologist David Gilmore finds just this pattern. There, the four-day celebration of Carnival is a "people's festival," celebrated and controlled primarily by the lower classes of the town. Although it is the most joyous and eagerly anticipated community event of the year for these classes, the *señoritos*, the rich, show their contempt by leaving town for the duration of the festivities. Participants are emotionally charged; jettisoning quotidian notions of shame, they are encouraged to follow their impulses. Indeed, they are encouraged to act in ways that are normally forbidden, dressing in clothes of the opposite sex, flirting openly, and behaving violently.[56]

Because the working class families of Fuenmayor are spread out over such a wide area, the Carnival assumes particular importance in building working-class solidarity. Only at Carnival time are all working-class people physically united, free from the direct supervision of the upper class or its agents. Carnival also permits the people to assert working-class values in dramatic fashion. As elsewhere, part of the rites involve ridiculing fellow villagers who have transgressed against these norms during the past year. Working-class values thus replace the laws of the state— laws associated with elite domination—as the basis for local rule. In spite of the presence of a few unarmed constables, on these days "the official state law with all its oppressiveness is replaced by the informal moral code of the poor, and those who remain in town must submit to its power."[57]

Rather than simply serving as a safety valve, as a reinforcement of the political hierarchy, Carnival in Fuenmayor further polarizes the community and sharpens the lines of class conflict. Although, in a certain sense, the villagers have driven the local elite out of town for the day, their absence is resented just the same. The townsmen cite the elite's failure to join with them in the festival as yet another example of its disdain for the working class. Historically, too, the fevered pitch of class antagonism engendered by local Carnival celebrations has led to spontaneous class violence, which has sometimes resulted in deaths. Franco knew what he was doing in outlawing Carnival rites.[58]

Popular rites of community solidarity, with their well-developed symbolism, their legacy of emotional fervor, and the power that comes with sharing with others in regular ritual performances, have the power that comes from communal effervescence, *joyeusetés collectives*.[59] It is indeed a power that can be used to deflect social tensions, but it also can be used for quite different purposes. For centuries, power holders have dreaded the rites' capacity for "exaltant subversion," and for good reason.[60] "*Carnaval fut aussi Révolte*," as Faure puts it.[61] History is dotted with acts of revolt spawned by the special atmosphere that communal rites provide. Yet, the revolutionary potential of ritual is not limited to the irrepressible spontaneity of local enthusiasms. Under the right circumstances, rites can take on a much more systematic and self-conscious role in bringing about political change.

8

Rituals of Revolution

With soaring spirits, the people of Paris descended on the city center for the consecration of the new order, the new French federation. Gathering at the Bastille on the first anniversary of its fall, 14 July 1790, fourteen thousand representatives of the National Guard and the armed forces formed groups beneath the eighty-three flags that proclaimed the departments from which they hailed. As the delirious crowds lining the streets shouted and sang, the men marched. It was a gray and rainy day, but few felt the cold.

The highlight was yet to come, for, as the marchers entered the natural amphitheater, they were greeted by three-hundred thousand wildly cheering countrymen, ablaze in their tricolor ribbons. A special gallery held the National Assembly, municipal officials, and the royal family. The vast central arena soon filled with the thousands of marching *fédérés*, the eldest member of each group proudly bearing the department flag. A special military detail held the royal standard aloft, as an artillery salute announced the opening of the ceremony.

On the central altar, Talleyrand, Bishop of Autun, assisted by a phalanx of priests, blessed the banners of the fédérés and the royal banner. The priests appeared more gaily clad than usual, with patriotic tricolored sashes across their robes. A mass was then said, but this was merely a preliminary to the great event, when Lafayette, heroic commander of the National Guard, stepped forward onto the new national altar. There, on behalf of the thousands of representatives of all France assembled beneath him, he pronounced the civic oath, proclaiming allegiance to uphold

151

the new constitution decreed by the national assembly. As he finished, by reciting the pledge "to live united with all the people of France through the indissoluble bonds of fraternity," the huge crowd beneath him roared "I swear it." Following the administration of a similar oath to the members of the national assembly, the elated multitudes looked on as a rather less enthusiastic king was compelled to swear an oath of his own. For the patriots of the revolution, it was an intoxicating day. As one national deputy wrote, "I do not believe there has ever been a more beautiful spectacle on the earth, or so many souls filled with the same joy at the same time."[1]

All through France the people rejoiced as they enacted similar ceremonies. Variations on the themes of loyalty to the new regime and popular unity were expressed in multifarious ways. In Strassburg, for example, the crowds gathered beneath an altar constructed atop a sixty-foot-high artificial knoll. On the altar, a Catholic priest and a Protestant minister, who spoke alongside the fédérés and the municipal officials, gushed forth with patriotic pride. To the accompanying roar of cannons and the beating of drums, the assembled fédérés took the same oath being administered to their compatriots in Paris at the same time. Thousands of ecstatic citizens joined them, crying "*Je le jure!*" and "*Vive la Nation! Vive la Loi! Vive le Roi!*"[2]

The value of ritual to revolutionary movements and to new regimes is based on the same factors that make it so important to all political sys-

tems: ritual fulfills important organizational needs, it helps provide legitimacy at the same time as it mystifies actual power relations, it facilitates
popular solidarity even where consensus is conspicuously absent, and it
leads people to conceive of their political universe in certain ways. In
some respects, ritual is even more important to revolutionary movements
and revolutionary regimes than it is to long-established political organizations or regimes. Radical political shifts must have strong support if they
are to be institutionalized, and this requires that people give up long-
established habits and previously held conceptions of their world.

But the best way to discover how ritual is employed in this fashion is
to take some examples of revolutions and revolutionary regimes and look
at the role ritual has played in them. The French Revolution and the rise of
Nazism, representing a democratic (or, from another perspective, bourgeois) revolution and a totalitarian movement, respectively, provide examples worth considering in detail. Briefer consideration of a number of
other revolutions and uprisings—from the American Revolution to the
demise of the Iranian shah—round out the picture.

The French Revolution

The ups and downs of the French Revolution are reflected in the huge
ritual apparatus which was, with amazing celerity, erected in the revolutionary decade at the end of the eighteenth century. Although the suc-
cesses and failures of the revolution cannot be understood simply in
terms of its contemporaneous ritual struggle, the rituals of the revolution
were far more than window dressing. The rites did not simply reflect the
political wars but were potent weapons for fighting them.

The leaders of the French Revolution were strikingly self-conscious
in creating and manipulating rites for political ends. In this they had two
sources of inspiration. Festivals had long served as a mechanism for mass
involvement in French politics, from meticulously choreographed royal
entries to rebellious village carnivals. In addition, several influential political theorists had attributed political value to popular celebrations. Indeed, Rousseau, in his recommendations to the Polish government, had
earlier called for the creation of civic festivals. These would have the
effect, he wrote, of "reinforcing the national character, of strengthening
the new tendencies," and giving "new energy to all the passions." Rousseau held, in terms that would later be taken up by Durkheim, that
participation in such festivals reduces the social barriers that separate
people and thus brings about social solidarity.[3]

The intense struggles of the first years of the revolution were waged through rituals as well as through arms. The rituals served not only to support a new solidarity, but to create new political loyalties and new political perceptions. In 1792, the year preceding the royal decapitation and the launching of the Reign of Terror, political antagonists sponsored competing public rites that were celebrated in the streets of Paris. The festival of Liberty, honoring military mutineers, and the festival of Simonneau, honoring the murdered mayor of Etampes, offer dramatic instances of this ritual struggle. Held within six weeks of each other, they pitted Jacobins against conservatives shortly before the Revolution was to reach its bloody climax.

The struggle between the forces of moderation and the revolutionaries was coming to a head. The same Lafayette who had led the National Guard in the oath to the new republic in Paris in 1790, led his guardsmen just a year later in the Massacre of the Champ de Mars on July 17, 1791. There he oversaw the shooting of unarmed petitioners who had gathered to demand that the king be put on trial and that a new government be formed. With the moderate constitutionalists in power, the revolutionaries were blocked from sponsoring a public rite to honor the victims, but they did succeed in organizing a festival to honor a similar group of martyrs, the Swiss military mutineers of 1790.

Fittingly, the villain of this story, General Bouillé, had been alarmed by the federation festival of 1790 which, he argued, "poisoned the spirit of the troops."[4] Just a month after that festival, several regiments stationed at Nancy rebelled against their aristocratic officers. Bouillé's troops were sent to Nancy, where they brutally crushed the uprising and imprisoned the rebels who survived the attack. Among the survivors were members of the Swiss regiment of Chateauvieux. The national assemblymen applauded the suppression of the mutiny, but partisans of the revolution were enraged. The imprisoned Swiss troops were part of the same regiment that had refused to fire on the Parisian crowds who had liberated the Bastille in 1789, a fact that gave their cause special symbolic weight.

Supporters of the imprisoned soldiers not only succeeded in inducing the authorities to free them from prison; they also persuaded the municipal officials of Paris to sponsor a festival in their honor. In petitioning the city authorities, the sponsors' motives were clear: "This touching festival will be everywhere the terror of tyrants, the hope and consolidation of patriots."[5] Conservatives were outraged at this commemoration of "murderers" and "public enemies," fulminating that it was an insult to the honor of the National Guard, an incitement to mutiny. Tension permeated the capital in the weeks preceding the celebration, the moderates stymied in their efforts to undermine the festival. The threat of violence hung over the approaching day.

The heroes of this festival of Liberty, the forty surviving Swiss soldiers, marched with their broken chains on display before them. A huge crowd marched and celebrated; the common people of Paris were out in force. The ceremonies bore the marks of careful Jacobin planning. Four men carried aloft tablets inscribed with the Declaration of the Rights of Man; busts of Rousseau, Voltaire, and Benjamin Franklin were paraded through the streets of Paris, and two sarcophagi were dedicated, one to the mutineers and the other to the National Guardsmen killed at Nancy. At the Bastille, leaders also dedicated a statue representing Liberty, which was adorned with scenes depicting the revolution. Along the march, to the horror of the monarchists and the delight of the Jacobins, a statue of Louis XV was crowned with a red cap and blindfolded as the procession passed.

For the participants the day was inspiring, but the conservatives dismissed it as a shabby and miserable affair, an "odious scandal" that, according to one royalist paper, "represented perfectly the triumph of crime." The Duchess of Tourzel, for her part, disparaged the fête as a "ridiculous and indecent promenade of miserable deserters." Yet the more astute conservative observers realized that the procession was a powerful stimulus to the revolutionary movement. Heads would roll.[6]

Recognizing the political power of the Jacobin festivals, conservatives quickly planned a ritual counterattack of their own. Just as the revolutionaries had seized on the symbolism of the freeing of the Swiss mutineers for their festival of "liberty," the constitutional monarchists embraced the funeral of the murdered mayor of Etampes, Jacques Simonneau, killed on March 3 of the same year. To the glorification of the rebels in the first festival, the conservatives opposed the glorification of the victims of rebellion. The mayor had been lynched by rioting peasants demanding that he control the price of grain.

Not long after Simonneau's death a battle began between the conservatives and the revolutionaries over the former's plans for public commemoration of the death. As war had broken out with Austria in April, the conservatives argued with even greater fervor that the message of the liberty festival, which encouraged insurrection, must be countered by its ritual antidote. In the aftermath of the first military losses, which the generals blamed on their troops' lack of discipline, conservative petitioners to the national assembly called for a public ceremony that would deal a "death blow" to the "enemies of the Constitution." It was "time to prove," the petitioners argued, "that the inflexible reign of law had finally come." In a report read to the assembly, a conservative champion of the rites put the matter clearly: national festivals "can excite disorder or calm it, command obedience and enforce respect for the law." Indeed, pronounced de Quincy, the festival in honor of Simonneau would be "a call to order more powerful . . . than the most menacing laws." Over the protests of the radicals, the assembly agreed to the request.[7]

Where the liberty festival had been a boisterous, ragtag affair with enthusiastic popular participation, the festival of Simonneau held just a few weeks later, on June 3, 1792, reflected its intended authoritarian message: the call for law and order. Although some (rather ponderous) classical themes were employed—liberal use was made of women clad in white Roman togas—the major element was the display of military might, with long lines of armed troops marching by. The only conspicuous civilian participation in the procession came from the public functionaries. The central theme, respect for law, was symbolized not just by the intimidating display of military force, but also by a host of symbols on parade: a huge sword, a book of law on a golden throne, and a giant statue of the Law, bearing a scepter, the statue carried aloft by tunic-clad slaves. Various commemorations of Simonneau rolled past as well, from a bust of the mayor and a model of the monument to be dedicated in his honor, to a bas-relief depicting his murder.

Leftist critics condemned the procession as an offensive military spectacle designed to humiliate the people. They showed special interest in the procession's symbolism. For example, in one of their more bizarre images, Simonneau celebrants had borne aloft an image of a shark, skewered on a spade. Across the shark's body was the phrase "respect for the law." Revolutionaries saw this as an attempt to intimidate the people, the shark representing the rebellious masses and the spade representing military might. But, argued one revolutionary paper, "we believe on the contrary that the spade is the people," and the skewered shark despotism, aristocracy, and religious fanatics.[8] Especially controversial was the bas-relief that showed Simonneau's murder at the hands of men armed with pikes, for the pike was the weapon emblematic of the revolutionaries. This representation was blasphemous to the left, who branded its perpetrators "counter-revolutionaries."[9] Four days following the giant spectacle, Robespierre rose in the national assembly to attack the festival, calling it not a fête of the nation, but a festival of public functionaries. It recalled, he argued, the ancien régime: bayonets and uniforms, "what kind of ornaments are these for festivals of a free people!"[10]

Robespierre himself was a ceaseless champion of festivals as a means of making the revolution. Indeed, in 1794 he proposed a decree in the national assembly to sponsor a series of public festivals, going so far as to establish a different festival for the tenth day of each of the thirty-six ten-day weeks that were instituted with the new calendar.[11]

The Festival of the Supreme Being, held in Paris on 8 June 1794, reflected Robespierre's attempts to regularize the rites of the state and to sacralize the regime, to replace the rites of the church and the monarchy with a holy system of revolutionary state rites. In a series of ceremonies planned to the tiniest detail, half a million people—virtually all of Paris—watched and participated in this attempt to establish a new status quo. Temporary stands were erected, huge monuments constructed, buildings along the parade route decorated, and a massive artificial mountain built. Robespierre, with a grand flourish, put the torch to a cardboard statue of Atheism, to reveal the unblemished image of Wisdom hidden beneath it. However, Wisdom—much to the Jacobins' dismay—showed more than a little trace of smoke damage. After two speeches by Robespierre and a procession, the revolutionary leader climbed a specially constructed hill, accompanied by the Convention, while the massive crowds below celebrated, singing revolutionary songs. The emotional apex came as the crowd, led by a mammoth band that included two hundred drummers, sang the recently composed "Marseillaise," intoning the last verse to the accompaniment of artillery salvos.

This rite marked the high point of the Jacobin regime. It was a huge, impressive festival, but at the same time, it highlighted Robespierre's assumption of dictatorial powers and, in the end, could not stave off his defeat.[12] Though Robespierre's head joined those of his recent victims, his visions of revolutionary rites lived on under the new government. Attacked from right and left, the Thermidorians who took power in 1794 largely accepted Robespierre's festival proposals. In some respects, they had even greater need to create new ritual to enlist popular support. Lacking the rich symbolism and ritual of the Catholics and royalists on the one hand, or popular revolutionary enthusiasm on the other, they deliberately set out to use festivals to build support for their middle course. Although the new curriculum to be instituted in the schools would provide political socialization for the youths, and the government-controlled press could influence the literate adults, festivals were needed to provide similar instruction for the illiterate masses.[13]

The ritual battle raged both among factions in the government and between the government and the church. In 1792 the state expropriated the rites of passage—from baptism through marriage to death—that had long tied the people to the church. The new rulers substituted the Declaration of Rights for the Bible as the sacrament to which allegiance should be sworn; revolutionary hymns replaced those of the church; and festivals marking the great events of the revolution replaced local saints' day processions. Indeed, for the seven-day calendar pivoting around the holy day of Sunday the government substituted the revolutionary ten-day calendar, which was punctuated by new secular festivals.[14]

The revolution set off a tremendous burst of spontaneous ritualization as well. Even though the most spectacular rites took place in the streets of Paris, no village in the country was unaffected. The simplest items of everyday life took on symbolic importance. Different costumes came to represent different political positions, and wearing the wrong color, the wrong trouser length, or the wrong hat could lead to a street brawl. Lynn Hunt, the French historian, notes that these everyday symbols did not just express the individual's political position but, by "making a political position manifest, they made adherence, opposition and indifference possible."[15]

The tricolor cockade, worn atop the head, provides a nice illustration. On the proper ritual occasions, wearing such a cockade was synonymous with expressing support for the revolution, and it evoked great emotion. In October 1789, a group of women marched on Versailles, incited by reports that soldiers there had trampled the tricolor cockade and were wearing in its place the white cockade of the Bourbons and the black of the aristocratic counter-revolution. At this time, political sides were not yet clearly formed, much less institutionalized; it was through the public display of such symbols that the political battle came to be defined. Through the rites, too, people developed their own sense of allegiances for the struggles ahead.[16]

The creation and manipulation of symbols occupied a crucial place in the French Revolution, but not all attempts at ritualization proved successful. There was a fine line between ritual forms that defined political groups and through which political struggle could be successfully waged, and those stillborn forms that simply appeared ridiculous. Partisans of the revolution, in their eagerness to replace rituals sponsored by the church and ancien régime with those proclaiming revolutionary loyalties, often stumbled over that line. The altars of confiscated churches were turned into altars for Marat or other revolutionary heroes. The adoption of a "patriotic sign of the cross" invoking Marat, Lepeletier, Liberty, or Death met an ignominious end in a number of towns and villages, while misguided patriots in one parish tried to show their revolutionary zeal by reconsecrating a "patriotic holy water font."[17]

The ritual of the French Revolution had its lighter moments, but, needless to say, it also had its grim side. Certainly one of the most celebrated revolutionary rites was the public beheading of enemies of the revolution. Indeed, with heroes and villains changing places at a dizzying pace, the government defined the enemy for the population through these rites. Murdering such individuals in the privacy of a jail cell could hardly have had the political effect of the guillotine. The scale of the bloody ceremonies certainly magnified this effect. In the year and a half of the Reign of Terror, 2,632 heads were sliced off for the edification of the population. Here it was the dying that was ritualized, not the burial. Indeed, following the decapitation of Louis XVI in January 1793, the only public funeral held was not for Louis, but for the national deputy who had been assassinated the night before. The assassin, a former royal bodyguard, had sought revenge for the deputy's vote in favor of the king's execution.[18]

The ritual of the French Revolution was designed not just to exalt but also to instruct, not just to create solidarity but also to instill terror. The guillotine was not the only instrument of intimidation. A variety of rites required people to swear their public support for the new regime. Just as fear drove King Louis XVI to swear allegiance to the new government at the festival of the federation in 1790, increasing numbers of people came under a similar threat at rituals conducted in succeeding years. Ozouf describes one such scene:

Everything works together to make this fear the real basis of the festival: the sacramental formula, written in large letters on the sacred altar of the nation; the steps to be climbed in order to take the oath; the heroic tension the body must imitate, while the arm is held straight up; and the silent coercion of the circle of spectators.[19]

The terror was evident on the faces of the participants who well knew the perils of eschewing the rite: some fainted, while others were stricken by a sudden paralysis as they were poised to sign.

Just how important was this whole complex of rites to the course of politics in France in these years? Some historians argue that the French Revolution shows how fragile an influence ritual has on the course of political events. They cite the collapse of the revolution after a decade of frantic ritualization, as well as the collapse of the ritual itself. Indeed, claimed Edgar Quinet, all of the revolutionary ritual did not succeed in "displacing a single village saint."[20] Mosse, likewise, argues that festivals cannot be "artificially created as part of the effort to unite the people behind their leaders," and he cites the demise of the revolutionary festivals with the demise of the revolution to support his claim.[21]

Yet, the fact that the cumbersome edifice of revolutionary ritual had crumbled by the turn of the nineteenth century does not prove that ritual lacked political significance. Quite the contrary. The leaders of the revolution found themselves in need of replacing the former conception of the political order—in which king, nobles, and church occupied center stage—with an entirely different one. There is no doubt that rituals played an important role in this process. The political struggle was waged in part through ritual, a fact that both reactionaries and revolutionaries recognized. Ritual was needed to define political organizations and to identify individuals with those organizations. It was employed to legitimize a wholly new regime and to delegitimize the ancien régime, to mystify an emerging dictatorship with symbols of democracy, and to create solidarity among people who had vastly different conceptions of what the whole enterprise was about. In the absence of a single figure who could, like the king, symbolize the state, the state came to be known through these ritual expressions.[22] The rites did not simply express previously existing popular perceptions of proper political relations and institutions; they also played a major role in creating these perceptions and ideals.[23]

These rites proved to be not so fleeting after all. The rituals generated in the revolutionary decade continued to play a role in French politics in the decades to come, with celebration of Bastille Day being one of the ways in which different governments and various opposition groups defined themselves. Half a century after the demise of the Revolution, the first public appearance of the new revolutionary government in 1848 consisted of a trip to the Place de la Bastille to proclaim the new Republic. The second occasion, a few days later, involved a funeral procession for the victims of the uprising that brought the new government to power; this procession ended at the Bastille. There, the martyrs were to be buried alongside their predecessors of the revolt of 1830. New symbols and new rites arose, but the political legacy of previous rituals lived on.[24]

Napoleon's suppression of the revolutionary festivals bespeaks not their political insignificance, but rather the close interrelationship between politics and ritual. With the new regime came different symbolic requirements, of which Napoleon was quite aware. The revolutionary festivals, marked by popular participation and the research for internal enemies, gave way to rites that glorified military might, conquest, and the defeat of foreign foes. Napoleon, too, had a minister of cults, whose report to the emperor in 1806 shows the ruler's continuing interest in political ritual after the revolution had been spent. Two grand national festivals were proposed: one dedicated to peace and justice, marking the new social order created by Napoleon; the other an annual festival honoring Napoleon himself, celebrated on the first Sunday following the anniversary of his coronation.[25] The cult of the revolution would be replaced by the cult of Napoleon and the latter, like the former, would meet an ignominious end.

The American Revolution

The role of ritual in the French Revolution has long been recognized, no doubt encouraged by the revolutionaries' own realization of its importance, yet the significance of ritual in the American Revolution remains little known and undervalued. Like other revolutionaries, however, the American patriots needed to delegitimate the established political order and inspire popular solidarity around a new series of political symbols. Scattered through the thirteen colonies, they also required some means of identifying themselves as participants in the same movement. Of course, the various documents that they drafted—and which would draw so much of the attention of historians later—were important in creating the new unity, the new identity, but here too ritual played a significant role, both among the elite and, especially, in relating elite action to the lives of the common people.

A major requirement of the revolution was that the mystique surrounding royal power be dispelled. This was especially problematic because for many years American patriots had—following a political precedent established millennia before—largely blamed the king's ministers and parliament, rather than the king himself, for the oppression they suffered. Indeed, up to 1776, gatherings of patriots included rituals of obeisance, such as toasts, to the king, while celebrations of the king's birthday continued to inspire popular enthusiasm.[26]

It was only with the Declaration of Independence that the symbolic break with the king came. To make such a radical shift in the popular conception of political relations, publication of the document was hardly sufficient. Throughout the colonies, public readings of the Declaration were followed by ritual killings of the king. The sovereignty of George III was destroyed as much by burning him in effigy, burying him in mock burials, and shattering statues showing his likeness as it was by formulation of the written document itself. In Savannah, Georgia, the largest gathering ever seen in the area conducted a "very solemn funeral procession" for the king. In New York City, following the reading of the Declaration, a crowd surrounded the gilded equestrian statue of the king, tore it apart, and ground it into the earth. In Boston, shop signs which happened to contain decorations of royal crowns or lions were tossed onto a bonfire. In Baltimore, patriots carried an effigy of the king through the streets of the city, climaxing their march by consigning it to flames. The patriots of the colonies, in short, found the best immediate means for destroying the king's authority to be through rituals of revolt.[27]

The use of ritual forms for organizational purposes, to communicate common allegiances and common political antagonisms, was especially important in a polity divided into separate colonies, each directly overseen from Britain. The adherence of the Virginian political leaders to the revolution, for example, was proclaimed in a series of rituals by which they connected themselves to events taking place hundreds of miles to the north. Representatives of the counties of Virginia gathered at Williamsburg, where the House of Burgesses declared June 1—the date when Parliament's closing of Boston harbor would begin to be enforced—to be a day of fasting and prayer. In retaliation for this symbolic act, the governor dissolved the assembly. There followed another rite the next day, a public signing of allegiance by eighty-nine of the burgesses to an association for common action in the crisis. In this they revived a ritual form of public protest that would later be taken up throughout the colonies in the revolution. On June 1, led by their speaker and someone carrying a mace, the burgesses marched in procession to the church in front of the governor's palace, where they held their fast-day service. Meanwhile, similar rites were being celebrated in many other Virginia parishes.[28]

But even before this time, Liberty tree observances anchored a variety of prerevolutionary rites. Following Boston's example, Stamp Act protests throughout the colonies involved the dedication of a Liberty tree, which subsequently became the focal point of many Boston protests and celebrations. Political commemorative plaques and flags adorned these trees, and they were as jealously protected as the tricolored cockades of the French. Indeed, New York's largest riot broke out when British soldiers attempted to cut down the Liberty Pole.

In the years preceding revolution, Liberty trees provided the focus for acts of rebellion that spread anti-British sentiment and encouraged rebel solidarity. Typically, the rituals involved the hanging of effigies that represented either individuals or unwelcome royal orders, such as the Stamp Act. As political tensions mounted, the tree became the preferred site for tarring and feathering ceremonies, used to intimidate loyalists and informers.[29]

In this period, it was not the patriots' actual violence against their enemies that rallied support or that most concerned the British and their allies; rather, it was the ritualized form in which aggression was carried out that gave the protests their power. The symbolic execution of a king in a large, enthusiastic public ritual had more political power than waylaying a loyalist in a back alley and beating him black and blue.[30] For an effective revolution to take place, people had to perceive themselves as oppressed, they had to see their oppression as caused by British domination, and they had to recognize an alternative political organization both as offering an effective revolutionary force and a desirable political future. In all these respects, ritual played an important part in bringing about the American Revolution.

The founding fathers were themselves aware of the need for ritual, not only for the revolution itself, but also in establishing a firm basis for the new government. Just after John Adams and his colleagues had decided to proclaim the independence of the colonies from Britain, Adams wrote that the date of the vote for independence "will be celebrated by succeeding generations as the great anniversary festival." He proclaimed: "It ought to be solemnized with pomp and parades, with shows, games, sports, guns, bells, bonfires, and illuminations, from one end of the continent to the other, from this day forward, forever more."[31]

Given Adams's views on the importance of political ritual, his later views on the ritualization of the presidency are not surprising: "Take away thrones and crowns from among men," he wrote in 1790, "and there will be an end of all dominion and justice." Indeed, he was not even happy with the title of "president," which seemed too ordinary, too little exalted. Soon thereafter, his successor's actions highlighted this link between the degree and kind of ritual that surrounds the presidency and the powers that would inhere in the office. Disdaining the elaborate ritual of Washington's inauguration, for his own inauguration in 1801 Jefferson chose instead to walk unostentatiously from his boarding house to the Capitol, where he delivered his inaugural address to a joint session of Congress. The political effect of this and other attempts to place the presidency on a less ritualistic basis was a decline in the power of the office, with the concomitant increase in the power of Congress. The return of the potent president would come only when another president interested in the symbols of office, Andrew Jackson, took over the White House.[32]

The Nazis

Although all political movements become known through their rituals and symbols, the identification of politics with ritual is perhaps nowhere more graphic than in the case of Nazism. Hitler himself became an icon,

the embodiment of two of the primary symbols of the Nazi movement:
the swastika armband and the Nazi salute. Even though the power of
Nazism was ultimately the power of an army, the creation of that power
was accomplished in no small measure by the use of ritual. The movement had its holy book in *Mein Kampf*, but there was little need for the
masses to read it, for, in George Mosse's words, "the ideas of *Mein Kampf*
had been translated into liturgical forms and left the printed page to
become mass rites of national, Aryan worship."[33] It is impossible to
conceive of the Nazi rise to power without its successful use of ritual.

Hitler, like Robespierre, was keenly aware of the need to develop
ritual forms if his revolution was to succeed. Among his earliest concerns
was the establishment of powerful symbols that could be used to identify
members of his movement, to communicate their strength, and attract
converts. Lamenting the lack of such identifying symbols in the early
post-World War I period, Hitler later noted: "The disadvantages were
above all that the party members lacked every outward sign of their
belonging together," symbols that "could be put up in opposition to the
International." Indeed, it was from observing the socialist enemy that
Hitler recognized the value of symbols and rituals to the revolutionary
cause. He tells of attending a Marxist mass demonstration in Berlin shortly after the war: "An ocean of red flags, red scarves and red flowers gave
this demonstration . . . a powerful appearance at least outwardly." But
the power was not just an external one, as Hitler went on to note: "I
personally could feel and understand how easily a man of the people
succumbs to the suggestive charm of such a grand and impressive
spectacle."[34]

Hitler subsequently devoted much attention to the creation of the
National Socialist symbols. He chose red for the Nazi flag because it was
the "most inciting color." The swastika was needed to give the movement its own unique identity. Hitler speaks of the "almost childlike joy"
he and his comrades had in 1920 when the first flag was stitched together;
the flag "had an effect," he enthused, "like that of a flaming torch."[35]

After that, a Nazi gathering could scarcely take place without the
display of the flag and the swastika. Indeed, without the symbols and
accompanying rites, it was not a Nazi gathering at all. Just two years later,
in 1922, Hitler arrived in Coburg for a parade through the city. When his
local organizers informed him that they had acceded to demands that the
Nazi flag not be unfurled in the march, he "flatly rejected," he puffed,
"such disgraceful conditions."[36] And well he might, for what good
would a demonstration do him without the red flag and the swastika?

As the movement developed, the rites were enriched, taking on symbolically molded historical associations. The death of sixteen Nazis in the abortive coup of 9 November 1923 was quickly transformed into a martyrdom and given palpable representation in the "Bloodflag" they had carried. The red of the flag came to represent the sacrificial blood of the movement martyrs and was treated as a holy relic. Indeed, the Nazis displayed this flag only twice a year: on the anniversary of the martyrdom and at the mass Reichsparty-day rallies at Nuremberg. On the latter occasions, the Nazis enacted an elaborate ritual, in which the flags and banners of each of the party units were sanctified by Hitler's touch, together with the touch of the original Bloodflag.[37]

For Hitler, mass rallies were crucial, both in attracting followers during the struggle for power and, later, in reinforcing his hold on power. The importance of the rallies, in Hitler's eyes, stemmed from the facts of mass psychology. "The individual," he wrote, "who in becoming an adherent of a new movement feels lonely . . . receives [in the mass meeting] for the first time the pictures of a greater community, something that has a strengthening and encouraging effect on most people." Surrounded by thousands of people in the rally, the individual "is carried away by the powerful effect of the suggestive intoxication." Continuing his lesson on collective psychology, Hitler argued that the fervent approval emanating from the masses of people who surrounded him demonstrated "the correctness of the new doctrine." "The man who comes to such a meeting doubting and hesitating," he wrote, "leaves it confirmed in his mind: he has become a member of a community."[38] Or, as the head of the storm troopers later put it, "Every brown troop marching under the swastika was a living call to the bystander: 'Come along, comrade.'"[39]

The apotheosis of these rites was the annual Reichsparty-day rally, staged for the first time in Munich in 1923, but held from 1927 to 1938 in Nuremberg. Here, the dedication and enthusiasm of the party's new members were reinforced and their perceptions of the world changed. At the same time, the Nazis sent out an emotionally powerful message of the inevitability of their victory.

From the first rally in 1923, many of the key ritual elements were in evidence. The rallies began with memorial services for the World War I dead, identifying Nazism with the symbolism of their sacrifice. Uniformed storm troopers marched, bearing a sea of Nazi flags. Indeed, the great majority of the eighty thousand participants in 1923 wore uniforms, giving the rally a martial flavor and recalling patriotic sentiments associated with the military and the recent war.[40]

By the end of the decade the ritual was more fully developed. At the 1929 rally, twenty-five new standards and eleven new storm flags paraded past Hitler, who touched each with the Bloodflag, as the assembled crowd thrice sang out "Germany, Awaken." But it was with the rise of Hitler to power that the rallies took on their gargantuan proportions, with vast public resources devoted to monumental construction to set the stage for the annual rites. The concept of the thousand-year Third Reich was to be made palpable through monumental settings rivaling those of ancient Egypt and Rome.[41]

A rally of one-hundred-sixty thousand Nazis marked the beginning of the new era in 1933. With the party leaders from around the country standing at attention in narrow rows, a mass of flag bearers rose from a rear embankment and marched in perfect formation through them. Later in the day, sixty thousand representatives of the Hitler Youth gathered for a similar spectacle of power. As the *New York Times* reported, "They moved by battalions. . . . As the flags swept by, a forest of swastikas almost a block long for each regiment, every flagstaff was wreathed with the green oak leaves of victory and every man's cap bore a flower or a knot of green." The rite's message was not lost on the reporter, who concluded: "Young Germany was showing its strength. And young Germany is very strong."[42]

During its formative years the Nazi movement used a variety of preexisting ritual elements to lend legitimacy to its organization as well as to build loyalties. This was especially noticeable in the constant use of commemorations of the war dead, as well as in the singing of the national anthem when the symbols of Nazism were displayed. When the Nazis came to power, they sought not only to build their own system of regular rituals, but also to undermine competing rites. Often, this meant trying to remold existing rites into expressions of Nazism.

May First, as the foremost ritual linking the working class to the socialist movement, was one of the first casualties of this ritual struggle. Rather than ban May Day observances, the Nazis transformed the day into a Festival of National Brotherhood, celebrating the new national solidarity under the Nazi regime. March 16, Remembrance Day for mourning the dead of the First World War, was likewise transformed into "Heroes' Remembrance Day," associated with the rebirth of the German army and the glorification of the military. The nation's flag—now the red flag with swastika—was no longer lowered to half-staff as a sign of mourning, but flown high as a sign of the new national pride.[43] Similar attempts at ritual transformation of secular and church-related celebrations, including Easter and Christmas, became increasingly frequent as the years passed.

The Nazis were less successful in taking over preexisting church-linked rites than they were in inventing rites of their own. Quite a bit of effort, for example, went into trying to wrest marriage and funeral rites from the churches, but with limited success. The Nazi wedding ceremony retained some traditional elements—such as the exchange of rings and the participation of godparents—while others were transformed. Bride and groom each received an engraved commemorative sheet with patriotic symbols and an appropriate saying of the Fuehrer; and in place of the charge to the newlyweds by the priest or minister, a local party officer stressed the duty of the couple to produce children for the service of the Fatherland. Yet, like their Soviet neighbors to the east, the Nazis got an unenthusiastic response.[44]

The mass rallies were the most dramatic Nazi rituals, but with the advent of the Third Reich it was the daily rites of loyalty to the regime that assumed the greatest importance in the Nazi penetration of society. Party members were required to wear the Nazi insignia at all times and to wear their party uniforms to public meetings and demonstrations. When a citizen was greeted in public with a Nazi salute, failure to respond with "Heil Hitler" carried grave consequences. There were few more powerful ways to oppose the regime than to refuse to cooperate in such a ritual; by the same token, the ritualized form allowed the regime to identify opponents or to destroy their self-respect. The power of the regime was communicated to the rest of the population not just through the enthusiastic salute of the true believer, but perhaps even more chillingly through the forced complicity of the skeptic.[45]

The Iranian Revolution

Some of the most dramatic revolutionary rallies of recent years took place in Iran in 1978 and led to the fall of a regime. The Iranian rites of resistance provide a graphic example of the power of the ritual manipulation of symbolism. They also reflect the long historical pedigree of these ritual means of political action. Indeed, the processions associated with the rites of Islam have been used for centuries to mobilize the Iranian population against the government.[46] Throughout this century, such mass rites were often a major factor in Iranian politics; they provided the only significant way that the masses of people could affect national-level political decisions. Crowd action was crucial in bringing about the Constitutional Revolution and in defeating the 1919 Anglo-Persian Agreement; mass demonstrations helped preserve the monarch in 1924 and, between 1941 and 1953, they were the primary political weapon used by the Tudeh Party and the National Front to exert pressure on the national decision makers.[47]

In 1978, revolutionary victory was precipitated by the performance of a powerful mass ritual, which was linked to the Islamic celebration of the martyrdom of Hussein at the hands of the evil Yazid, believed to have occurred thirteen centuries earlier. Chelkowski describes this mass demonstration in dramatic terms:

Rhythmically striking their breasts with their hands, the demonstrators— more than a million strong—march along the main avenues of Tehran. Those in the lead, dressed in white burial shrouds, chant the story of the mutilation and massacre of Muhammed's grandson Hussein and Hussein's family and followers by the army of the accursed Caliph Yazid in the month of Muharram in the year 680. As they sing, they intersperse their litany with a list of wrongs suffered by the Iranian people under Shah Muhammed Reze Pahlavi.[48]

For years, the leaders of the revolt against the shah had cultivated the symbolic equation between the shah and Yazid, and they had equated the sacrifice required of Islam with the sacrifice needed to overthrow the evil government. The 1978 mass ritual made this symbolic equation in a manner that was not only dramatic but also designed to rouse people's emotions to a feverish pitch as they were led to meet the repressive forces of the shah. The marchers, rather than inflicting injury on themselves in the traditional rite of self-flagellation, confronted the armed forces of the shah, dressed symbolically in burial shrouds to proclaim their readiness for the ultimate sacrifice. Those killed in these demonstrations were publicly mourned forty days later by crowds throughout Iran. These rites led to further killing of demonstrators, keeping the cycle of antigovernment rites, and with them the revolution, alive.[49]

Rites and Rebellion

When people are oppressed by the overwhelming force of a militarily superior power, and especially when they have no traditional mechanism for large-scale political organizing, ritual can provide a basis for resistance and revolt. Indeed, lack of a hierarchically organized political organization and military inferiority are often closely related; many foreign occupying powers are able to make do with relatively few armed men, thus operating at a great numerical disadvantage. What the oppressed lack is organization, and colonial regimes seek to prevent modern forms of indigenous organization from arising.

In such circumstances, organization is best catalyzed either by preexisting ritual specialists and the transformation of preexisting rites, or by leaders who pioneer new ways of generating ritual forms. The rites provide a basis for common identification and communication, for a new definition of political relations, and the delegitimating of the existing power relations.

Mahatma Gandhi pioneered such rites of resistance, first in South Africa and then in India. The ability of the British to rule the vast Indian subcontinent with a relative handful of soldiers of its own depended in good part on the religious, regional, caste, and other divisions that prevented a national opposition movement from forming. At a time when violent anti-British action was likely to elicit little popular support and be ruthlessly suppressed, and with formal political organization difficult in the face of class, caste, regional and religious barriers, Gandhi recognized the potency of ritual action.

In the late 1920s, Gandhi issued an eleven-point manifesto which, itself, would have little political effect. Although the main demands were independence and the end of British rule, Gandhi decided to focus on what was a minor point by comparison, the demand that the salt tax and colonial salt monopoly be ended. His choice of symbols was shrewd. By ritually attacking the salt tax, he challenged Britain's right to rule; yet any colonial attempts to suppress the salt tax protest would appear disproportionate and inflammatory.

In March 1929, Gandhi set off on his month-long, 240-mile pilgrimage to the coastal town of Dandi, where he would make salt from the sea. Such a pilgrimage followed various ritual precedents, and Gandhi made use of all the symbolism at his disposal. Seventy-eight carefully selected male supporters accompanied him, representing most areas, different religions, castes, and ages. They stopped at one village in the morning and at another at night, asking only for the simplest foods. In part, the voyage highlighted the contrast with the travels through the countryside of the colonial officials, who feasted amidst the general want. At each village Gandhi spoke, using the pilgrimage to educate the villagers along the route as well as to reach thousands of others indirectly through the press. According to all accounts, the march was impressive, led by the austere, yet confident and peaceful figure, staff in hand.

As the pilgrimage continued, it drew increasing attention, and thousands crowded into the towns where the procession stopped. This excitement placed great pressure on the village headmen, who acted as agents of colonial power, for Gandhi had called upon them all to resign. In the end, over two hundred of them did. When, following great popular anticipation, Gandhi reached the sea and boiled salt out of the water, he was arrested, as he had planned. Protest demonstrations and riots subsequently erupted in various parts of the country, and sympathy for the independence movement grew in Britain itself. Similar salt tax protest rites were quickly enacted elsewhere in India. It would still be years before independence was won, but the evocative flaunting of colonial laws and colonial legitimacy, as well as the impetus given to local Congress committees, played a major role in the revolutionary struggle.[50]

In all parts of the colonial world, old ritual forms were revived and combined with new elements in the conflict of the powerless against the European authorities. Seeing that they were no military match for the Europeans, people thought that if they just took the right ritual steps, victory would be theirs. In North America in the nineteenth century the Ghost Dance rituals reflected this common pattern. Participation in these rites, the Plains Indians believed, would protect them from the bullets of the American cavalry. Rarely has the symbolic world of ritual come up so directly against physical realities, as bullets pierced the ritual shield and the blood of the Indians washed away their carefully constructed symbolic universe.[51]

Similar ritual responses to colonialism swept the African continent and the Pacific islands. One such movement arose in Kenya in the first years of this century. After disastrous attempts at military resistance against the British colonial forces, the Gusii, a people who had no previous centralized political organization, turned to ritual means of organized resistance. The cult of Mumbo, based on traditional beliefs and practices, was transformed to meet the new colonial situation. Like other movements that dotted the colonial world, Mumboism rejected European customs and called for a return to Gusii traditions. Careful observance of prescribed ritual, participants believed, would lead to the new millennium, from which the Europeans would be banished. They thought that no harm could come to anyone who wore a Mumbo cloak and cap made of animal skins. The British recognized this as a challenge to their authority, and colonial officers who encountered the Mumbo vestments seized and burned them. With their ritual garb thus suppressed, members who worked around colonial authorities took to wearing a more modest badge of goatskin under their clothes.[52]

Such ritualized movements of resistance were not simply ways of harmlessly displacing native opposition to colonialism. In the 1940s in western Kenya, for example, not far from the Gusii, there arose a resistance movement called Dini ya Msambwa. The movement united members of the twenty-one politically independent, but linguistically and culturally related, groups of Luhya people. The powerful rites used to organize the revolt were accompanied by more material acts of rebellion, including the burning down of colonial buildings.

The use and power of ritual in this revolt can be illustrated by the pilgrimage made by five thousand Dini ya Msambwa members in 1947. Dressed in traditional warrior's garb and led by the prophetic leader of the movement, Masinde, they proceeded to Lugulu fort, where in 1895 their ancestors had fought a battle against the British. At the site of that now sacred place of resistance, Masinde led his followers in an elaborate rite. The slain warriors of a half-century before had been left unburied; Masinde and his followers began by performing proper burial rites, thus appeasing the unhappy spirits of the dead. After sacrificing a black ram, Masinde recalled the truce with the British that had followed the unsuccessful battle. Taking a bottle containing a sheet of paper symbolizing the truce agreement, he announced, "I make this sacrifice to commemorate the truce between the whites and the Bukusu [a Luhya group] at the end of the war." He buried the bottle, then dug it up, poured ram's blood over it, burned the symbolic document and smashed the bottle. Lest the meaning of the rite be unclear, he proclaimed that by his sacrificial rite the truce with the government was broken and the power of the whites was ended. The rite, combining traditional and Christian symbols, helped spur the people on to insurrection.[53]

Reliance on ritual to express and organize rebellion against repressive regimes continues to this day in Africa, where the white run South African government prevents the black majority from organizing political opposition in other ways. Nowhere is this more dramatically expressed than in the funerals of blacks slain by the police, through which a mass resistance movement is being built. Indeed, this is a tactic used by revolutionary movements throughout the world.

A brief glance at the political use of funeral rites in 1985 illustrates just how powerful a political device they have become in the South African struggle against white rule. On April 13, for example, a mass funeral was held for twenty-seven blacks—many of them youths—killed by police. Most of the victims had been killed when police opened fire on mourners who had gathered for a previous funeral. The sixty thousand participants in the rite, according to the newspaper account, "mixed solemnity with politics, mourning with exhortation and clenched fists with the soft swelling of African singing." The coffins were draped in the black, green, and gold colors of the outlawed African National Congress.[54] Emotions ran high.

Although these rites certainly allow people to ventilate their anger and their rage at their own powerlessness, they should not be seen as simple safety valves permitting the regime to continue without serious threat. In the absence of preexisting forms of national political organization, and given the government's repression of more direct attempts to organize such national protest, much less revolt, the funerals allow a national leadership to arise, and they create a common identity, building a broader antigovernment solidarity. They also help create an alternative conception of a future political universe, and they instill strong emotions of resistance to the government.

Just as in the French and American revolutions, ritual is used in South Africa not only to build solidarity, but also to instill fear and communicate an alternative source of power. Few more chilling examples of such symbolism are to be found than the "necklace," a tire doused in gasoline, used to immolate government collaborators. Such political enemies could be more simply (and safely) done away with in private, but the use of the necklace in public executions has transformed the humble tire into an unexpected symbolic weapon. At a funeral for eighteen blacks killed in September, for example, forty thousand people gathered, their emotions aroused. Following the rites, in which the crowd chanted "Long live the necklace!", two white passersby had the misfortune of running into people leaving the funeral and were brutally murdered. At another funeral the same day, a priest arrived just in time to rescue a terrified young black man, thought by members of the crowd to be a police informer, who had been bound with a rubber tire necklace and was about to be burned alive.[55]

That these funerals are more than expressions of outrage, that they are also important elements in defining and organizing political opposition and revolt, was also evident in another funeral held in October. Following a killing during riots in Cape Town, fifteen thousand people marched in a huge funeral procession. The political significance of the event lay in the fact that the dead man was a Muslim, and the procession was led by Muslim clerics. The marchers, holding hands, chanted "Allahu Akbar!" ("God is Great"). Interspersed throughout the procession were men carrying the African National Congress flag and others carrying placards bearing ANC slogans and verses from the Koran. This rite obviously reflected growing political opposition in the formerly quiescent Muslim community, and for this reason was viewed with great concern by the government. But it was more than that, for it was also very much part of the building of the resistance, of the creation of political opposition.[56] It signaled a new course of action and called for a new set of political attitudes among the Muslim population.

The South African government looked on these funeral rites with mounting alarm. In July 1985, in spite of the symbolic importance given by the world community to free observance of funerals, the government ordered a ban on outdoor funerals in areas of political unrest. Also forbidden were funeral services for more than one person at a time. The display of flags and banners was outlawed and presiding ministers were forbidden from making any political statements during the rites. Noted the *New York Times* reporter from Johannesburg, "Some black commentators have said they regard the funerals as a safety valve that permits the expression of anger, but the police seem to have seen them as fanning fires of organized dissent."[57] Seldom have the arid debates of armchair theorists been so clearly echoed by the protagonists of political struggle.

Ritual struggle against the black liberation movement in South Africa involves not only white attempts to suppress black rituals, but also the use of powerful political rites among the whites as well. Commemorations of the great symbolic events of Afrikaner history, such as the Great Trek and Battle of Blood River in the nineteenth century, remain important means of reinforcing political solidarity and claiming legitimacy against ever-increasing threats. And even right-wing resistance to the Pretoria government is given its most dramatic expression through ritual, as evidenced by the rally held in May 1986 commemorating Republic Day. It was then, on the twenty-fifth anniversary of South Africa's proclamation of independence from Britain, that the largest gathering of right-wing opponents of President Botha's proposed racial reforms was held. Eight thousand Afrikaners gathered beneath the huge Pioneer Monument. Murals on the monument portray the movement inland of the first Afrikaner settlers in the seventeenth century. At the ceremonies, scores of men attired in paramilitary uniforms hoisted the banner of the Afrikaner Resistance Movement. The red flag has a swastika-like black emblem in the center, more than a little reminiscent of another flag, from another time. Some symbols are hard to kill.[58]

. . . with a flag one can do anything, even lead a people into the promised land.

—THEODORE HERZL[1]

One sings the Marseillaise *for its words, of course, but one sings it especially for the mass of emotions that it stirs in our subconscious.*

—MAURICE BARRÈS (1902)[2]

9

The Rites of Power

After examining political rites in what may seem like a tremendous variety of people, places, and historical periods, I think it is time to ask what lessons these cases offer about the nature of political life. In trying to bury the naive notion that politics is simply the outcome of different interest groups competing for material resources, I want to avoid the opposite fallacy, that of portraying people as zombies imprisoned in a symbolically created universe they are powerless to change.

The fact that symbols and rites are crucial to politics does not mean that people simply view the world in the way their culture and its guiding myths dictate. What *is* crucial, though, is the fact that power must be expressed through symbolic guises. Symbolism is necessary to prop up the governing political order, but it is also essential in overthrowing it and replacing it with a different political system. Where do these new symbolic systems come from? If we are simply prisoners of the dominant symbol system, if it is the symbol system that determines our perceptions of the world, our interpretation of political life, how does change come about?

Here it is hard to resist the biological analogy. Evolution can only take place where genetic diversity exists, so that with environmental change certain genes, previously rare, become increasingly common. Genetic diversity itself is produced in a population both through spontaneous innovations (mutations) and through the movement of individuals from one population to another (genetic drift). In a comparable, but by no means identical way, symbolic diversity exists in all societies, and the diversity is replenished through symbolic invention and through contact with other populations having other symbol systems. Our symbol system, then, is not a cage which locks us into a single view of the political world, but a melange of symbolic understandings by which we struggle, through a continuous series of negotiations, to assign meaning to events.[3]

A struggle such as this implies the existence of conflicts of interest among people. The conflicts can take place within a political framework that is itself relatively unquestioned, as when many compete to fill a limited number of available positions of power. Here the symbol system itself provides the impetus for the conflict, as well as the terms in which the conflict will be fought. There can also, however, be conflict over which symbolic understandings are appropriate: what roles should exist, what the "issues" are, and which are worth fighting over. Part of the cultural struggle is a struggle over the dominant symbolic paradigm, the struggle for hegemony. It is a battle that never ceases, for, in Fox's words, "domination has to be constantly re-created."[4] It is the struggle of the privileged to protect their positions by fostering a particular view of people's self-interest. It is a process that involves defining people's identity for them. How else can people's strong devotion to such abstract entities as the nation or people's willingness to die for this unseen identity be explained?[5]

But a view of culture that does not account for interaction between our symbol system and the physical world of human activity is bound to lead to a mystical anthropology, a world without any cross-cultural regularities, one in which historical change is completely fortuitous. People's symbols, and their behavior, do change, sometimes with startling rapidity, and these changes are very much linked to external events.

One example will serve to relieve this abstract discussion: the course of British royal ritual in the nineteenth century. On the surface, these rites seem to argue for the durability of symbolism, and especially ritual, in the face of massive changes in the material world. However, the splendiferous elaboration of ritual that so colorfully marks the British royal family today represents not a simple continuation of a long-held tradition, but a re-elaboration of old symbols to meet changing political conditions.

Throughout most of the nineteenth century, the rites surrounding the family events of British royalty were rather modest, and no one could

seriously argue that they bound the entire population in political communion. In 1830, when William attended the funeral of his predecessor,
George IV, he talked his way through most of the service and then unceremoniously walked out before it was over. His own coronation was a
hurried affair, the subject of snide comments among the elite. Nor did
William enjoy any more ritual glory at his own funeral. The long ceremony was tedious, and some participants laughed, gossiped, and
snickered not far from the coffin. During Victoria's subsequent coronation, the clergymen, who had not rehearsed the rite, lost their place, the
archbishop of Canterbury could not get the small ring on the queen's
pudgy finger, and two of the trainbearers chattered away, oblivious to the
ceremony.[6]

It was only in the last quarter of the nineteenth century that royal
ceremonial reacquired its public magnificence, its pomp magnified for the
masses. This corresponded to the monarchy's final loss of power, the rise
in domestic class conflict, and the need to provide a unifying symbol for
the colonies. Other sources of political power, previously in competition
with the Crown for influence, were no longer threatened by the ritual
elaboration of royal prestige. The nonroyal elite could whole-heartedly
support the symbolic re-creation of the sacred ruler, which helped prop
up the hierarchical social structure. The rites gave the people a feeling of
stability, as well as a measure of pride by tying them into a larger imagined tradition of greatness. To understand the power of the rites it is
necessary to examine the power of the symbols; but to understand why
the rites developed as they did one must look at the struggle for power
that has taken place in Britain, and at who controls these ritual productions.[7]

If no celebratory fireworks were shot off during the dark years of the
Second World War, when London prepared for German air attacks, the
change in ritual action could hardly be explained by symbolic constraints.
The material world does indeed impinge on the world of symbolism.
Geertz argues that: "The real is as imagined as the imaginary,"[8] and it is
true that we can only perceive and understand the world around us
through mental processes that present the world to us in a highly limited
way. But we live in a world that needn't obey our imaginings. In trying to
understand in what ways it won't, we come to see the vulnerability of
symbols. In highly stratified societies, elites must work hard to foster
symbolic systems among people whose experience insidiously undermines them, for the best that elites can hope to do is shore up a predomi-
nant symbolic construction of how society should work. They can never
eliminate all loose ends, all contradictions in the symbols themselves, nor

all vestiges of alternative symbol systems. Fragments of other systems, as well as internal symbolic contradictions, are forever threatening to replace discredited views of the political universe.[9]

Have We Outgrown Political Ritual?

Throughout Africa, South America, and Asia, missionaries face difficult decisions about how to handle traditional rites. If they try to suppress the rites, they risk the people's wrath and undermine their own efforts to win a place in the community. On the other hand, to allow the people to continue with their alternative ritual system is to admit failure, to leave the field to the competitor. Typically, the missionaries solve this liturgical conundrum by doing what they can to insinuate their church into the celebration of preexisting rites.

If the beleaguered missionaries occasionally feel uneasy about all this, they may take comfort from the fact that their ecclesiastical predecessors faced much the same predicament in Europe. In Russia, for example, the Shrovetide celebration began as an indigenous holiday designed to hasten the coming of the spring, but was ultimately taken over—though never fully tamed—by the Russian Orthodox Church, which found a place for this rite of sun worship in its holy calendar.[10] In France, the priests were constantly faced with popular rites that the church could control only with the greatest difficulty. For example, through the nineteenth century, in periods of drought, the peasants of Nièvre organized processions to the Fountain of Nôtre Dame de Fauboulain to seek rain. The local priest was willing to lead the pilgrims in various prayers along the way, but he was less enthusiastic about the climax of the rite. On arrival at the fountain, each member of the procession took off a shoe, filled it with fountain water, and poured the water over the priest's head.[11] When the church, for reasons of propriety or perceived symbolic incongruity, refused to sanction such rites, popular hostility gushed forth.

Quaint stories such as this, with their benighted peasants and patronizing priests, bring to mind the common image of ritual as something that more sophisticated peoples have largely outgrown. In Malinowski's influential model, as more of nature is understood, there is less need for ritual; people replace much of magic with science. They no longer need to use rites to try to control the world around them, since science robs life of many of its mysteries.[12]

Max Gluckman concluded from his African research that ritualization of social relations is a feature of small-scale societies only.[13] Subsequently, other scholars, though recognizing the importance of political ritual to modern state societies, have clung to the notion that the value of such rites lies primarily in their appeal to the ignorant rather than to the educated, to the masses rather than to the elite.[14] Typical is Lane's claim that state rituals in the Soviet Union are targeted for those who "have been unable *fully* to develop their critical faculties." Ritual is used to overcome conflict in the Soviet Union, she claims, "in relation to the culturally more backward or immature social strata who do not perceive of inequality as a basic conflict in their society." From this, she concludes that ritual "can only successfully gloss over conflicts (or resolve ambiguities) in societies, or sectors of society, which accept their social order uncritically."[15]

The condescending view that ritual is something that can pull the wool over the eyes of the credulous, while serving the well-informed as a tool for exploiting the ill-educated, has been around for a long time. But did Reagan's trip to Bitburg have meaning only for the poorly educated? Did Carter's failure to attend Tito's funeral have no significance for the Yugoslav elite, who of course realized that this was only a ritual, not the real stuff of politics? Did the draft-card burning ceremonies have no meaning to their highly-educated participants or to the political elite who directed the Vietnam war?

Political rites are important in all societies, because political power relations are everywhere expressed and modified through symbolic means of communication. Of course, certain kinds of political rites are more important in some political contexts than others. Aronoff, for example, speculates that political rites are most common in new regimes that are dominated by a single party, as found in many African states.[16] Indeed, the creation of a new nation requires a massive effort at symbolic construction, of creating a sense of unity, of identification with a new, abstract entity, the nation. Here ritual can play a major role. Given the difficulty people with no previous conception of national identity have in making the notion symbolically real to themselves, it is not surprising that such efforts often involve creation of personified images of the state. Rites of new nations thus often revolve around the image of the heroic figure leading his people to the promised land.[17]

Conversely, the struggle of groups seeking to delegitimize the new order involves a fierce struggle over symbolism. The Ethiopian flag and ubiquitous portraits of Mengitsu, the nation's leader, are anathematized in Eritrea while they are ritually venerated in Addis Ababa. Singing a national anthem to Sri Lanka in Jaffna can be hazardous for a Tamil. If the struggle for national identity is waged in part through symbols and accompanying rites, so too is the revolutionary struggle for liberation. The true nation that is to be liberated is as much a symbolic product as the false nation that is to be dismembered.

Thus, in the new nations, it is not just the regime that is in the business of cultural management, but all players in the political scene. Insofar as the concept of the nation is problematic, the need to create rituals to bolster or destroy it is politically crucial. It is a lesson to be learned from Ireland, from the Sudan, from the efforts to create an independent Quebec or an autonomous Punjab. No matter how culturally artificial or historically serendipitous the new national entity, it must be endowed with a sacred unity and made to seem a natural social unit. Such is the case in Indonesia, with its scores of component islands extending over thousands of miles and enveloping totally unrelated peoples. Playing rather loose with history, Indonesian political leaders speak of the three-hundred-fifty years of colonialism that Indonesia has endured, even though the whole notion of Indonesia is a twentieth-century invention, and much of what is now included in the country was conquered by the Dutch colonialists only at the end of the last century.[18] Without rites and symbols, there are no nations.

On the Effectiveness of Political Rites

The power of the rite is based in good part on the potency of its symbols and its social context. Political rites can be spectacular failures or, more routinely, simply fail to be spectacular. Many observers over the centuries have linked the success of a political rite to the degree of popular enthusiasm it generates. Elites attempting to design effective political rites have, accordingly, been advised to design them in a way that will get people emotionally involved.

This is certainly the advice that Soviet officials have recently been getting. The success of spontaneous rites in the early post-revolutionary period, with the "chaotic enthusiasm and communal feeling" that they engendered, is compared unfavorably with today's routinized state rites.[19] One scholar cautioned that the "artificial process of imposing new customs does not evoke much enthusiasm among the population." A Russian folklore expert opined, in this regard, that "our new holidays and rites are threatened by a danger . . . the possibility that they will become rather desiccated and conventional, and turn into tedious bureaucratic measures."[20] "Without faith," writes Struve, "there is no rite."[21]

Although seemingly incontrovertible, this is an overly narrow view of the nature and importance of political ritual. To pursue this point, it is worth looking at a Soviet example offered by a scholar who holds this opinion. Lane chronicles the transformation of the mass rites commemorating May Day and the October revolution. What once aroused delirious popular emotions has turned into a bureaucratically organized affair that has little room for spontaneous individual involvement. "Even committed communists," she writes, "admit that the demonstration has become a 'mere ritual.'" What could be a better example of the "unimaginative uniformity" of the rites than the canned music to which the parading soldiers strut?[22]

Here, then, is the consummate case of the bureaucratized, routinized state rite. But what does it mean to say that this has degenerated into "mere ritual"? What can be made of the fact that, in spite of all the heavy-handed state management of the rite, "its sheer volume made it nevertheless impressive, not only for the foreign observers but also for the Soviet people who had turned out in great numbers to witness it with interest"?[23] In fact, the rites continue to have an important political effect, with their dramatic display of military might, the prominent place occupied by the national leadership, the sea of red flags and banners, and the venerated portraits of the founding fathers. Why else, after all, would the Soviet leaders go to so much trouble and expense each year to assure that just these effects are maintained?

People's emotional involvement in political rites is certainly a key source of their power, but there are many other emotions besides joy. As is evident in the cases of Aztec cannibalism, the Nazi salute, and the French revolutionary oath, political rites are also effective when they inspire fear. The effectiveness of rituals also depends on the cognitive messages they so effectively convey, and here too there need be no collective effervescence for the messages to be sent and received. When diplomats from eleven Western countries attended a massive funeral for a dozen South Africans killed by police in December 1985, they may have felt euphoric or they may have been scared to death. Either way, their participation in the ritual sent a strong message to the South African government, to the people of South Africa, and to the people of their own countries. And whatever emotion the royal subject felt as he bowed before the king, it is clear what emotion the king was likely to feel should the subject fail to bow before him. In short, not only do we commune through ritual, we also use ritual to define our relations with others. Political rites often help to allay our fears, but they can also create anxieties that we would not otherwise have.[24]

If rites can be powerful weapons of the elite, they also represent one

of the most potent weapons of the powerless. Lacking the formal organization and the material resources that help perpetuate the rule of the elite,
the politically deprived need a means of defining a new collectivity. This
collectivity, created through rituals and symbols, not only provides people with an identity different from that encouraged by the elite, but also
serves as a means to recruit others to their side. An insurgent force that
lacks its own distinctive symbolism and rites is not likely to get very far.
By the same token, regimes seeking to suppress insurgent movements
pay very serious attention to their opponents' rites and symbols. Thus,
Ukrainian nationalists in the 1960s charged the Soviet government with
"symbolcide" for its systematic efforts to erase all symbols of Ukrainian
independence. Said one Ukrainian, "It is impossible to break people, to
make slaves out of them, until you steal their holy days from them, and
until you trample upon their temples."[25] There could be no Mau Mau
movement without Mau Mau rituals, nor any popular anti-Vietnam war
movement without its public rites.

Ritual, Symbols, and the Nature of Political Life

The call to place politics on a more rational basis has a long history in the
West, rising to international prominence with the philosophers of the
Enlightenment. In this view, there is little place for ritual in politics, for
rites are the products of passion, not reasoned reflection.[26] People must
be freed from their "irrational obsessions."[27] Machiavelli, in a less re-
forming spirit, argued that "Men in general make judgments more by
appearances than by reality, for sight alone belongs to everyone, but
understanding to few." Accordingly, he advised the rulers to "keep the
people occupied with festivals and shows."[28] Yet, for the rationalists, it
was precisely this ignorant tenacity of the masses to judge by "appearances" rather than by "reality" that had to be overcome.

　　With the rise of Mussolini and Hitler, Western observers again pointed fearfully to the insidious role of political rites in seducing a credulous
people. Cassirer went so far as to identify political rituals with the abdica-
tion of moral responsibility, claiming that "in all primitive societies ruled
and governed by rites individual responsibility is an unknown thing."[29]
The world of political rites is a world of political idolatry, and a "world
with no idols," opined Light, "would not be such a bad place to live in.
Illusion is a curse."[30]

　　But if illusion is a curse, it is a curse from which no prince's kiss will
free us. There can be no politics without symbols, nor without accompanying rites. Nor can there be a political system based simply on rational

principles, freed from symbolic connotations. What may be emerging is a world in which all people think that their political system and their political conceptions are rational. Gilbert and Sullivan's play *H.M.S. Pinafore* with its chorus, "Yet in spite of all temptations, to belong to other nations, he remains an Englishman, he remains an Englishman," comes especially to mind. Political allegiances flow not from culture-free judgments but from symbolically nourished conceptions of the order of the universe.[31]

Some observers have recognized this but, with Freud, envision a future in which society will have evolved to a higher, more rational plane. Bagehot put the matter more colorfully, if more ambiguously: "Royalty is a government in which the attention of the nation is concentrated on one person doing interesting actions. A Republic is a government in which the attention is divided between many, who are all doing uninteresting actions. Accordingly, so long as the human heart is strong and the human reason weak, Royalty will be strong because it appeals to diffused feeling, and Republics weak because they appeal to understanding."[32] Yet, not only will people always be influenced by their emotions, they also will never be able to make judgments independent of the symbols they use, symbols that can be powerfully conditioned through rites.

In the United States, as elsewhere, the rationalist bias remains strong, and the power of political rites is downplayed and often misunderstood. No less acute an observer than John Kenneth Galbraith, for example, in examining the quadrennial American political party conventions in 1960, seemed positively peeved that people did not all share his recognition that the rites were a vestige of the past and could not survive much longer. The convention, he wrote, "is an occasion when almost nothing happens. At the same time it is the centre of a remarkable conspiracy to prevent this elementary fact from being known." It "has lost nearly all of its original functions and gained no new ones." Indeed, for Galbraith the modern nation has little use for political rites, though the recognition of their demise prompts a nostalgic, if patronizing, note: "We have few ceremonies, few rituals in the United States with a legitimate historical base. The conventions were about the best we had. So everyone hates to see them go—or to admit that, like the cavalry charge, they have gone."[33]

Jimmy Carter, infected with this same liberal spirit, made a big show at the beginning of his presidency of shedding a number of the rites that had developed around the presidency. He eschewed the cavalcade back to the White House after his inauguration, walking back instead; he removed the gold braids from the epaulets of the White House guards, and he suppressed the flourishes that accompanied the president's every formal entrance.[34] He soon learned, though, that the power of these rites, of these symbols, was not to be trifled with. If by deritualizing the office he became "one of the people," he paid for it by being popularly perceived as lacking the charisma, the sacred aura, that presidents should have.

What could be more telling than the case of the French Revolution, whose leaders, dedicating their efforts to the elimination of superstitions and the crowning of Reason, rushed to create rites of Reason? The battle of Reason against Ignorance was fought through symbols and rites. The tricolored French flag, symbol of a nation liberated from the obfuscations and oppression of the Church and aristocracy, was created the day after the fall of the Bastille in 1789. When Napoleon was exiled to Elba in 1814, one of the first acts of the reactionary government was to restore the white flag. A year later, on his return from exile, Napoleon quickly replaced the white with the tricolor. Alas, this totemic tug-of-war continued the following year, for one of the casualties of Napoleon's defeat at Waterloo was the revolutionary flag, replaced once more with the white flag of aristocratic France. Yet, though driven underground, ritual use of the tricolored flag continued to have a powerful effect in focusing democratic political loyalties and rallying opposition to the regime. When the battle that would again overthrow the old regime was being waged in July 1830, the rebels' efforts were given a big lift when some of their colleagues stole up to the tops of Nôtre Dame and city hall and hoisted the forbidden tricolored flag. The raising of the flag did not simply announce a political change, it was one of the instruments of struggle. Its effect on the rebels, wrote one observer, was "electric."[35]

A century later, in Fascist Italy, people were bound to the regime through a panoply of rites of obeisance, from the Roman salute to the Day of Faith in 1935, when all Italians were urged to show their loyalty to the regime by giving their wedding rings to the state, to be melted down to help finance the African colonial march. The socialists and communists had been severely repressed, their leaders languishing in prisons or in exile abroad. In those dark days, what gave Mussolini's opponents in the working-class areas of northern Italy most hope, what stirred their anti-Fascist sentiments most powerfully, was the sight of the red flag, mysteriously hung each May Day from the factory smokestacks. The symbolic vehicles bearing an alternative understanding of political reality, an alternative basis of social solidarity, were kept alive amidst a fearful repression; the rites of resistance were all the anti-Fascists had left.

If Galbraith detected the disappearance of ritual in modern political life, he was looking in the wrong places or, more likely, failing to see the layers of rites in which modern political life is enveloped. This is understandable, since our own rites, our own symbols, are the most difficult to see. They seem like such natural ways of behaving, such obvious ways of representing the universe, that their symbolic nature is hidden. Here, indeed, is one of the sources of power of rites and symbols, for insofar as they become dominant they create a convincing world; they deflect attention from their contingent nature and give us confidence that we are seeing the world as it really is. It is hard to argue with a flag, especially if you do not have another flag of your own; hard to argue with a song, unless you have another anthem to sing; and hard to argue with the view of the world embodied in the funeral rites of a popular leader, a fact both Communists and Christian Democrats realized to their horror when Aldo Moro's family stole away in the night with his blood-stained body.

Notes

Chapter 1

1 Vogt and Abel (1977); Hamill (1966).
2 Reynolds (1978: 134).
3 Norbeck (1977); Sahlins (1981). On politics and sacrality, see also Bergesen (1977: 221).
4 Shils (1966: 447).
5 The foremost anthropological exponent of the importance of ritual in all political systems is Abner Cohen (1974, 1981). Mackenzie (1967: 290), a political scientist, declared: "It seems an obvious idea that someone should tackle the subject of political rituals in the Western world, yet nothing (so far) has come of it." Although there have been a handful of attempts to examine modern political rites in the West since, to date not much progress has been made in putting this all in a larger framework.
6 Here I follow Clifford Geertz's (1966: 5) broad use of the concept of the symbol. In this view, a symbol refers to "any object, act, event, quality, or relation which serves as a vehicle for a conception," and the conception constitutes the meaning of the symbol.
7 Arnold (1935: 17).
8 Berger (1967: 22).
9 Berger (1967: 24).
10 Burke (1966: 5).
11 Cassirer (1946); Bauman (1973).
12 Carlyle (1908: 45–46, 54).
13 Kessler (1978: 244–45).

14 Nieburg (1973: 54).
15 Lerner (1941: 235).
16 Duncan (1962: 245–46).
17 Walzer (1967: 194).
18 Anderson (1983: 14–15). The idea that polities are governed by "master fictions" is Geertz's (1977). For a discussion of this usage, see Wilentz (1985).
19 Novak (1974: 23), Turner (1974: 55).
20 Singer (1982: 76).
21 Sahlins (1981: 70) recounts this story, citing an earlier version in Lévi-Strauss (1966: 239n). Radcliffe-Brown (1940: xxiii) also sheds light on the problem of reification in politics, writing that "There is no such thing as the power of the State; there are only, in reality, powers of individuals—kings, prime ministers, magistrates, policemen, party bosses, and voters." On the development of children's political conceptions, see Niemi (1973: 121–22).
22 The exceptions include Murray Edelman (1964) and some of those most influenced by his work, such as Bennett (1980). In addition, a few political scientists, such as Aronoff (1980) and Laitin (1986), have been directly influenced by symbolic study in anthropology. However, this line of work has remained outside the main stream in both political science and political sociology, as its practitioners recognize. In Laitin's (1986: 171) words, "The systematic study of politics and culture is moribund."
23 Cohen (1974: 8; 1979: 87).
24 Cohen (1974: 7) has also made this point. I do not want to leave the impression that quantitative studies have no place in political study, for such work is certainly of great value in dealing with certain problems.
25 Geertz (1964: 53).
26 Turner (1974: 140–41).
27 Walzer (1968: 36). It may seem surprising to quote Marx in conjunction with an attack on materialist approaches to the study of politics, but there is no contradiction here. In some ways, as Cohen (1979: 11) notes, the study of political symbolism is "essentially the child of Marxism, for it was Marx who initiated the systematic analysis of culture in relation to the power structure." Gramsci's attempts to produce a more sophisticated Marxian analysis of the relationship between ideological and material bases of political power are also of interest here. See Gramsci (1971) and, for commentary on Gramsci's famous concept of hegemony, see Boggs (1976), Kertzer (1979), Fox (1985) and Laitin (1986).
28 See, for example, Firth (1951: 222).
29 Durkheim (1915: 37, 41).
30 Nadel (1954: 99) should be mentioned as one of the earlier anthropologists to focus on the formalized, repetitive nature of ritual rather than limiting the term to action involving religious phenomena.
31 Ritual can also be seen as a quality of certain social behavior that is found where there is an important symbolic element present. In this perspective, actions are not categorized as either ritual or not, but rather both the ritual and nonritual aspects of particular human activities are examined (Leach 1954: 12–13). See also Da Matta (1977: 256–57).
32 Thus, Gluckman (1965: 251) distinguished between "ritual" and "ceremonial"; for a similar distinction see Binns (1980: 586). Referring to Gluckman's distinction, Aronoff (1979: 277–78) clarifies his own use of ritual as a means of analyzing Israeli

politics by specifying that "when I speak of ritual in the modern political context I
am referring to secular, ritual-like activity in which mystical notions are absent."

33 Further discussion of some of these definitional issues are found in Mead
(1973: 87–88); Munn (1973: 580); Lukes (1975: 290); Goody (1977); Rappaport
(1979: 174–77); Lewis (1980); Lane (1981); and Silverman (1981: 164).

34 On the political significance of spatial symbolism, see Kuper (1972: 420–21). Trexler's (1973: 126–27) analysis of the sacralization of city hall in Renaissance Florence
provides valuable insight into this process.

35 Leach (1966: 404); Rappaport (1979: 175–76).

36 Myerhoff (1977: 200) also makes this point. From a Freudian point of view, an
individual may engage in ritual behavior even though his action is not intelligible
to anyone else. In such cases, of course, the analyst attributes symbolic meaning to
the standardized, repetitive action, even though it is idiosyncratic. However, I
exclude such idiosyncratic forms of behavior from what I consider as ritual action
in this book. For a discussion of such "neurotic ritual," see Freud (1907).

37 Cassirer (1955: 38–39).

38 Nieburg (1973: 30).

39 Myerhoff (1984: 152).

40 Moore (1975: 234).

41 On the physiological bases of the power of ritual, see d'Aquili and Laughlin (1979)
and Lex (1979).

42 See Rappaport (1979: 188).

43 Cohen (1974: 4; 1979: 102–03); Bennett (1979: 109n). Ortner (1975: 167) has made a
related point that is worth noting here:

We cannot, if we understand the ritual fully, emerge with a clear-cut assertion of
the primacy of the social or cultural or psychological dimension of its meaning. It is
the ingenuity of ritual symbolism constantly to transpose these into one another,
to solve problems in each mode by means of forms derived from other modes and
thus to show, ultimately, both their irreducible interdependence and the means of
moving between them.

44 Along these lines, Lewis (1977: 2) has written that "Symbols and sentiments feed
upon each other and their fruitful interplay lies at the heart of social behaviour."
Fernandez, in dealing with this question of the relationship between ritual and
emotional arousal, views the metaphorical properties of ritual as enabling people
to bring about changes they desire in "the way they feel about themselves and the
world in which they live" (1971: 56).

45 Arnold (1935: iii). This dramatistic perspective has been more fully developed in
Goffman's (1959) works. The use of masks in so many rituals around the world
may be seen as a manifestation of this dramatistic quality (Tonkin 1979).

46 Mosse (1975: 168).

47 Lewis (1980: 33).

48 I follow Cohen (1981: 156) here in defining a drama as "a limited sequence of
action, defined in space and time, which is set aside from the ordinary flow of
purposeful social activity."

49 Bennett (1977: 227).

50 Victor Turner (1967) has been the one to develop most fully the concept of condensation in this context.

51 Munn (1973: 580) discusses the multivocality of ritual symbolism. Turner (1967: 50)
    uses the term multivocality to refer to the fact that "a single symbol may stand for
    many things."
52 Lewis (1980: 9). On this point, too, see Sperber's (1975) attack on semiotic analysis
    of symbolism.
53 On the creative potential in ritual, see Munn (1973: 592), Moore (1977: 167), and
    Moore and Myerhoff (1977: 5).
54 Mead (1973: 90–91).
55 Skinner (1981: 37) has made a similar point. See also Lane (1981: 2) and Bennett
    (1980: 170).
56 Douglas (1966: 62).
57 Bennett (1980: 168).
58 Quoted in Pocock (1964: 14). More recently, Gramsci (1971: 339) has made a similar
    argument:

> The most important element is undoubtedly one whose character is determined
> not by reason but by faith. But faith in whom, or what? In particular in the social
> group to which he belongs, in so far as in a diffuse way it thinks as he does. The
> man of the people thinks that so many like-thinking people can't be wrong, not so
> radically, as the man he is arguing against would like him to believe; he thinks
> that, while he himself, admittedly, is not able to uphold and develop his argu-
> ments as well as the opponent, in his group there is someone who could do this
> and could certainly argue better than the particular man he has against him; and
> he remembers, indeed, hearing expounded, discursively, coherently, in a way
> that left him convinced, the reason behind his faith.

59 In Pocock (1964: 6).
60 In Binns (1980: 594).

Chapter 2

1   Venomous descriptions of this KKK rite are found in *Life* magazine (27 May 1946):
    "The Ku Klux Klan tries a comeback," pp. 42–44, and *Time* (20 May 1946), p. 20.
    For the KKK oath, see the Committee on Un-American Activities (1967).
2   A number of students of organizational behavior have begun examining the cru-
    cial role played by rituals in all kinds of organizations, including large corpora-
    tions. See Pfeffer (1981); Deal and Kennedy (1982); Martin (1982); and DiMaggio
    and Powell (1983).
3   Cohen (1974: 30).
4   Burke (1959: 263).
5   Burke (1959: 267).
6   Lane (1981: 94). Another of the intended effects of this rite was undoubtedly to
    bolster the legitimacy of Brezhnev by associating him with Lenin.
7   On children's developing concepts of flag and country, see Weinstein (1957).
8   In this context Ortner (1973: 1340) recalls a billboard she saw, proclaiming "our
    flag, love it or leave."
9   On this point, see Agulhon (1979: 30–31). For an instructive Turkish example of
    this personification, see Frey (1968).
10 For a description of the Montagnard rites, see Margadant (1979) and Berenson

(1984). For a similar republican secret oath of this period, see McPhee (1977: 248–49).

11   The anthropological literature on rites of passage is voluminous. For the classic statement, see van Gennep (1960). On rites of passage into political organizations, see Borhek and Curtis (1975).

12   In making this point, Cohen (1974) uses the term *distinctiveness* in this sense.

13   Arnold (1937:25).

14   Goldberg (1981:110).

15   See Wechsler (1985:136) on the use of Mao's body by the Chinese government. For Lenin, see Tumarkin (1983). On the "routinization of charisma" more generally, see the classic work of Max Weber (1968).

16   Fortes (1940, 1945). See also Evans-Pritchard (1964) and Fortes and Evans-Pritchard (1940:21–22).

17   Richards (1940).

18   Knauft (1985:327–28) and Kelly (1977).

19   This can also be seen in ancient Greece and Italy, where what identified the members of a city was the fact that they performed the rites to their protecting deity together (Fustel de Coulanges 1901:193–211).

20   Evans-Pritchard (1949); Turner (1957:292), Fry (1976), Cohen (1981:127–28); Packard (1981).

21   Wechsler (1985:6–7).

22   On the changing Chinese calendar, see Wechsler (1985:212).

23   Thompson (1985:40).

24   To protect their privacy, Hicks and Kertzer (1972) used the pseudonym "Monhegan" for this Indian group. For the same reason, their exact location is not provided.

25   Geertz (1980:76–77). For a good example of how ritual authority can be transformed into broader political authority in small-scale societies, see Packard (1981).

26   On these imperial rites in the provinces of the Roman Empire, see Fishwick (1978), Price (1984), and Taylor (1931).

27   Geertz (1977:159).

28   Graham and Johnson (1979:3). There is a large historical literature on European royal entries. Of special interest here is Apostolidès' (1981) study of the royal entries of Louis XIV. But see also Bergeron (1971) and Strong (1973).

29   Geertz (1977:162).

30   Moore (1977:154).

31   Ozouf (1975; 1976:62–63).

32   Gerlach and Hine (1970:58).

33   Hooglund (1980).

34   Cohen (1974:78).

35   These induction rituals can be viewed as a special aspect of the more general phenomenon of rites of passage (van Gennep 1960; Turner 1969) which are universally employed in publicly marking changes in social status.

36   Fortes (1962:86).

37   Cassirer (1955:41).

38   As Anglo (1969:11) argues, "These ceremonies were no mere embellishment of political realities; they were, in fact, the instruments employed to erect the entire Tudor dynasty upon a sure foundation."

39   Seth Mydans, "Violence increases: The standoff goes on—Separate government

named by rebels," and Clyde Haberman, "Rebels inaugurate Aquino as president," both in *New York Times* (25 February 1986), pp. 1, 13.

40 This account of Shilluk kingship rites is taken from Evans-Pritchard (1964: 205–06). For a comparable series of rites by which the chief of the Bemba, in Rhodesia, is invested, see Richards (1940: 99).

41 Giesey (1985: 48; 1960: 177). The classic study of the king's two bodies is Kantorowicz (1957).

42 This ban on the heir attending the funeral procession of his father was sometimes difficult for the successor to abide. At the funeral of Francis I in 1547, for example, Henry II snuck into Paris to witness his father's magnificent funeral procession from a house along the route. He warned his compatriots never to reveal his presence there (Giesey 1960: 48).

43 This reflects a symbolic element of royalty that has a wide distribution through the world. The king of Bunyoro, in Uganda, for example, could not even attend his own mother's funeral in 1953, for the king must not come into contact with death (Beattie 1960: 26).

44 Giesey (1960: 60).

45 Hanley (1983: 333).

46 Jackson (1984: 46–47).

47 The transformation of the accession ceremonies into a liturgical rite can be traced in western Europe to the coronation of Charles the Bald as king of Lorraine in 869 and that of Louis the Stammerer as king of West Francia in 877 (Jackson 1984: 203–04).

48 Nelson (1976: 108–09).

49 Cherniavsky (1961: 90–91). This rite has an even longer history. For example, a similar ritual of self-crowning has been described for the Spanish kingdom of Navarre in the fourteenth century by Woolley (1915: 134–35).

50 Bennett (1979: 132) argues that the subsequent presidential pardon of Nixon by his successor robbed the rituals of their dramatic resolution. On rituals of degradation, see Garfinkel (1956). Gronbeck (1978) has further developed Garfinkel's ideas with respect to the political realm.

51 Lane (1981: 217–18). Such rites of delegitimation have a long history. For example, following the break from Philip V of Macedonia, the Athenians decreed an end to all festivals and monuments honoring him and his ancestors. His name was erased from inscriptions and he was to be cursed in the Athenians' annual prayer for their city (Price 1984: 40).

52 Wechsler (1985: 24–25).

53 This description of the Roman triumphal entries is based on Scullard (1981: 213–17).

54 Indeed, this use of ritual displays to indicate status relations can be traced biogenetically to a broad range of animal behavior. See, for example, Lorenz (1964; 1966), Huxley (1966), and Laughlin, McManus, and d'Aquili (1979).

55 Bernardi (1986: 185).

56 Meeker (1972: 263–64).

57 Quoted in Vittorio Mimmi, "Sulla marcia della pace, nuova polemica Psi-Pci," *La Repubblica* (15 October 1986), p. 7.

58 This was the account of Gorbachev's motives given in the Italian press at the time. Whether these were in fact his motives is not crucial here; the point is that political

observers thought the botched ceremony was a reasonable explanation of the ambassador's dismissal.

59 I am indebted to Bergeron (1971:1) for this quote.
60 Strong (1973:121–22).
61 Ranger (1980).
62 Ranger (1980:354–55).
63 Kurtz (1978:184).
64 I rely here primarily on the account of Motolinia, the Spanish colonial observer of these rites, as found in the manuscripts edited by Foster (1950:63–64). Also see Kurtz (1978), Aho (1977), and Conrad and Demarest (1984).

Chapter 3

1   My description of the Bunyoro rites surrounding the Mukama is based on Beattie (1960:27–29).
2   This quote, by Daniel Malan, head of the "Purified" National Party, is taken from Thompson (1985:40). My description of this event is based on Thompson (1985:39–40, 144–45).
3   Durkheim (1915). The quote, referring to Durkheim's position, is from Leach (1954:15).
4   Balandier (1970:99–101). Hunt (1977:143), adopting just such a Durkheimian view, observes, "Insofar as societies tend to deify, sacralize and idolize their own social condition as the condition of the cosmic order, secular rituals would always be tinged with sacred aspects, with deeply buried divine symbolism. . . ."
5   On the rites of the Roman and the Athenian senates, see Fustel de Coulanges (1901:216–17).
6   Bettelheim (1960:86).
7   This account of the rites surrounding Lenin is taken from Lane (1981:210–13).
8   Abercrombie and Turner (1978).
9   Piven (1976:302).
10 Bloch (1974:79).
11 Turner (1967:30). On the continuing necessity for political systems to be legitimated through symbolic means, see Smith (1978).
12 See Hall (1972; 1979) on political impression management.
13 Ranger (1980:350–55).
14 Cohen (1974:53).
15 Deal and Kennedy (1982:72).
16 Edelman (1977:161).
17 Seneviratne (1978:120–22).
18 Hayes (1960:66).
19 Sanson (1976:126–37).
20 See Kertzer (1980).
21 Kessler (1978) discusses one such case of this use of Islamic ritual in Malaysia.
22 Lane (1981:137–38). On the rise of Christianity in Russia, see Brian-Chaninov (1931).
23 Oberg (1940:156).
24 Wechsler (1985:87).
25 Holtom (1972:45).

26 On the Hindu rites, see Inden (1978). The identification of the health of the king's body with the health of the nation became a classic anthropological theme through Frazer's treatment of the divine king in his *The Golden Bough* (1925).

27 Adler (1982: 395).

28 Norbeck (1977: 70–71). The account of the dishes of the Japanese emperor is based on the account of a late seventeenth-century European visitor to the court.

29 On the horses of Spanish rulers, see Ruiz (1985).

30 Geertz (1977: 168).

31 Cohen (1974: 32; 1981: 3–4, 8–10).

32 Crick (1982: 303).

33 Greisman and Mayes (1977: 60). See also Bloch (1977a; 1980).

34 Scott (1975).

35 Unger (1974: 126–27); Lukes (1975: 305).

36 Bennett (1980).

37 Olsen (1970: 98). Olsen's study, based on a Norwegian community, challenges the common use of decision-making models by political scientists to examine the municipal budgeting process. In a fascinating analysis, he concludes that "decision-making does not seem to be a very important aspect of what is going on" (1970:99). The title of his article is revealing: "Local budgeting, decision-making or a ritual act?" On ritual in municipal government, also see Dahl (1961: 133).

38 Johnson (1978).

39 This point is argued by Aronoff (1977: 96).

40 Nieburg (1973: 55) has gone so far as to argue that "Improvement of one's own legitimacy is . . . the main function of political symbolic action. . . ."

41 Fortes (1962: 86). On the social tensions engendered by role transition rites, see Foner and Kertzer (1978; 1979).

42 Bloch (1977a: 139).

43 On the role of ritual in structuring social reality, see Moore and Myerhoff (1977: 3–4).

44 Rosaldo (1968).

45 Hocart (1927: 7).

46 Valeri (1985: 140–52). On the rites surrounding the rulers of ancient Hawaii, see also Sahlins (1985). Such was the power of the Aztec ruler that commoners were forbidden to look on his countenance, prostrating themselves in his presence (Kurtz 1978: 175).

47 Fairman (1958); Engell (1967).

48 On the Persians and Romans see Taylor (1931: 3, 195). For the reference to Virgil, see Fustel de Coulanges (1901: 233).

49 Starkey (1977: 194).

50 Figures on the royal touch are from Bloch (1973: 204, 212).

51 Starkey (1977: 192–94) and Bloch (1973: 65).

52 On the Soviet parade as a rite of popular submission, see Binns (1980: 598).

53 Gluckman (1963).

54 Gluckman (1963: 127).

55 Lane (1981: 23).

56 For another criticism of Gluckman's thesis, see Norbeck (1963). For a sixteenth-century English example of rites of reversal, see Pythian-Adams (1976).

57 Quoted in Duncan (1968: 182).

58 Kertzer (1974).
59 See Turner (1969: 176–77).

Chapter 4

1 The "aisles of grief" quote is from MacGeorge Bundy, cited in Manchester (1967: 570). My description of the Kennedy funeral rites is based on Manchester's moving account, as well as on Grosvenor (1964), and "The family in mourning," *Time* (6 December 1963), pp. 27a–27b.
2 Durkheim (1915: 230).
3 Durkheim's views on the role of ritual in producing social solidarity build on those expressed before him by Robertson Smith. For Smith, ritual was the key to religion, and the archetypical rite consisted of people getting together to eat and drink. Smith (1907: 267) concluded, in this vein, that "the whole force of ancient religion is directed, so far as the individual is concerned, to maintain the civic virtues of loyalty and devotion to a man's fellows at a pitch of confident enthusiasm. . . ."
4 For a recent anthropological application of this Durkheimian approach to the ritual marking of community boundaries, see Rasnake (1986).
5 Durkheim (1915: 418).
6 Durkheim (1915: 427).
7 Radcliffe-Brown (1952: 157) claims that he formulated this perspective independently of Durkheim, while he was working on his Andaman Island dissertation in 1908 (but only published in 1922).
8 Fortes and Evans-Pritchard (1940: 17–18).
9 Turner (1957: 290, 302). He puts this thesis succinctly: "A society continually threatened with disintegration is continually performing reintegrative ritual" (1957: 303).
10 For a different and more critical view of Durkheim's use of psychology, see Beidelman (1966: 403).
11 Munn (1973: 583).
12 Munn (1973: 605).
13 Michelet's quote is from his book, *Le peuple,* cited in Rearick (1977: 60).
14 Winthrop (1857: 335).
15 As it turns out, the native people of Australia have a devilishly complex kinship system at the heart of their society. Social scale and social complexity are not so simply related.
16 Subsequent anthropologists have not all agreed with him on this point.
17 Bergesen (1977: 221). On the archetypal political myth of the evil national enemy, see Edelman (1969: 235). On rites of nationalism, see Hayes (1960: 167–68).
18 Lerner (1941: 236).
19 On the sacrality of the U.S. Constitution, see Bennett (1975: 87).
20 Novak is quoted in Fairbanks (1981: 215). See also Brogan (1968: 357). The American civil religion debate was triggered by Bellah (1967; 1968).
21 Warner used the pseudonym of Yankee City for Newburyport.
22 Warner (1974: 90).
23 Warner (1974: 111). On the Soviet use of the war dead to foster national solidarity around the government, see Lane (1981: 145–46).

24 Shils and Young (1953:80). For a stinging rebuttal of this view of the coronation, see Birnbaum (1955).
25 Blumler et al. (1971:151).
26 Joseph Lelyveld, "Pledge of truth and faith by a duke and a duchess," *New York Times* (24 July 1986), p. 6. For a Durkheimian view of the rites of British royalty performed abroad, see Cleveland's (1973) perceptive study of the royal tour of New Zealand.
27 Robertson Smith (1907:16).
28 Leach (1954:13–14).
29 Cassirer (1946:24). The remark by E. Doutte comes from p. 602 of *Magie et Religion dans l'Afrique du Nord* (Algiers: Typographie Adolphe Jordan, 1909).
30 Quoted in Nieburg (1973:32).
31 Rappaport (1979:194–95).
32 Fernandez (1965:923; 1977).
33 Converse (1964).
34 Lukes (1975). See also Mann (1970).
35 Gluckman (1965:252); Cohen (1974:36–37); Bennett (1979:117–18). However, see chapter 5 for a discussion of the theory of cognitive dissonance.
36 Goldschlager (1982:17–18).
37 Lane (1981:141).
38 Sanson (1973:455). My account of the conflict over the Joan of Arc commemorations is based on this source.
39 Quoted in Haynes Johnson's preface to Lowe (1967:18).
40 Blumer (1974:9–11).
41 Sproull (1981:210).
42 Turner (1969:96, 128–29). See Siegel (1969:282–83) for a critical discussion of Turner's thesis.
43 Hayes (1960:166–67); Shafer (1972:214–15); Aronoff (1980:7).
44 Da Matta (1977:247).
45 Snyder (1976:272–73).
46 Dahl (1961:113).
47 I follow here the interpretation offered by Silverman (1981).

Chapter 5

1 Hedrick Smith, "Delicate Reagan path," *New York Times* (6 May 1985), p. 10; Bernard Weinraub, "Reagan joins Kohl in brief memorial at Bitburg graves," *New York Times* (6 May 1985), p. 1.
2 For an account of the ceremonies surrounding Charles's entry into Bologna, see Terlinden (1960), Chastel (1960) and Strong (1984:78–80).
3 Bandura (1977:160).
4 Nisbett and Ross (1980:7).
5 Tesser (1978:293). There are a number of different terms used by various cognitive psychologists to refer to the same basic principle. Schema is the most widely used.
6 Neisser (1976:55).
7 Fiske and Kinder (1981:173).
8 Fiske and Kinder (1981:176).
9 Hamilton (1981:139); Tesser (1978:290–98).

10 Tesser (1978: 307).
11 Higgins and King (1981: 71).
12 Higgins and King (1981: 80). The role of each of these factors in rendering schemas accessible is still a matter of controversy among psychologists.
13 Tversky and Kahneman (1974).
14 Nisbett and Ross (1980: 7).
15 Wilder (1981).
16 Tesser (1978: 294–95).
17 Cantor (1981).
18 The power of the cognitive drive for consistency remains a matter of considerable debate. While some psychologists argue that conflict between schemas or conflict between observations and schemas leads inexorably to schema revision, others argue that there is no inherent drive toward cognitive consistency. For example, Tedeschi et al. (1971: 692) suggest that people are socialized to learn that they must give other people the impression of being cognitively consistent, and it is this social force that works toward cognitive consistency rather than any inherent process.
19 Wilder (1981).
20 Nisbett and Ross (1980: 43). I am also indebted to these authors for the quote from Stalin.
21 McGuire, McGuire, and Winton (1979: 79).
22 Nisbett and Ross (1980: 172).
23 This example is adapted from Abelson and Kanouse (1966: 171–72).
24 For one of the few conscious attempts to use the language of cognitive psychology in studying ritual, see McManus, Laughlin, and d'Aquili (1979).
25 Schutz (1967: 84).
26 Needham (1963: vii).
27 Douglas (1966). Her discussion of schema is found on page 36.
28 Edelman (1971: 83).
29 Crocker (1977).
30 Moore and Myerhoff (1977: 18).
31 Bloch (1975: 22).
32 Nieburg (1973: 44) makes a similar point.
33 Hamill (1966: 216), Turner (1974: 125). Exemplary royal punishment was well developed in sixteenth-century France, where public executions drew large crowds to see the tongues of blasphemers slit, the hands of desecrators sliced off, and the corpses of traitors quartered, with the parts marched in public display through the city (Davis 1973: 62).
34 For a discussion of the use of symbolism by President Carter in the Iranian hostage crisis, see Hahn (1984).
35 Geertz (1966: 28).
36 Also see Aronoff (1977: 88).
37 This argument has previously been made by Lukes (1975: 301–2).
38 Da Matta (1977: 259).
39 Here I am paraphrasing Young's (1986: 105) comments on political monuments.
40 Bloch (1974; 1977b; 1980); Silverman (1981).
41 Rockhill (1905: 35–36).
42 Snyder (1976: 196–98).

43   Kuper (1978: 301–4).
44   Edelman (1971: 158). See also Bennett (1980).
45   Weatherford (1981); Gronbeck (1978: 167).
46   Bergesen (1977: 223). On rites of denunciation, see Garfinkel (1956).
47   See Garrow (1978).
48   Bennett (1979).
49   Habermas (1986: 44).
50   These remarks come from a presidential press conference, and are reproduced in "Responses of the President to queries on the German visit," *New York Times* (19 April 1985), p. 13.
51   James M. Markham, "Kohl says he urged Reagan to visit a Nazi camp," *New York Times* (17 April 1985), p. 14.
52   Meir Merhav, "Honouring evil," *Jerusalem Post* (3 May 1985), reprinted in Hartman (1986).
53   Kohl's remarks were delivered at the U.S. air base at Bitburg following the cemetery ceremonies. The text is reproduced in "Transcript of speech by Kohl at U.S. air base," *New York Times* (6 May 1985), p. 8.
54   *Chicago Tribune* (4 May 1985).
55   In addition to the sources previously cited, this discussion of the Bitburg rites is based on the following accounts in the *New York Times*: Bernard Weinraub, "Aides review Reagan's plan to visit German war graves" (13 April 1985), pp. 1, 4; David Kaiser's op-ed piece, "No wreath for Hitler's army" (18 April 1985), p. 27; Anthony Lewis, "Appointment at Bitburg" (25 April 1985), p. 27; Flora Lewis, "History doesn't die" (26 April 1985), p. 31; and James M. Markham, "Bitburg visit: Is 'reconciliation' needed?" (2 May 1985), p. 16. Also of use were Eckardt (1986), Hilberg (1986), and Rosenfeld (1986).
56   McManus (1979: 227).
57   Edelman (1971: 45–46).
58   Gramsci (1971: 339).
59   Edelman (1969: 232).
60   Norman (1975: 83).
61   Snyder and Swann (1976: 1041).
62   Bagehot (1914: 147).
63   This is cited in a similar context by Cohen (1979: 98).
64   Festinger (1957: 2–3). On cognitive dissonance, see also Wicklund and Brehm (1976).
65   Festinger (1957: 11).
66   Bettelheim (1960: 290–91).
67   Bettelheim (1960: 292).
68   Hobsbawm (1984: 67).
69   Lewis (1977: 2).
70   See Ortner (1978: 5–6).
71   Of relevance here are the findings of some experimental psychologists that the more a person thinks about another person, an idea, or a thing, the more intensified that person's feelings become. See Tesser (1978: 298–99).
72   Lane (1981: 32).
73   Turner (1974: 56).
74   Bandura (1977: 65).
75   Burke (1950: 58).

Chapter 6

1 Douglas Robinson, "Many draft cards burned—eggs tossed at parade," *New York Times* (16 April 1967), pp. 1–2.
2 Scribner (1978: 304).
3 Duncan (1962: 264–65).
4 Bryant (1976: 15).
5 Muir (1981: 232–35).
6 Muir (1981: 190).
7 Wechsler (1985: 143–60).
8 Bryant (1976: 18).
9 Hanley (1983: 287–91).
10 Elias (1983: 86–88).
11 Weatherford (1981: 267).
12 Weatherford (1981: 65–66).
13 This point is made by Weatherford (1981: 36).
14 Some congressional candidates, such as William Cohen of Maine, have taken this metaphor very seriously, engaging in long hikes through their districts or states.
15 Novak (1974: 41, 47).
16 Gillespie (1980: 110–11).
17 Aronoff (1986: 114–15). This discussion is based on Aronoff's account.
18 This is a bit of a simplification, as there was always considerably more flexibility in the determination of descent group membership than is implied in a system in which genealogy unambiguously determines membership. In addition, marriage alliances can also be important in determining status. However, for present purposes this is of no great importance.
19 Abu-Zahra (1972). For a more traditional anthropological analysis of the use of ritual to prop up the dominance of village descent groups in the Islamic world, see Peters (1963).
20 Hardgrave (1979: 151).
21 This account of the Nadar struggle is based on Hardgrave (1979). For a similar example, involving the attempts of a caste of cowherds in northern India to change their status by wearing the sacred threads associated with the lofty twice-born status, see Srinivas (1966: 16). There, too, violent assault by members of the higher castes greeted their efforts. For a discussion of how the rituals of domination continue to be used by the Tamils of Jaffna, Sri Lanka, to keep the untouchables in their place, see Pfaffenberger (1980).
22 Davis (1980), on whom I base my description of the Bengali case, offers a similar analysis of the relationship between economic changes and political change in India. For another instructive example of intercaste struggle through ritual, see Blustain (1980).
23 This is not the place to enter into a discussion of theories of why rites of passage are universal. See Van Gennep (1960) for the classical statement of this problem.
24 Supek (1980: 289, 320).
25 Lane (1981: 242).
26 Serge Schemann, "New Soviet rituals seek to replace Church's," *New York Times* (15 March 1983), pp. 1, 6.
27 On Soviet state efforts to replace the churches in sponsoring rites of passage, see Lane (1981), Unger (1974), and McDowell (1974).

28 Bucci (1969:37). The emergence of the Italian nation in the nineteenth century itself involved a long battle between Church and state over marriage rites, with each refusing to recognize the validity of the other's ceremonies. For details, see Kertzer and Hogan (n.d.).

29 For a fuller discussion of the battle over rites of passage in Albora, and in Italy in general, see Kertzer (1980). Here I describe the situation existing in Albora in 1971–72.

30 Children, though, may also have weekly contact with a priest through the hour of religious instruction mandated at all public schools. However, under the terms of the agreement between state and Vatican that went into effect in 1986, each family has the choice of whether to send their child to such instruction.

31 Senin-Artina (1983).

32 Taylor (1931:79–80).

33 This last phrase, and this account, are drawn from Biondi (1973:226).

34 Biondi (1973:224–25).

35 Lane (1981:279).

36 This occurred in San Francisco in March 1983.

37 Even the Pentagon demonstration in 1967 began in the center of Washington, linking the demonstrators to the nation's symbolic core.

38 Berger (1968:755).

39 Berger (1968:754).

40 Lee (1980:602).

41 James M. Markham, "Bitburg visit: Is 'reconciliation' needed," *New York Times* (2 May 1985), p. 16.

42 Wallace Turner, "Antiwar demonstrations held outside draft boards across U.S.; 119 persons arrested on coast," *New York Times* (17 October 1967), p. 3.

43 Cook (1976:110).

44 E. W. Kenworthy, "10 leaders of protest urge laws to end racial inequality," *New York Times* (29 August 1963), pp. 1, 16; James Reston, "'I have a dream . . .' Peroration by Dr. King sums up a day the Capital will remember," *New York Times* (29 August 1963), pp. 1, 17.

45 Reynolds (1978).

46 Jo Thomas, "Ulster tension focuses on street called the Tunnel," *New York Times* (5 July 1985), p. 2; Tim Jones, "Lambeg drums tightened for the Ulster tribal march," *The Times* (London) (5 July 1985), p. 4; Tim Jones, "RUC ready for Ulster marches," *The Times* (London) (12 July 1986), p. 2; "23 policemen injured in clashes across Ulster," *New York Times* (13 July 1985), p. 4.

Chapter 7

1 This account is based on Chagnon (1983).

2 Huxley (1966:250).

3 Lorenz (1964:48–49; 1966).

4 Lorenz (1966:281).

5 It is even possible to acknowledge a phylogenetic legacy, a genetic predisposition toward certain kinds of stylized behavior, without falling into the trap of seeing human ritual as simply a more elaborate version of nonhuman "ritualization." See Smith (1979) for a discussion of this point.

6 See Calder (1966) on the use of symbols of identity in the ritualization of warfare. See Reay (1959: 291) for a description of rites of war preparation in New Guinea.

7 Patterson (1969). For a dramatic case of the use of sports symbolism in internal political struggles, see Kessler's (1978: 143–45) account of soccer in Malaysia.

8 Norbeck (1963: 1265).

9 Dramatic cases of the ritualization of warfare are found among the Dani of New Guinea (Heider 1970) and the Tiwi of Australia (Hart and Pilling 1960). Although I use the present tense here, such indigenous forms of warfare were among the first casualties of colonialism in non-state societies. While common in the past, they are rare today, at least in this form.

10 Muir (1981: 212–13).

11 Davis (1973).

12 Marriott (1966: 211).

13 Hunt (1977: 144–45).

14 Edelman (1971); Malinowski (1945).

15 Bennett (1977).

16 Lee (1980: 618).

17 Turner (1957: 289).

18 Turner (1957: 301–2).

19 Gluckman (1962: 47).

20 On judicial ritual in Western societies, see Arnold (1935).

21 Linton (1933: 156–57), quoted in Roberts (1965: 187).

22 Roscoe (1911: 341).

23 On the reasons why ritual is employed in dealing with crises, see Gluckman (1965: 265), Berger and Luckmann (1966: 143), Crocker (1973: 49), and Turner (1974: 39).

24 The opening of the movie "Il caso Moro" in November 1986 provides an indication of this. Denunciations of the film by Christian Democratic party leaders were first-page news in Italy for several days, as were mutterings about filing suit against the film makers, and efforts to keep the film's highly respected star, Gian Maria Volonté, from appearing on state-controlled television. The film failed to portray the events in the way the government leaders had labored painfully to create.

25 Moss (1981: 272).

26 Moss (1981: 273–74) has noted this similarity between the kidnappings and rites of passage.

27 Katz (1980: 26–28); Moss (1981: 277). For an analysis of the Moro kidnapping in terms of social drama, see Wagner-Pacifici (1986).

28 Quoted in Katz (1980: 243).

29 An instructive parallel can be found in the case of Lenin's death, though the political circumstances were very different. Upon his death, Lenin's widow made a public appeal to the state officials. She wrote, "Do not allow your mourning for Ilich to take the form of external reverence for his person. Do not raise memorials to him, name palaces after him, etc.: to all this he attached so little importance in his life; all this was burdensome to him." Yet, for reasons in part similar to those of the Italian political leaders following Moro's death, this was a request that the Soviet authorities would refuse to honor. With the old leader dead, it was crucial that his symbolism be actively employed to legitimate the new leadership and to tie in their actions with those of the legendary hero. Thus, rather than eschew

Lenin's ritualization, the Soviet authorities quickly changed the name of Petrograd to Leningrad, made the day of Lenin's death an annual national holiday, set up monuments to Lenin in all the large cities, and preserved Lenin's body in a mausoleum to which millions of citizens could make sacred pilgrimages (Binns 1980: 599).

30   Douglas C. McGill, "Golden Temple in Amritsar: Sikhism's most sacred shrine," *New York Times* (4 June 1984), p. 6.

31   Michael Hamlyn, "How Sikh's holy shrine became a 'killing ground'," *The Times* (London) (15 June 1984), p. 26.

32   See, among many other journalistic accounts of the Sikh reactions to the Golden Temple raid, Michael Hamlyn, "Anxious wait in Delhi for reactions from Punjab," *The Times* (London) (8 June 1984), p. 10; "Sikhs in Temple hold out; More violence is reported," *New York Times* (9 June 1984), p. 4; James M. Markham, "Temple raid puts Sikhs 'in a very foul mood'," *New York Times* (12 June 1984), p. 6; and "Angry Sikhs stage rallies across India," *New York Times* (18 June 1984), p. 3.

33   William K. Stevens, "Mrs. Gandhi visits captured temple," *New York Times* (24 June 1984), p. 4.

34   Mohan Ram, "The temple restored," *Far Eastern Economic Review* (11 October 1984), p. 47.

35   See Michael Hamlyn, "Platform of death will become new shrine for pilgrims," *The Times* (London) (5 November 1984), p. 5; Bob Secter and Rone Tempest, "Thousands see Gandhi's son 'consign her body to sacred flames'," *Los Angeles Times* (3 November 1984), p. 8; James M. Markham, "Beside New Delhi river, 2 scenes of mourning," *New York Times* (4 November 1984), p. 12; "Funeral held," *Facts on File* vol. 44 #2296 (16 November 1984), pp. 845–46.

36   James M. Markham, "Gandhi's ashes placed at family estate," *New York Times* (10 November 1984), p. 3; Rone Tempest, "Son scatters Indira Gandhi's ashes on Himalayas," *Los Angeles Times* (12 November 1984), p. 12.

37   Quoted by Davis (1971: 41). Davis herself challenges any simple safety-valve view of these rites.

38   The safety valve view of carnivals is discussed in Scribner (1978).

39   Muir (1981: 156).

40   Muir (1981: 157).

41   Burke (1983: 15).

42   Davis (1971: 68).

43   Davis (1971: 69).

44   Berenson (1984: 207).

45   Berenson (1984: 213).

46   Bezucha (1975: 238–39).

47   Bezucha (1975: 242–43).

48   McPhee (1977: 241–42).

49   McPhee (1977: 242–43).

50   Bercé (1976: 66–67).

51   Burke (1983).

52   McPhee (1977: 243).

53   McPhee (1977: 244–45).

54   Kaplan (1984: 173).

55   Brandes (1980: 90).

56 Gilmore (1975: 339–40). For an analysis of the reversal of class positions that takes place in the Brazilian carnival, see Da Matta (1977).
57 Gilmore (1975: 344).
58 Gilmore (1975: 344). See also Gilmore (1987: 96–125). The history of May Day, mandated in 1889 by the Second International as an international worker's holiday, presents similar issues of rites of class solidarity that have been sometimes interpreted as a safety valve keeping the capitalist system going, rather than a threat to the system. See Mosse (1975: 167–68); Hobsbawm (1984: 76–79); Perrot (1984); and Dommanget (1972). On a comparable rite of European working class solidarity, the Durham Miner's Gala, see Rodger (1981).
59 This felicitous term is from Bercé (1976: 73).
60 This term, used by Jean Duvignaud, is quoted in Rearick (1977: 437).
61 Faure (1978: 92).

Chapter 8

1 Quoted in Shafer (1943: 92). My description of this initial *fête de la Fédération* in Paris is based on Dunn (1939: 9–10) and Sanson (1976: 13–14).
2 The Strassburg ceremonies are described in Shafer (1943: 86–87).
3 A discussion of Rousseau's writings on civil festivals is found in Duvignaud (1965: 239), from which the quote used here is also taken. Note that Mathiez (1904: 77) claims that the idea of organizing a "civic cult" came to the leaders of the French Revolution not from political theory, but from spontaneous local rites that sprang up in the federations around the country beginning in 1789.
4 Quoted from the general's memoirs, in Dowd (1948: 54).
5 Quoted in Dowd (1948: 56).
6 This account of the festival of 15 April 1792 is based on Dowd (1948) and Ozouf (1976). Quotations are from Dowd (1948: 62).
7 Quotes are from Dowd (1948: 68–69).
8 This is taken from the account of the festival found in the *Révolutions de Paris*, extracted in Ozouf (1976: 86).
9 Quoted in Dowd (1948: 75).
10 From Robespierre's remarks to the national assembly on 7 June 1792, quoted by Ozouf (1976: 89). My description of the festival of Simonneau is based on this source as well as Dowd (1948) and Mathiez (1904: 56–58).
11 See Kohn (1967: 327).
12 This account of the Festival of the Supreme Being is based on Brinton (1934), Ozouf (1976), and Dowd (1948).
13 See Ozouf (1976: 236–38), Dunn (1939: 132) and Kohn (1967: 83–86).
14 Many observers have noted the similarities between this system of revolutionary ritual and belief and that of religion, especially Catholicism. See Mathiez (1904: 62), Soboul (1957: 199), Kohn (1967: 42), and Ozouf (1976: 322–25).
15 Hunt (1984: 53).
16 Hunt (1984: 57–59).
17 Brinton (1934: 154–57).
18 Guillotine statistics are found in Duvignaud (1965: 248). On the state funeral for the deputy Michel Le Peletier de Saint-Fargeau, see Dowd (1948: 99–100).
19 Ozouf (1975: 383).

20 Quoted in Ozouf (1976: 316).
21 Mosse (1971: 172). See also Soboul (1957: 213).
22 The problems posed by lack of a suitable human representation of the state are discussed by Agulhon (1985). Emblematic was the quandary faced by the revolutionary regime regarding what to do with the coins of the realm. The picture of the king could scarcely be retained, yet whose likeness could replace his in this new democratic society? It was unimaginable to mint coins without any person's image, and so it was decided to use the allegorical head of Liberty (1985: 188).
23 Hunt (1984), with a debt to Clifford Geertz, attributes similar importance to ritual in the French Revolution.
24 Agulhon (1979: 67).
25 The report of Portalis, *ministre des Cultes à l'Empereur*, is reproduced in Bercé (1976: 225–27). On Napoleon's attitude toward national festivals, see Kohn (1967: 86).
26 Shaw (1981: 14).
27 These events are described in Jordan (1973: 306–07) and Shaw (1981: 15).
28 Isaac (1976: 367).
29 Shaw (1981: 181–84) and Jordan (1973: 305).
30 Shaw (1981: 20–21) has made this point.
31 In Inglis (1967–69: 22).
32 Novak (1974: 21).
33 Mosse (1975: 10).
34 Hitler (1939: 730–31).
35 Hitler (1939: 736, 734, 506–7).
36 Hitler (1939: 806).
37 Taylor (1981: 508–9).
38 Hitler (1939: 715–16).
39 Ernst Roehm, cited in Unger (1974: 83).
40 Burden (1967: 26–29).
41 Burden (1967: 50–57).
42 Quoted in Burden (1967: 73). Leni Riefenstahl's famous film, "Triumph of the Will," was made at the Reichsparty-day rally in Nuremberg in 1934. It includes all the aspects of the ceremonies discussed here, and it gives a powerful impression of the emotional impact of the rites. For a discussion of the film, see Barsam (1975).
43 Unger (1974: 171) and Taylor (1981: 506).
44 Unger (1974: 176–82).
45 Unger (1974: 86–87).
46 Chelkowski (1980: 35) cites such cases back to the seventeenth century.
47 Abrahamian (1968: 191–92).
48 Chelkowski (1980: 30).
49 Chelkowski (1980: 37). See also Hooglund (1981).
50 This description of the salt-tax protest is based on Brown (1977).
51 On the Ghost Dance and its associated native American revolt, see Mooney (1965).
52 On the Mumbo cult, see Wipper (1977).
53 Masinde's sacrificial remarks are reported in Wipper (1977: 142–43). I rely here on Wipper's account. There is a large anthropological literature on the related phenomenon of the religions of the oppressed. For the classical studies, see Lanternari (1963) and Worsley (1968).

54 Quote is from Richard Bernstein, "60,000 blacks at South African funeral," *New York Times* (14 April 1985), p. 3. See also Ray Kennedy, "Four die after township mass funeral," *The Times* (London) (15 April 1985), p. 7.
55 Ray Kennedy, "Two whites murdered in ambush by mourners after mass funeral," *The Times* (London) (2 September 1985), p. 6.
56 Ray Kennedy, "Besieged white kills black in Cape attack," *The Times* (London) (21 October 1985), p. 1.
57 Alan Cowell, "South Africa bans mass funerals for the victims of black unrest," *New York Times* (1 August 1985), p. 1.
58 Alan Cowell, "Rightists defiant at Pretoria rally," *New York Times* (1 June 1986), p. 7.

Chapter 9

1 Herzl was here justifying the amount of effort he had devoted to designing a flag for a nation that did not yet exist. His remarks are quoted in Mosse (1976:49).
2 Quoted in E. Weber (1977:172–73).
3 Turner (1985:154) writes of culture in this vein as "an endless series of negotiations among actors about the assignment of meaning to the acts in which they jointly participate."
4 Fox (1985:204).
5 See Bennett (1979:107).
6 This account is based on Cannadine (1985).
7 Bloch (1986) makes a good case for the importance of distinguishing between determinants of a ritual's content and the determinants of its political functions.
8 Geertz (1980:136).
9 Bloch (1977b; 1986), attempting to cope with this issue of the relationship between the material world and symbolic constructions that guide people's lives, argues that people have two different cognitive systems: a naturalist system tied directly to the material world and differing little from culture to culture, and a culturally variable system of symbols, such as is employed in ritual. He laments that "Unfortunately many anthropologists, fascinated as usual by the exotic, have only paid attention to the world as seen in ritual." And he goes on to conclude: "they have confounded the systems by which we know the world with the systems by which we hide it" (1977b:290). I agree with his general point that there are some important regularities in cultures around the world and that these are ultimately based in regularities of the material world. However, I find his dichotomy simplistic and unconvincing. There is no such simple division between our "everyday communication," which Bloch claims is based on direct perception of nature, and "ritual communication," which he describes in terms of "static and imaginary models of . . . society." Everyday understandings are highly constrained by "imaginary models" just as the material world weighs heavily in ritual communication. We do not alternate between a naturalistic perception of the universe and a mystifying symbolic view; the natural world seeps in through our symbolic lenses, not in spite of them.
10 Lane (1981:132).
11 Berenson (1984:61).
12 Malinowski (1948).

13   See Gluckman (1962: 38; 1965: 261–62).
14   For some of the reasons given for the importance of ritual in communication among the illiterate, see McPhee (1977: 244).
15   Lane (1981: 26, 32). This argument is also presented in Lane (1984).
16   Aronoff (1979: 306).
17   On the need for ritualization in new states, see Apter (1963) and Verba (1965: 530).
18   Anderson (1983: 19).
19   Binns (1980: 588).
20   Struve (1968: 760).
21   Struve (1968: 763).
22   Lane (1981: 185–86).
23   Lane (1981: 186).
24   This last point was made, in a somewhat different context, by Radcliffe-Brown (1952: 148–49) in his attack on Malinowski's anxiety-reduction theory of ritual.
25   Kowalewski (1980: 102).
26   In this regard, see Fernandez's (1977: 103) comments on Locke.
27   Lipsitz (1968: 533).
28   Machiavelli is quoted in Muir (1981: 74–75).
29   Cassirer (1946: 285).
30   Light (1969: 198).
31   Borhek and Curtis (1975: 105) refer to these lines from Gilbert and Sullivan in a somewhat similar context.
32   Bagehot (1914: 107).
33   Galbraith (1960).
34   Hahn (1984: 275).
35   Agulhon (1985: 190).

References

[References to journalistic sources are to be found in the notes]

Abelson, Robert P., and David E. Kanouse. 1966. Subjective acceptance of verbal generalizations. In Shel Feldman, ed., *Cognitive Consistency*, pp. 171–97. New York: Academic.

Abercrombie, Nicholas, and Bryan S. Turner. 1978. The dominant ideology thesis. *British Journal of Sociology* 29: 149–70.

Abrahamian, E. 1968. The crowd in Iranian politics, 1905–1953. *Past and Present* 41: 184–210.

Abu-Zahra, Nadia M. 1972. Inequality of descent and egalitarianism of the new national organizations in a Tunisian village. In Richard Antoun and Iliya Harik, eds., *Rural Politics and Social Change in the Middle East*, pp. 267–86. Bloomington: Indiana University Press.

Adler, Alfred. 1982. *Le mort est le masque du roi: La royauté des Moundang du Tchad*. Paris: Payot.

Agulhon, Maurice. 1979. *Marianne au combat: Imagerie et symbolique républicaine en France de 1789 à 1880*. Paris.

———. 1985. Politics, images and symbols in post-revolutionary France. In Sean Wilentz, ed., *Rites of Power*, pp. 177–205. Philadelphia: University of Pennsylvania Press.

Aho, James A. 1977. Huitzilopochtili's feast: Sacramental warfare in ancient Mexico. *Sociological Symposium* 18: 84–107.

Anderson, Benedict. 1983. *Imagined Communities: Reflections on the Origin and Spread of Nationalism*. London: Verso.

Anglo, Sydney. 1969. *Spectacle, Pageantry, and Early Tudor Policy*. Oxford: Clarendon Press.

Apostolidès, Jean-Marie. 1981. *Le roi-machine: Spectacle et politique au temps de Louis XIV*. Paris: Editions de Minuit.

Apter, David E. 1963. Political religion in the new nations. In Clifford Geertz, ed., *Old Societies and New States*, pp. 57–104. Glencoe: Free Press.

Arnold, Thurmon W. 1935. *The Symbols of Government*. New Haven: Yale University Press.

———. 1937. *The Folklore of Capitalism*. New Haven: Yale University Press.

Aronoff, Myron J. 1977. *Power and Ritual in the Israel Labor Party*. Assen: Van Gorcum.

———. 1979. Ritual and consensual power relations: The Israel Labor party. In S. Lee Seaton and Henri J. M. Claessen, eds., *Political Anthropology: The State of the Art*, pp. 275–310. The Hague: Mouton.

———. 1980. Ideology and interest: The dialectics of politics. In Myron J. Aronoff, ed., *Ideology and Politics, Political Anthropology*, volume 1, pp. 1–30. New Brunswick, New Jersey: Transaction.

———. 1986. Establishing authority: The memorialization of Jabotinsky and the burial of the Bar-Kochba bones in Israel under the Likud. In Myron J. Aronoff, ed., *The Frailty of Authority, Political Anthropology*, volume 5, pp. 105–30. New Brunswick, New Jersey: Transaction.

Bagehot, Walter. 1914. *The English Constitution*. New York: Appleton.

Balandier, Georges. 1970. *Political Anthropology*. New York: Pantheon.

Bandura, Albert. 1977. *Social Learning Theory*. Englewood Cliffs, New Jersey: Prentice-Hall.

Barsam, Richard Meran. 1975. *Triumph of the Will*. Bloomington: Indiana University Press.

Bauman, Zygmunt. 1973. *Culture as Praxis*. London: Routledge and Kegan Paul.

Beattie, John. 1960. *Bunyoro: An African Kingdom*. New York: Holt, Rinehart and Winston.

Beidelman, T. O. 1966. Swazi royal rituals. *Africa* 36: 373–405.

Bellah, Robert N. 1967. Civil religion in America. *Daedalus* 96: 1–21.

———. 1968. Response to comments on "Civil religion in America." In Donald R. Cutler, ed., *The Religious Situation, 1968*, pp. 388–93. Boston: Beacon.

Bennett, W. Lance. 1975. Political sanctification: The civil religion and American politics. *Social Science Information* 14: 79–106.

———. 1977. The ritualistic and pragmatic bases of political campaign discourse. *Quarterly Journal of Speech* 63: 219–38.

———. 1979. Imitation, ambiguity, and drama in political life: Civil religion and the dilemmas of public morality. *Journal of Politics* 41: 106–33.

———. 1980. Myth, ritual and political control. *Journal of Communication* 30: 166–79.

Bercé, Yves-Marie. 1976. *Fête et révolution: Des mentalités populaires du XVIe au XVIIIe siècle*. Paris: Hachette.

Berenson, Edward. 1984. *Populist Religion and Left-Wing Politics in France, 1830–1852*. Princeton: Princeton University Press.

Berger, John. 1968. The nature of mass demonstrations. *New Society*, no. 295 (23 May), pp. 754–55.

Berger, Peter L. 1967. *The Sacred Canopy: Elements of a Sociological Theory of Religion*. New York: Doubleday.

——, and Thomas Luckmann. 1966. *The Social Construction of Reality*. Garden City, New York: Doubleday.

Bergeron, David M. 1971. *English Civil Pageantry*. London: Edward Arnold.

Bergesen, Albert J. 1977. Political witch hunts: The sacred and the subversive in cross-national perspective. *American Sociological Review* 42: 220–33.

Bernardi, Tiziana. 1986. Analisi di una cerimonia pubblica. L'incoronazione di Carlo V a Bologna. *Quaderni Storici* 61: 171–199.

Bettelheim, Bruno. 1960. *The Informed Heart*. Glencoe: Free Press.

Bezucha, Robert J. 1975. Mask of revolution: A study of popular culture during the Second French Republic. In Roger Price, ed., *Revolution and Reaction*, pp. 236–53. London: Croom Helm.

Binns, Christopher A. 1980. The changing face of power: Revolution and accommodation in the development of the Soviet ceremonial system, part 1. *Man* 14: 585–606.

Biondi, Dino. 1973. *La fabbrica del Duce*. Florence: Valecchi.

Birnbaum, Norman. 1955. Monarchs and sociologists: A reply to Professor Shils and Mr. Young. *Sociological Review* 3: 5–23.

Bloch, Marc. 1973. *The Royal Touch: Sacred Monarchy and Scrofula in England and France*. Translated by J. E. Anderson. London: Routledge and Kegan Paul.

Bloch, Maurice. 1974. Symbols, song, dance and features of articulation: Is religion an extreme form of traditional authority? *European Journal of Sociology* 15: 55–81.

——. 1975. Introduction. In Maurice Bloch, ed., *Political Language and Oratory in Traditional Society*, pp. 1–28. London: Academic.

——. 1977a. The disconnection between power and rank as a process: An outline of the development of kingdoms in Central Madagascar. *Archives Européennes de Sociologie* 18: 107–48.

——. 1977b. The past and the present in the present. *Man* 12: 278–92.

——. 1980. Ritual symbolism and the nonrepresentation of society. In Mary L. Foster and Stanley H. Brandes, eds., *Symbol as Sense*, pp. 93–102. New York: Academic.

——. 1986. *From Blessing to Violence: History and Ideology in the Circumcision Ritual of the Merina of Madagascar*. Cambridge: Cambridge University Press.

Blum, Albert A. 1961. Collective bargaining: Ritual or reality? *Harvard Business Review* 39: 6: 63–69.

Blumer, Herbert. 1974. Social movements. In R. Serge Denisoff, ed., *The Sociology of Dissent*, pp. 4–20. New York: Harcourt, Brace.

Blumler, J. G., J. R. Brown, A. J. Ewbank, and T. J. Nossiter. 1971. Attitudes to the monarchy: Their structure and development during a ceremonial occasion. *Political Studies* 19: 149–71.

Blustain, Harvey S. 1980. Caste, ideology, and power in north central Nepal. In Myron J. Aronoff, ed., *Ideology and Politics, Political Anthropology*, volume 1, pp. 127–50. New Brunswick, New Jersey: Transaction.

Boggs, Carl. 1976. *Gramsci's Marxism*. London: Pluto Press.

Borhek, James T., and Richard F. Curtis. 1975. *A Sociology of Belief*. New York: Wiley.

Brandes, Stanley H. 1980. Giants and big-heads: An Andalusian metaphor. In Mary L. Foster and Stanley H. Brandes, eds., *Symbol as Sense*, pp. 77–92. New York: Academic.

Brian-Chaninov, Nicolas. 1931. *The Russian Church*. Translated by Warre Wells. New York: Macmillan.

Brinton, Crane. 1934. *A Decade of Revolution, 1789–1799*. New York: Harper.

Brown, Judith M. 1977. *Gandhi and Civil Disobedience*. Cambridge: Cambridge University Press.

Bryant, Lawrence M. 1976. *Parlementaire* political theory in the Parisian royal entry ceremony. *Sixteenth Century Journal* 7: 15–24.

Bucci, P. Vincent. 1969. *Chiesa e Stato: Church-State Relations in Italy within the Contemporary Constitutional Framework*. The Hague: Martinus Nijhoff.

Burden, Hamilton T. 1967. *The Nuremburg Party Rallies, 1923–1939*. New York: Praeger.

Burke, Kenneth. 1950. *A Rhetoric of Motives*. New York: Prentice-Hall.

———. 1959. *Attitudes toward History*. Los Altos: Hermes.

———. 1966. *Language as Symbolic Action*. Berkeley: University of California Press.

Burke, Peter. 1983. The Virgin of the Carmine and the revolt of Masaniello. *Past and Present* 99: 3–21.

Calder, P. R. 1966. Ritualization in international relations. *Philosophical Transactions of the Royal Society*, series B, 251: 451–56.

Cannadine, David. 1985. Splendor out of court: Royal spectacle and pageantry in modern Britain, c. 1820–1977. In Sean Wilentz, ed., *Rites of Power*, pp. 206–43. Philadelphia: University of Pennsylvania Press.

Cantor, Nancy. 1981. A cognitive-social approach in personality. In Nancy Cantor and John F. Kihlstrom, eds., *Personality, Cognition, and Social Interaction*, pp. 23–44. Hillsdale, New Jersey: Erlbaum.

Carlyle, Thomas. 1908. *Sartor Resartus, On Heroes, Hero-worship and the Heroic in History*. London: J. M. Dent.

Cassirer, Ernst. 1946. *The Myth of the State*. New Haven: Yale University Press.

———. 1955. *The Philosophy of Symbolic Forms*, volume 2, *Mythical Thought*. Translated by Ralph Manheim. New Haven: Yale University Press.

Chagnon, Napoleon. 1983. *Yanomamo: The Fierce People*. Third edition. New York: Holt, Rinehart.

Chastel, André. 1960. Les entrées de Charles Quint en Italie. In Jean Jacquot, ed., *Fêtes et cérémonies au temps de Charles Quint*, pp. 197–206. Paris: Editions du Centre National de la Recherche Scientifique.

Chelkowski, Peter J. 1980. Iran: Mourning becomes revolution. *Asia* 3: 30–37, 44–45.

Cherniavsky, Michael. 1961. *Tsar and People: Studies in Russian Myths*. New Haven: Yale University Press.

Cleveland, Les. 1973. Royalty as symbolic drama: The 1970 New Zealand tour. *Journal of Commonwealth Political Studies* 11: 28–45.

Cohen, Abner. 1969. *Custom and Politics in Urban Africa*. Berkeley: University of California Press.

———. 1974. *Two-Dimensional Man*. Berkeley: University of California Press.

———. 1979. Political symbolism. *Annual Review of Anthropology* 8:87–113.

———. 1981. *The Politics of Elite Culture*. Berkeley: University of California Press.

Committee on Un-American Activities. 1967. *The Present-Day Ku Klux Klan Movement*. Washington, D.C.: Government Printing Office.

Conrad, Geoffrey W., and Arthur A. Demarest. 1984. *Religion and Empire: The Dynamics of Aztec and Inca Expansion*. Cambridge: Cambridge University Press.

Converse, Philip E. 1964. The nature of belief systems in mass publics. In David E. Apter, ed., *Ideology and Discontent*, pp. 206–61. New York: Free Press.

Cook, Rhodes. 1976. *National Party Conventions, 1831–1972*. Washington, D.C.: Congressional Quarterly.

Crick, Malcolm. 1982. Anthropology of knowledge. *Annual Review of Anthropology* 11:287–313.

Crocker, J. Christopher. 1973. Ritual and the development of social structure: Liminality and inversion. In James D. Shaughnessy, ed., *The Roots of Ritual*, pp. 47–86. Grand Rapids, Michigan: Eerdmans.

———. 1977. The social functions of rhetorical forms. In J. David Sapir and J. Christopher Crocker, eds., *The Social Use of Metaphor*, pp. 33–66. Philadelphia: University of Pennsylvania Press.

Dahl, Robert A. 1961. *Who Governs?* New Haven: Yale University Press.

Da Matta, Roberto. 1977. Constraint and license: A preliminary study of two Brazilian national rituals. In Sally F. Moore and Barbara G. Myerhoff, eds., *Secular Ritual*, pp. 244–64. Amsterdam: Van Gorcum.

d'Aquili, Eugene G., and Charles D. Laughlin, Jr. 1979. The neurobiology of myth and ritual. In Eugene G. d'Aquili, Charles D. Laughlin, Jr., and John McManus, eds., *The Spectrum of Ritual: A Biogenetic Structural Analysis*, pp. 152–82. New York: Columbia University Press.

Davis, Marvin. 1980. Two dimensional politics: Political action and meaning in rural West Bengal. In Myron J. Aronoff, ed., *Ideology and Politics, Political Anthropology*, volume 1, pp. 57–96. New Brunswick, New Jersey: Transaction.

Davis, Natalie Z. 1971. The reasons of misrule: Youth groups and charivaris in sixteenth-century France. *Past and Present* 50:41–75.

———. 1973. The rites of violence: Religious riot in sixteenth-century France. *Past and Present* 59:51–91.

Deal, Terrence E., and Allan A. Kennedy. 1982. *Corporate Cultures: The Rites and Rituals of Corporate Life*. Reading, Mass.: Addison-Wesley.

DiMaggio, Paul J., and Walter W. Powell. 1983. The iron cage revisited: Institutional isomorphism and collective rationality in organizational fields. *American Sociological Review* 48:147–60.

Dommanget, Maurice. 1972. *Histoire du premier mai*. Paris: Editions de la Tête de Feuilles.

Douglas, Mary. 1966. *Purity and Danger*. New York: Praeger.

Dowd, David L. 1948. *Pageant-Master of the Republic: Jacques-Louis David and the French Revolution*. Lincoln: University of Nebraska Press.

Duncan, Hugh D. 1962. *Communication and the Social Order*. New York: Bedminster Press.

————. 1968. *Symbols in Society*. New York: Oxford University Press.

Dunn, Seymour B. 1939. *The National Festival in the French Revolution, 1794–1797*. Ph.D. diss., Cornell University.

Durkheim, Emile. 1915 (1974). *The Elementary Forms of the Religious Life*. Translated by Joseph Swain. Glencoe: Free Press.

Duvignaud, Jean. 1965. La fête civique. In Guy Dumur, ed., *Histoire des spectacles*, pp. 238–64. Paris: Gallimard.

Eckardt, A. Roy. 1986. The Christian world goes to Bitburg. In Geoffrey Hartman, ed., *Bitburg in Moral and Political Perspective*, pp. 80–89. Bloomington: Indiana University Press.

Edelman, Murray. 1964. *The Symbolic Uses of Politics*. Urbana: University of Illinois Press.

————. 1969. Escalation and ritualization of political conflict. *American Behavioral Scientist* 13: 231–46.

————. 1971. *Politics as Symbolic Action*. Chicago: Markham.

————. 1977. The language of participation and the language of resistance. *Human Communication Research* 3: 159–70.

Elias, Norbert. 1983. *The Court Society*. Translated by Edmund Jephcott. New York: Pantheon.

Engell, Ivan. 1967. *Studies in Divine Kingship in the Ancient Near East*. Second edition. Oxford: Blackwell.

Evans-Pritchard, E. E. 1949. *The Sanusi of Cyrenaica*. Oxford: Clarendon Press.

————. 1964. *Social Anthropology and Other Essays*. New York: Free Press.

Fairbanks, James D. 1981. The priestly functions of the presidency. *Presidential Studies Quarterly* 11: 214–32.

Fairman, H. W. 1958. The kingship rituals of Egypt. In S. H. Hooke, ed., *Myth, Ritual, and Kingship*, pp. 74–104. Oxford: Clarendon.

Faure, Alain. 1978. *Paris Carême-prenant. Du Carnaval à Paris au 19e siècle*. Paris: Hachette.

Fernandez, James W. 1965. Symbolic consensus in a Fang reformative cult. *American Anthropologist* 67: 902–29.

————. 1971. Persuasions and performances: On the beast in every body . . . and the metaphors of everyman. In Clifford Geertz, ed., *Myth, Symbol and Culture*, pp. 39–60. New York: Norton.

————. 1977. The performance of ritual metaphors. In J. David Sapir and J. Christopher Crocker, eds., *The Social Use of Metaphor*, pp. 100–31. Philadelphia: University of Pennsylvania Press.

Festinger, Leon. 1957. *A Theory of Cognitive Dissonance*. Evanston, Illinois: Row, Peterson.

Firth, Raymond. 1951. *Elements of Social Organization*. London: Watts.

Fishwick, Duncan. 1978. The development of provincial ruler worship in the western Roman Empire. *Aufstieg und Niedergang der romischen Welt,* part 2, 16: 1202–53.

Fiske, Susan T., and Donald R. Kinder. 1981. Involvement, expertise, and schema use: Evidence from political cognition. In Nancy Cantor and John F. Kihlstorm, eds., *Personality, Cognition and Social Interaction,* pp. 171–90. Hillsdale, New Jersey: Erlbaum.

Foner, Anne, and David I. Kertzer. 1978. Transitions over the life course: Lessons from age-set societies. *American Journal of Sociology* 83: 1081–1104.

——. 1979. Intrinsic and extrinsic sources of change in life course transitions. In Matilda White Riley, ed., *Aging from Birth to Death,* pp. 121–36. Boulder, Colorado: Westview Press.

Fortes, Meyer. 1940. The political system of the Tallensi of the Northern Territories of the Gold Coast. In Meyer Fortes and E. E. Evans-Pritchard, eds., *African Political Systems,* pp. 239–71. London: Oxford University Press.

——. 1945. *The Dynamics of Clanship among the Tallensi.* London: Oxford University Press.

——. 1962. Ritual and office in tribal society. In Max Gluckman, ed., *Essays on the Ritual of Social Relations,* pp. 53–88. Manchester: Manchester University Press.

——, and E. E. Evans-Pritchard. 1940. Introduction. In Meyer Fortes and E. E. Evans-Pritchard, eds., *African Political Systems,* pp. 1–24. London: Oxford University Press.

Foster, Elizabeth Andros, ed. 1950. *Motolinia's History of the Indians of New Spain.* Berkeley: The Cortes Society.

Fox, Richard G. 1985. *Lions of the Punjab: Culture in the Making.* Berkeley: University of California Press.

Frazer, James G. 1925. *The Golden Bough.* Abridged edition. New York: Macmillan.

Freud, Sigmund. 1907. Obsessive actions and religious practices. In James Strachey, ed., *The Standard Edition of the Complete Psychological Works of Sigmund Freud,* volume 9, pp. 117–27. London: Hogarth Press.

Frey, Frederick W. 1968. Socialization to national identification among Turkish peasants. *Journal of Politics* 30: 934–65.

Fry, Peter. 1976. *Spirits of Protest: Spirit-Mediums and Articulation of Consensus among the Zezuru of Southern Rhodesia (Zimbabwe).* Cambridge: Cambridge University Press.

Fustel de Coulanges. 1901. *The Ancient City: A Study of the Religion, Laws, and Institutions of Greece and Rome.* Tenth edition. Boston: Lee and Shepard.

Galbraith, John Kenneth. 1960. Conventional signs. *The Spectator* (29 July) 205: 174–75.

Garfinkel, Harold. 1956. Conditions of successful degradation ceremonies. *American Journal of Sociology* 61: 420–24.

Garrow, David J. 1978. *Protest at Selma.* New Haven: Yale University Press.

Geertz, Clifford. 1964. Ideology as a cultural system. In David E. Apter, ed., *Ideology and Discontent,* pp. 47–76. New York: Free Press.

———. 1966. Religion as a cultural system. In Michael Banton, ed., *Anthropological Approaches to the Study of Religion*, pp. 1–46. London: Tavistock.

———. 1977. Centers, kings, and charisma: Reflections on the symbolics of power. In Joseph Ben-David and Terry N. Clark, eds., *Culture and its Creators*, pp. 150–71. Chicago: University of Chicago Press.

———. 1980. *Negara: The Theatre State in Nineteenth-Century Bali*. Princeton: Princeton University Press.

Gerlach, Luther P., and Virginia H. Hine. 1970. *People, Power, Change: Movements of Social Transformation*. Indianapolis: Bobbs-Merrill.

Giesey, Ralph E. 1960. *The Royal Funeral Ceremony in Renaissance France*. Geneva: Droz.

———. 1985. Models of rulership in French royal ceremonial. In Sean Wilentz, ed., *Rites of Power*, pp. 41–64. Philadelphia: University of Pennsylvania Press.

Gillespie, Joanna B. 1980. The phenomenon of the public wife: An exercise in Goffman's impression management. *Symbolic Interaction* 3: 109–26.

Gilmore, David. 1975. *Carnaval* in Fuenmayor: Class conflict and social cohesion in an Andalusian town. *Journal of Anthropological Research* 31: 331–49.

———. 1987. *Aggression and Community: Paradoxes of Andalusian Culture*. New Haven: Yale University Press.

Gluckman, Max. 1962. *Les rites de passage*. In Max Gluckman, ed., *Essays on the Rituals of Social Relations*, pp. 1–52. Manchester: Manchester University Press.

———. 1963. *Order and Rebellion in Tribal Africa*. London: Cohen and West.

———. 1965. *Politics, Law and Ritual in Tribal Society*. Oxford: Blackwell.

Goffman, Erving. 1959. *Presentation of Self in Everyday Life*. Garden City, New York: Anchor.

Goldberg, Robert A. 1981. *Hooded Empire: The Ku Klux Klan in Colorado*. Urbana: University of Illinois Press.

Goldschlager, Alain. 1982. Towards a semiotics of authoritarian discourse. *Poetics Today* 3: 11–20.

Goody, Jack. 1977. Against 'ritual': Loosely structured thoughts on a loosely defined topic. In Sally F. Moore and Barbara G. Myerhoff, eds., *Secular Ritual*, pp. 25–35. Assen: Van Gorcum.

Graham, Victor E., and W. McAllister Johnson. 1979. *The Royal Tour of France by Charles IX and Catherine de'Medici: Festivals and Entries, 1564–1566*. Toronto: University of Toronto Press.

Gramsci, Antonio. 1971. *Selections from the Prison Notebooks*. Translated by Quintin Hoare and Geoffrey Smith. London: Lawrence and Wishart.

Greisman, H. C., and Sharon S. Mayes. 1977. The social construction of unreality: The real American dilemma. *Dialectical Anthropology* 2: 57–67.

Gronbeck, Bruce E. 1978. The rhetoric of political corruption: Sociolinguistic, dialectical, and ceremonial processes. *The Quarterly Journal of Speech* 64: 155–72.

Grosvenor, Melville B. 1964. The last full measure. *National Geographic* 125: 307–55.

Habermas, Jürgen. 1986. Defusing the past: A politico-cultural tract. In Geoffrey Hartman, ed., *Bitburg in Moral and Political Perspective*, pp. 43–51. Bloomington: Indiana University Press.

Hahn, Dan F. 1984. The rhetoric of Jimmy Carter, 1976–1980. *Presidential Studies Quarterly* 14: 265–88.

Hall, Peter M. 1972. A symbolic interactionist analysis of politics. *Sociological Inquiry* 42: 35–75.

———. 1979. The presidency and impression management. In Norman K. Denzin, ed., *Studies in Symbolic Interaction*, volume 2, pp. 283–305. Greenwich, Connecticut: JAI Press.

Hamill, Hugh M., Jr. 1966. *The Hidalgo Revolt*. Gainesville: University of Florida Press.

Hamilton, David L. 1981. Illusory correlation as a basis for stereotyping. In David L. Hamilton, ed., *Cognitive Process in Stereotyping and Intergroup Behavior*, pp. 117–45. Hillsdale, New Jersey: Erlbaum.

Hanley, Sarah. 1983. *Le Lit de Justice of the Kings of France: Constitutional Ideology in Legend, Ritual and Discourse*. Princeton: Princeton University Press.

Hardgrave, Robert L. 1979. *Essays in the Political Sociology of South India*. New Delhi: Usha Publications.

Hart, C. W. M., and Arnold R. Pilling. 1960. *The Tiwi of North Australia*. New York: Holt, Rinehart.

Hayes, Carlton J. 1960. *Nationalism: A Religion*. New York: Macmillan.

Heider, Karl. 1970. *The Dugum Dani: A Papuan Culture in the Highlands of West New Guinea*. Chicago: Aldine.

Hicks, George L., and David I. Kertzer. 1972. Making a middle way: Problems of Monhegan identity. *Southwestern Journal of Anthropology* 28: 1–24.

Higgins, E. Tory, and Gillian King. 1981. Accessibility of social constructs: Information-processing consequences of individual and contextual variability. In Nancy Cantor and John F. Kihlstorm, eds., *Personality, Cognition and Social Interaction*, pp. 69–122. Hillsdale, New Jersey: Erlbaum.

Hilberg, Raul. 1986. Bitburg as symbol. In Geoffrey Hartman, ed., *Bitburg in Moral and Political Perspective*, pp. 15–26. Bloomington: Indiana University Press.

Hitler, Adolf. 1939. *Mein Kampf*. New York: Reynal & Hitchcock.

Hobsbawm, E. J. 1984. *Worlds of Labour: Further Studies in the History of Labour*. London: Wiedenfeld and Nicolson.

Hocart, A. M. 1927. *Kingship*. London: Oxford University Press.

Holtom, Daniel C. 1972. *The Japanese Enthronement Ceremonies with an Account of the Imperial Regalia*. Reprint of 1928 edition. Tokyo: Sophia University.

Hooglund, Mary. 1980. One village in the revolution. *Middle East Research and Information Project Reports*, no. 87, pp. 7–12.

———. 1981. Ritual and revolution in Iran. In Myron J. Aronoff, ed., *Culture and Political Change, Political Anthropology*, volume 2, pp. 75–100. New Brunswick, New Jersey: Transaction.

Hunt, Eva. 1977. Ceremonies of confrontation and submission: The symbolic dimension of Indian-Mexican political interaction. In Sally F. Moore and Barbara G. Myerhoff, eds., *Secular Ritual*, pp. 124–47. Assen: Van Gorcum.

Hunt, Lynn. 1984. *Politics, Culture and Class in the French Revolution*. Berkeley: University of California Press.

Huxley, Julian. 1966. Introduction. *Philosophical Transactions of the Royal Society*, series B, 251: 249–71.

Inden, Ronald. 1978. Ritual, authority and cyclic time in Hindu kingship. In J. F. Richards, ed., *Kingship and Authority in South Asia*, pp. 28–73. Madison: University of Wisconsin South Asian Studies.

Inglis, K. S. 1967–1969. Australia Day. *Historical Studies* 13: 20–41.

Isaac, Rhys. 1976. Dramatizing the ideology of revolution: Popular mobilization in Virginia, 1774 to 1776. *William and Mary Quarterly* 33: 357–85.

Jackson, Richard A. 1984. *Vive le roi! A History of the French Coronation from Charles V to Charles X*. Chapel Hill: University of North Carolina Press.

Johnson, Willis. 1978. *The Year of the Longley*. Stonington, Maine: Penobscot Bay Press.

Jordan, Winthrop D. 1973. Family politics: Thomas Paine and the killing of the king, 1776. *Journal of American History* 60: 294–308.

Kantorowitz, Ernst H. 1957. *The King's Two Bodies: A Study in Mediaeval Political Theology*. Princeton: Princeton University Press.

Kaplan, Temma. 1984. Civic rituals and patterns of resistance in Barcelona, 1890–1930. In Pat Thane, Geoffrey Crossick, and Roderick Floud, eds., *The Power of the Past*, pp. 173–93. Cambridge: Cambridge University Press.

Katz, Robert. 1980. *Days of Wrath, The Ordeal of Aldo Moro*. Garden City, New York: Doubleday.

Kelly, Raymond. 1977. *Etoro Social Structure*. Ann Arbor: University of Michigan Press.

Kertzer, David I. 1974. Politics and ritual: The Communist festa in Italy. *Anthropological Quarterly* 47: 374–89.

_____. 1979. Gramsci's concept of hegemony: The Italian Church-Communist struggle. *Dialectical Anthropology* 4: 321–28.

_____. 1980. *Comrades and Christians: Religion and Political Struggle in Communist Italy*. Cambridge: Cambridge University Press.

_____, and Dennis P. Hogan. n.d. *Social Dimensions of Demographic Change: The Transformation of Nineteenth-Century Italy*. In preparation.

Kessler, Clive S. 1978. *Islam and Politics in a Malay State*. Ithaca: Cornell University Press.

Knauft, Bruce M. 1985. Ritual form and permutation in New Guinea: Implications of symbolic process for socio-political evolution. *American Ethnologist* 12: 321–40.

Kohn, Hans. 1967. *Prelude to Nation-States: The French and German Experience, 1789–1815*. Princeton: Van Nostrand.

Kowalewski, David. 1980. The protest uses of symbolic politics: The mobilization functions of protester symbolic resources. *Social Science Quarterly* 61: 95–113.

Kuper, Hilda. 1972. The language of sites in the politics of space. *American Anthropologist* 74: 411–25.

_____. 1978. *Sobhuza II: Ngwenyama and King of Swaziland*. New York: Africana.

Kurtz, Donald V. 1978. The legitimation of the Aztec state. In H. Claessen and P. Skalnik, eds., *The Early State*, pp. 169–89. The Hague: Mouton.

Laitin, David. 1986. *Hegemony and Culture*. Chicago: University of Chicago Press.

Lane, Christel. 1981. *The Rites of Rulers*. Cambridge: Cambridge University Press.

———. 1984. Legitimacy and power in the Soviet Union through socialist ritual. *British Journal of Political Science* 14: 207–17.

Lanternari, Vittorio. 1963. *The Religions of the Oppressed*. Translated by Lisa Sergio. New York: Alfred A. Knopf.

Laughlin, Charles D., Jr., John McManus, and Eugene G. d'Aquili. 1979. Introduction. In Eugene G. d'Aquili, Charles D. Laughlin, Jr., and John McManus, eds., *The Spectrum of Ritual: A Biogenetic Structural Analysis*, pp. 1–50. New York: Columbia University Press.

Leach, Edmund. 1954. *Political Systems of Highland Burma*. Boston: Beacon.

———. 1966. Ritualization in man in relation to conceptual and social development. *Philosophical Transactions of the Royal Society*, series B, 251: 403–8.

Lee, Alfred M. 1980. Nonviolent agencies in the Northern Ireland struggle, 1969–1979. *Journal of Sociology and Social Welfare* 7: 601–23.

Lerner, Max. 1941. *Ideas for the Ice Age*. New York: Viking.

Lévi-Strauss, Claude. 1966. *The Savage Mind*. Chicago: University of Chicago Press.

Lewis, Gilbert. 1980. *Day of Shining Red: An Essay on Understanding Ritual*. Cambridge: Cambridge University Press.

Lewis, Ioan M. 1977. Introduction. In Ioan M. Lewis, ed., *Symbols and Sentiments*, pp. 1–24. London: Academic.

Lex, Barbara W. The neurobiology of myth and ritual. In Eugene G. d'Aquili, Charles D. Laughlin, Jr., and John McManus, eds., *The Spectrum of Ritual: A Biogenetic Structural Analysis*, pp. 117–52. New York: Columbia University Press.

Light, Ivan H. 1969. The social construction of uncertainty. *Berkeley Journal of Sociology* 14: 189–99.

Linton, Ralph. 1933. *The Tanala: A Hill Tribe of Madagascar*. Chicago: Field Museum of Natural History, Anthropological Series.

Lipsitz, Lewis. 1968. If, as Verba says, the state functions as a religion, what are we to do then to save our souls? *American Political Science Review* 62: 527–53.

Lorenz, Konrad. 1964. Ritualized fighting. In J. D. Carthy and F. J. Ebling, eds., *The Natural History of Aggression*, pp. 39–50. London: Academic.

———. 1966. Evolution of ritualization in the biological and cultural spheres. *Philosophical Transactions of the Royal Society*, series B, 251: 273–84.

Lowe, David. 1967. *Ku Klux Klan: The Invisible Empire*. New York: Norton.

Lukes, Steven. 1975. Political ritual and social integration. *Sociology* 9: 289–308.

Mackenzie, W. J. M. 1967. *Politics and Social Science*. Baltimore: Penguin.

Malinowski, Bronislaw. 1945. *Magic, Science, and Religion*. Glencoe: Free Press.

Manchester, William. 1967. *The Death of a President*. New York: Harper and Row.

Mann, Michael. 1970. The social cohesion of liberal democracy. *American Sociological Review* 35:423–39.

Margadant, Ted. 1979. *French Peasants in Revolt: The Insurrection of 1851*. Princeton: Princeton University Press.

Marriott, McKim. 1966. The feast of love. In Milton Singer, ed., *Krishna: Myths, Rites, and Attitudes*, pp. 200–12. Honolulu: East-West Center Press.

Martin, Joanne. 1982. Stories and scripts in organizational settings. In Albert H. Hastorf and Alice M. Isen, eds., *Cognitive Social Psychology*, pp. 255–305. New York: Elsevier.

Mathiez, Albert. 1904. *Les origines des cultes révolutionnaires (1789–1792)*. Paris: Société Nouvelle de Librairie et d'Edition.

McDowell, Jennifer. 1974. Soviet civil ceremonies. *Journal for the Scientific Study of Religion* 13:265–79.

McGuire, William J., Claire V. McGuire, and Ward Winton. 1979. Effects of household sex composition on the salience of one's gender in the spontaneous self-concept. *Journal of Experimental Social Psychology* 15:77–90.

McManus, John. 1979. Ritual and human social cognition. In Eugene G. d'Aquili, Charles D. Laughlin, Jr., and John McManus, eds., *The Spectrum of Ritual: A Biogenetic Structural Approach*, pp. 216–48. New York: Columbia University Press.

————, Charles D. Laughlin, Jr., and Eugene d'Aquili. 1979. Concepts, methods, and conclusions. In Eugene G. d'Aquili, Charles D. Laughlin, Jr., and John McManus, eds., *The Spectrum of Ritual: A Biogenetic Structural Approach*, pp. 342–62. New York: Columbia University Press.

McPhee, Peter. 1977. Popular culture, symbolism and rural radicalism in nineteenth-century France. *Journal of Peasant Studies* 5:238–53.

Mead, Margaret. 1973. Ritual and social crisis. In James D. Shaughnessy, ed., *The Roots of Ritual*, pp. 87–102. Grand Rapids, Michigan: Eerdmans.

Meeker, Michael E. 1972. The great family aghas of Turkey: A study of a changing political culture. In Richard Antoun and Iliya Harik, eds., *Rural Politics and Social Change in the Middle East*, pp. 237–66. Bloomington: Indiana University Press.

Mooney, James. 1965. *The Ghost-Dance Religion and the Sioux Outbreak of 1890*. Reprinted from 1896 edition. Chicago: University of Chicago Press.

Moore, Sally F. 1975. Epilogue: Uncertainties in situations, indeterminacies in culture. In Sally F. Moore and Barbara G. Myerhoff, eds., *Symbol and Politics in Communal Ideology*, pp. 210–39. Ithaca: Cornell University Press.

————. 1977. Political meetings and the simulation of unanimity: Kilimanjaro 1973. In Sally F. Moore and Barbara G. Myerhoff, eds., *Secular Ritual*, pp. 151–72. Assen: Van Gorcum.

————, and Barbara G. Myerhoff. 1977. Introduction: Secular ritual, forms and meanings. In Sally F. Moore and Barbara G. Myerhoff, eds., *Secular Ritual*, pp. 3–24. Assen: Van Gorcum.

Moss, David. 1981. The kidnapping and murder of Aldo Moro. *Archives Européennes de Sociologie* 22:265–95.

Mosse, George L. 1971. Caesarism, circuses, and monuments. *Journal of Contemporary History* 6: 167–82.

———. 1975. *The Nationalization of the Masses*. New York: Fertig.

———. 1976. Mass politics and the political liturgy of nationalism. In Eugene Kamenka, ed., *Mass Politics and the Political Liturgy of Nationalism*, pp. 38–54. New York: St. Martin's.

Muir, Edward. 1981. *Civic Ritual in Renaissance Venice*. Princeton: Princeton University Press.

Munn, Nancy D. 1973. Symbolism in ritual context: Aspects of symbolic action. In John J. Honigmann, ed., *Handbook of Social and Cultural Anthropology*, pp. 579–612. Chicago: Rand McNally.

Myerhoff, Barbara. 1977. We don't wrap herring in a printed page: Fusion, fictions and continuity in secular ritual. In Sally F. Moore and Barbara G. Myerhoff, eds., *Secular Ritual*, pp. 199–226. Assen: Van Gorcum.

———. 1984. A death in due time: Construction of self and culture in ritual drama. In John J. MacAloon, ed., *Rite, Drama, Festival, Spectacle*, pp. 149–78. Philadelphia: ISHI.

Nadel, S. F. 1954. *Nupe Religion*. London: Routledge and Kegan Paul.

Needham, Rodney. 1963. Introduction. In Emile Durkheim and Marcel Mauss, *Primitive Classification*, pp. vii–xlviii. Translated by Rodney Needham. Chicago: University of Chicago Press.

Neisser, Uri. 1976. *Cognition and Reality*. San Francisco: Freeman.

Nelson, Janet L. 1976. Symbols in context: Rulers' inauguration rituals in Byzantium and the West in the early Middle Ages. In Derek Maker, ed., *The Orthodox Churches and the West*, pp. 97–119. Oxford: Blackwell.

Nieburg, H. L. 1973. *Culture Storm: Politics and the Ritual Order*. New York: St. Martin's.

Niemi, Richard G. 1973. Political socialization. In Jeanne N. Knutson, ed., *Handbook of Political Psychology*, pp. 117–38. San Francisco: Jossey-Bass.

Nisbett, Richard, and Lee Ross. 1980. *Human Inference: Strategies and Shortcomings of Social Judgment*. Englewood Cliffs: Prentice Hall.

Norbeck, Edward. 1963. "African rituals of conflict." *American Anthropologist* 65: 1254–79.

———. 1977. A sanction for authority: Etiquette. In Raymond D. Fogelson and Richard N. Adams, eds., *The Anthropology of Power*, pp. 67–76. New York: Academic.

Norman, Ross. 1975. Affective-cognitive consistency, attitudes, conformity, and behavior. *Journal of Personality and Social Psychology* 32: 83–91.

Novak, Michael. 1974. *Choosing our King: Powerful Symbols in Presidential Politics*. New York: Macmillan.

Oberg, K. 1940. The kingdom of Ankole in Uganda. In Meyer Fortes and E. E. Evans-Pritchard, eds., *African Political Systems*, pp. 121–62. London: Oxford University Press.

Olsen, Johan P. 1970. Local budgeting: Decision-making or a ritual act? *Scandinavian Political Studies* 5: 85–118.

Ortner, Sherry B. 1973. On key symbols. *American Anthropologist* 75: 1338–46.

———. 1975. Gods' bodies, gods' food: A symbolic analysis of a Sherpa ritual.

In Roy Willis, ed., *The Interpretation of Symbolism*, pp. 133–69. New York: Wiley.

―――. 1978. *Sherpas through their Ritual*. Cambridge: Cambridge University Press.

Ozouf, Mona. 1975. Space and time in the festivals of the French Revolution. *Comparative Studies in Society and History* 17: 372–84.

―――. 1976. *La fête révolutionnaire, 1789–1799*. Paris: Gallimard.

Packard, Randall. 1981. *Chiefship and Cosmology: An Historical Study of Political Competition*. Bloomington: Indiana University Press.

Patterson, Orlando. 1969. The cricket ritual in the West Indies. *New Society* 352: 97–98.

Perrot, Michelle. 1984. The First of May 1890 in France: The birth of a working-class ritual. In Pat Thane, Geoffrey Crossick, and Roderick Floud, eds., *The Power of the Past*, pp. 143–71. Cambridge: Cambridge University Press.

Peters, Emrys. 1963. Aspects of rank and status among Muslims in a Lebanese village. In Julian Pitt-Rivers, ed., *Mediterranean Countrymen*, pp. 159–200. Paris: Mouton.

Pfaffenberger, Bryan. 1980. Social communication in Dravidian ritual. *Journal of Anthropological Research* 36: 196–219.

Pfeffer, Jeffrey. 1981. Management as symbolic action: The creation and maintenance of organization paradigms. In L. L. Cummings and Barry M. Staw, eds., *Research in Organizational Behavior*, volume 3, pp. 1–52. Greenwich, Connecticut: JAI Press.

Piven, Frances Fox. 1976. The social structuring of political protest. *Politics and Society* 6: 297–326.

Pocock, J. G. A. 1964. Ritual, language, power: An essay on the apparent meanings of ancient Chinese philosophy. *Political Science* 16: 3–31.

Price, S. R. F. 1984. *Rituals and Power: The Roman Imperial Cult in Asia Minor*. Cambridge: Cambridge University Press.

Pythian-Adams, Charles. 1976. Ceremony and the citizen: The communal year at Coventry 1450–1550. In Peter Clark, ed., *The Early Modern Town*, pp. 106–28. London: Longman.

Radcliffe-Brown, A. R. 1940. Preface. In Meyer Fortes and E. E. Evans-Pritchard, eds., *African Political Systems*, pp. x–xxiii. London: Oxford University Press.

―――. 1952. *Structure and Function in Primitive Society*. Glencoe: Free Press.

Ranger, Terrence. 1980. Making Northern Rhodesia imperial: Variation on a royal theme. *African Affairs* 79: 349–73.

Rappaport, Roy A. 1979. *Ecology, Meaning and Religion*. Richmond, California: North Atlantic Books.

Rasnake, Roger. 1986. Carnival in Yura: Ritual reflections on *ayllu* and state relations. *American Ethnologist* 13: 662–80.

Rearick, Charles. 1977. Festivals in modern France: The experience of the Third Republic. *Journal of Contemporary History* 12: 435–60.

Reay, Marie. 1959. *The Kuma. Freedom and Conformity in the New Guinea Highlands*. Melbourne: Melbourne University Press.

Reynolds, Frank E. 1978. Legitimation and rebellion: Thailand's civic religion and the student uprising of October, 1973. In Bardwell L. Smith, ed., *Religion and Legitimation of Power in Thailand, Laos, and Burma*, pp. 134–46. Chambersburg, Penn.: ANIMA Books.

Richards, Audrey I. 1940. The political system of the Bemba tribe, northeastern Rhodesia. In Meyer Fortes and E. E. Evans-Pritchard, eds., *African Political Systems*, pp. 82–120. London: Oxford University Press.

Roberts, John M. 1965. Oaths, autonomic ordeals, and power. *American Anthropologist* 67: 186–212.

Rockhill, William W. 1905. *Diplomatic Audiences at the Court of China*. London: Luzac.

Rodger, Ian. 1981. Rhetoric and ritual politics: The Durham Miners' Gala. In Robert Paine, ed., *Politically Speaking*, pp. 43–63. Philadelphia: ISHI.

Rosaldo, Renato I., Jr. 1968. Metaphors of hierarchy in a Mayan ritual. *American Anthropologist* 70: 524–36.

Roscoe, J. 1911. *The Baganda*. London: Macmillan.

Rosenfeld, Alvin H. 1986. Another revisionism: Popular culture and the changing image of the Holocaust. In Geoffrey Hartman, ed., *Bitburg in Moral and Political Perspective*, pp. 90–102. Bloomington: Indiana University Press.

Ruiz, Teofilo F. 1985. Unsacred monarchy: The kings of Castile in the late Middle Ages. In Sean Wilentz, ed., *Rites of Power*, pp. 109–44. Philadelphia: University of Pennsylvania Press.

Sahlins, Marshall. 1981. *Historical Metaphors and Mythical Realities*. Ann Arbor: University of Michigan Press.

———. 1985. *Islands of History*. Chicago: University of Chicago Press.

Sanson, Rosemonde. 1973. La fête de Jeanne d'Arc en 1894: Controverse et célébration. *Revue d'Histoire Moderne e Contemporaine* 20: 444–63.

———. 1976. *Les 14 juillet: Fêtes et conscience nationale (1789–1975)*. Paris: Flammarion.

Schutz, Alfred. 1967 (1932). *The Phenomenology of the Social World*. Translated by George Walsh and Frederick Lehnert. Evanston: Northwestern University Press.

Scott, James. 1975. Exploitation in rural class relations: A victim's perspective. *Comparative Politics* 7: 489–532.

Scribner, Bob. 1978. Reformation, carnival and the world turned up-side down. *Social History* 3: 303–29.

Scullard, H. H. 1981. *Festivals and Ceremonies of the Roman Republic*. Ithaca: Cornell University Press.

Seneviratne, H. L. 1978. *Rituals of the Kandyan State*. Cambridge: Cambridge University Press.

Senin-Artina, Giovanna. 1983. *Il matrimonio tra enciclopedie giuridiche e prassi sociale*. Seminari di storia delle istituzioni religiose e relazioni tra Stato e Chiesa, Facoltà di Scienze Politiche. Florence: Università degli Studi di Firenze.

Shafer, Boyd C. 1943. When patriotism became popular: A study of the festivals of federation in France in 1790. *The Historian* 5: 2: 77–96.

————. 1972. *Faces of Nationalism: New Realities and Old Myths*. New York: Harcourt, Brace.

Shaw, Peter. 1981. *American Patriots and the Rituals of Revolution*. Cambridge: Harvard University Press.

Shils, Edward. 1966. Ritual and crisis. *Philosophical Transactions of the Royal Society*, series B, 251: 447–50.

————, and Michael Young. 1953. The meaning of coronation. *Sociological Review* 1: 63–81.

Siegel, James T. 1969. *The Rope of God*. Berkeley: University of California Press.

Silverman, Sydel. 1981. Rites of inequality: Stratification and symbol in central Italy. In Gerald D. Berreman, ed., *Social Inequality: Comparative and Development Approaches*, pp. 163–80. New York: Academic.

Singer, Milton B. 1982. Emblems of identity: A semiotic exploration. In Jacques Maquet, ed., *On Symbols in Anthropology*, pp. 73–132. Malibu, California: Undena.

Skinner, Quentin. 1981. The world as a stage. *New York Review of Books* 26: 6(16 April): 35–37.

Smith, Bardwell L. 1978. Kingship, the Sangha, and the process of legitimation in Anuradhapura Ceylon. In Bardwell L. Smith, ed., *Religion and Legitimation of Power in Sri Lanka*, pp. 73–95. Chambersburg, Penn.: ANIMA Books.

Smith, W. John. 1979. Ritual and the ethology of communicating. In Eugene G. d'Aquili, Charles D. Laughlin, Jr., and John McManus, eds., *The Spectrum of Ritual: A Biogenetic Structural Analysis*, pp. 51–79. New York: Columbia University Press.

Smith, W. Robertson. 1907. *Lectures on the Religions of the Semites*. London: Adam and Charles Black.

Snyder, Louis L. 1976. *Varieties of Nationalism: A Comparative Study*. New York: Holt, Rinehart.

Snyder, Mark, and William B. Swann, Jr. 1976. When actions reflect attitudes: The politics of impression management. *Journal of Personality and Social Psychology* 34: 1034–42.

Soboul, Albert. 1957. Sentiments religieux et cultes populaires pendant la révolution: Saintes patriotes et martyrs de la liberté. *Annales Historique de la Révolution Français* 29: 193–213.

Sperber, Daniel. 1975. *Rethinking Symbolism*. Cambridge: Cambridge University Press.

Sproull, Lee S. 1981. Beliefs in organizations. In Paul C. Nystrom and William H. Starbuck, eds., *Handbook of Organizational Design*, vol. 2, pp. 203–24. London: Oxford University Press.

Srinivas, M. N. 1966. *Social Change in Modern India*. Berkeley: University of California Press.

Starkey, David. 1977. Representation through intimacy: A study in the symbolism of monarchy and court office in early-modern England. In Ioan Lewis, ed., *Symbols and Sentiments*, pp. 187–224. London: Academic.

Strong, Roy. 1973. *Splendor at Court: Renaissance Spectacle and the Theater of Power*. Boston: Houghton Mifflin.

———. 1984. *Art and Power: Renaissance Festivals, 1450–1650*. Berkeley: University of California Press.

Struve, Nikita. 1968. "Pseudo-religious rites in the USSR." In Donald R. Cutler, ed., *The Religious Situation, 1968*, pp. 757–64. Boston: Beacon.

Supek, Olga. 1980. The meaning of Carnival in Croatia. *Anthropological Quarterly* 56: 90–94.

Taylor, Lily Ross. 1931. *The Divinity of the Roman Emperor*. Middletown, Conn.: American Philological Association.

Taylor, Simon. 1981. Symbol and ritual under National Socialism. *British Journal of Sociology* 32: 504–20.

Tedeschi, James T., Barry R. Schenker, and Thomas V. Bonoma. 1971. Cognitive dissonance: Private ratiocination or public spectacle? *American Psychologist* 26: 685–95.

Terlinden, Vicomte. 1960. La politique italienne de Charles Quint et le 'Triomphe' de Bologne. In Jean Jacquot, ed., *Fêtes et cérémonies au temps de Charles Quint*, pp. 29–43. Paris: Éditions du Centre National de la Recherche Scientifique.

Tesser, Abraham. 1978. "Self-generated attitude changes." In Leonard Berkowitz, ed., *Advances in Experimental Psychology*, volume 11, pp. 290–338. New York: Academic.

Thompson, Leonard M. 1985. *The Political Mythology of Apartheid*. New Haven: Yale University Press.

Tonkin, Elizabeth. 1979. Masks and powers. *Man* 14: 237–48.

Trexler, Richard. 1973. Ritual behavior in Renaissance Florence: The setting. *Medievalia et Humanistica* 4: 125–44.

Trice, Harrison M., James Belasco, and Joseph A. Alutto. 1969. The role of ceremonial in organizational behavior. *Industrial and Labor Relations Review* 23: 40–51.

Tumarkin, Nina. 1983. *Lenin Lives! The Lenin Cult in Soviet Russia*. Cambridge: Harvard University Press.

Turner, Victor. 1957. *Schism and Continuity in an African Society*. Manchester: Manchester University Press.

———. 1967. *The Forest of Symbols*. Ithaca: Cornell University Press.

———. 1969. *The Ritual Process*. Chicago: Aldine.

———. 1974. *Dramas, Fields, and Metaphors*. Ithaca: Cornell University Press.

———. 1985. *On the Edge of the Bush*. Tucson: University of Arizona Press.

Tversky, Amos, and Daniel Kahneman. 1974. Judgment under uncertainty: Heuristics and biases. *Science* 185: 4157: 1124–31.

Unger, Aryeh. 1974. *The Totalitarian Party: Party and People in Nazi Germany and Soviet Russia*. Cambridge: Cambridge University Press.

Valeri, Valerio. 1985. *Kingship and Sacrifice: Ritual and Society in Ancient Hawaii*. Translated by Paula Wissing. Chicago: University of Chicago Press.

van Gennep, Arnold. 1960. *The Rites of Passage*. Translated by Monika Vizedom and Gabrielle Caffee. Chicago: University of Chicago Press.

Verba, Sidney. 1965. Conclusion: Comparative political culture. In Lucian W. Pye and Sidney Verba, eds., *Political Culture and Political Development*, pp. 512–60. Princeton: Princeton University Press.

Vogt, Evon Z., and Suzanne Abel. 1977. On political rituals in contemporary Mexico. In Sally F. Moore and Barbara G. Myerhoff, eds., *Secular Ritual*, pp. 173–88. Assen: Van Gorcum.

Wagner-Pacifici, Robin E. 1986. *The Moro Morality Play: Terrorism as Social Drama*. Chicago: University of Chicago Press.

Walzer, Michael. 1967. On the role of symbolism in political thought. *Political Science Quarterly* 82: 191–205.

———. 1968. Politics in the welfare state. *Dissent* 15: 26–40.

Warner, W. Lloyd. 1974 (1953). An American sacred ceremony. In Russell E. Richey and Donald G. Jones, eds., *American Civil Religion*, pp. 89–111. New York: Harper & Row.

Weatherford, J. McIver. 1981. *Tribes on the Hill*. New York: Rawson, Wade.

Weber, Eugen. 1977. Who sang the Marseillaise? In Jacques Beauroy, Marc Bertrand and Edward T. Gargan, eds., *The Wolf and the Lamb: Popular Culture in France*, pp. 161–73. Saratoga, California: Anma Libri.

Weber, Max. 1968. *Max Weber on Charisma and Institution Building*. Chicago: University of Chicago Press.

Wechsler, Howard J. 1985. *Offerings of Jade and Silk: Ritual and Symbol in the Legitimation of the T'ang Dynasty*. New Haven: Yale University Press.

Weinstein, Eugene A. 1957. Development of the concept of the flag and the sense of national identity. *Child Development* 28: 167–74.

Wicklund, Robert A., and Jack W. Brehm. 1976. *Perspectives on Cognitive Dissonance*. Hillsdale, New Jersey: Erlbaum.

Wilder, David A. 1981. Perceiving persons as a group: Categorization and intergroup relations. In David L. Hamilton, ed., *Cognitive Processes in Stereotyping and Intergroup Relations*, pp. 213–58. Hillsdale, New Jersey: Erlbaum.

Wilentz, Sean. 1985. Introduction. In Sean Wilentz, ed., *Rites of Power*, pp. 1–12. Philadelphia: University of Pennsylvania Press.

Winthrop, Robert C. 1857. Oration at the inauguration of Benjamin Franklin, in his native city, September 17, 1856. *North American Review* 175: 334–63.

Wipper, Audrey. 1977. *Rural Rebels: A Study of Two Protest Movements in Kenya*. Nairobi: Oxford University Press.

Woolley, Reginald M. 1915. *Coronation Rites*. Cambridge: Cambridge University Press.

Worsley, Peter. 1968. *The Trumpet Shall Sound*. Second edition. New York: Schocken.

Young, James E. 1986. Memory and monument. In Geoffrey Hartman, ed., *Bitburg in Moral and Political Perspective*, pp. 103–13. Bloomington: Indiana University Press.

Index

Abel, Suzanne, 185
Abelson, Robert, 51
Abercrombie, Nicholas, 191
Aborigines, 64, 65
Abrahamian, E., 202
Abu-Zahra, Nadia, 197
Accession ritual, 46
Adams, John, 163
Addis Ababa, Ethiopia, 178
Adler, Alfred, 192
Africa, 73, 170–71, 178. See also West Africa; East Africa; and individual countries
African National Congress, 171, 172
Afrikaner Resistance Movement, 173
Afrikaners: Great Trek, 36–37
Age groups, 130
Agulhon, Maurice, 188, 202, 204
Aho, James, 191
Alabama, 92
Allen, Frederick Lewis, 72
Alliance, 125
Ambiguity: of symbols, 11; of communication, 128–29
American Revolution, 70, 122, 161–63, 172
Americans: political opinions of, 6
Amherst, Lord, 87–88
Ancestor worship, 18, 110–11
Anderson, Benedict, 6, 186, 204
Andreotti, Giulio, 140

Andrew, Prince (of Britain), 66
Anglo, Sydney, 189
Anglo-Persian Agreement, 167
Ankole, 46
Anthem, 37; of Likud youth, 110; in South Africa, 20; Afrikaner, 37; origins of, 73; of Swaziland, 89; Nazi, 166; Sri Lankan, 178
Anthropologists: study of ritual, 3
Anticlerics, 147
Antiwar movement, 102–03, 181
Antony, Mark, 118
Anxiety, 131–32, 180
Apostolidès, Jean-Marie, 189
Apter, David, 204
Arab unity, 96
Arlington military cemetery, 61
Arms negotiations, 90
Arnold, Thurmon, 3, 10, 185, 187, 189, 199
Aronoff, Myron, 178, 186, 192, 194, 195, 197, 204
Ash Wednesday, 148
Ashes: scattering of, 144
Assassination: of Indira Gandhi, 140–44
Athens, 190
Australia, 64, 65, 193, 199
Austria, 155
Authority, 24; investiture of, 51
Aztecs, 33–34, 180

Baganda, 134
Bagehot, Walter, 97, 182, 196, 204
Balandier, Georges, 191
Baltimore, Maryland, 162
"Bandiera Rossa," 45
Bandura, Albert, 79, 194, 196
Baptism: Soviet, 116; Italian Communist,
    117; as Montagnard, 17
Barotseland, 22
Barrès, Maurice, 174
Barsam, Richard, 202
Basques, 76
Bastille (Paris), 151, 154, 160, 183
Bastille Day, 71, 160
Battle of Blood River, 173
Battle of the Boyne, 123
Bauman, Zygmunt, 185
Beattie, John, 190, 191
Begin, Menachim, 109–10
Behaviorism, 79
Beidelman, T. O., 193
Beijing, China, 18
Belafonte, Harry, 102
Belief: and ritual, 67–69; and solidarity,
    75–76; political, 95–97
Bellah, Robert, 65, 193
Bemba, 19
Ben-Gurion, David, 109–10
Bengal, 113
Bennett, W. Lance, 186, 187, 188, 190, 192,
    193, 194, 196, 199, 203
Bercé, Yves-Marie, 200, 201, 202
Berenson, Edward, 188, 200, 203
Bergen-Belsen concentration camp, 77, 95,
    121
Berger, John, 120, 198
Berger, Peter, 185, 199
Bergeron, David, 189, 191
Bergesen, Albert, 91–92, 185, 193, 196
Berlin, Germany, 164
Berlinguer, Enrico, 138, 140
Bernardi, Tiziana, 190
Berne, Switzerland, 146
Bettelheim, Bruno, 38, 98, 191, 196
Bezucha, Robert, 200
Binns, Christopher, 186, 188, 192, 200, 204
Biondi, Dino, 198
Birmingham, Alabama, 92
Birnbaum, Norman, 194
Bismarck, 99
Bitburg cemetery, 77, 90, 92–95
Black Power, 23–24
Black shirts: in Italy, 119
Bloch, Marc, 192
Bloch, Maurice, 40, 51, 85, 191, 192, 195,
    203

Bloodflag, 165–66
Bloody Sunday, 121
Blumer, Herbert, 72, 194
Blumler, J. G., 194
Blustain, Harvey, 197
Bodily adornment: in U.S., 107;
    Yanomamo, 125–26; and war, 129, 130
Body: of king, 47
Boggs, Carl, 186
Bologna, Italy, 31, 55; coronation of
    Charles V at, 77–78; rites of passage in,
    117–18
Borhek, James, 189, 204
Boston, Massachusetts, 122, 161, 162
Botha, Pieter Willem, 173
Bouillé, General, 154
Bourbons, 158
Brain, 79
Brandes, Stanley, 149, 200
Brandt, Willy, 57
Brazil, 73–74, 125; use of soccer in, 129
Brehm, Jack, 196
Breslau, Germany, 99
Brezhnev, Leonid, 16
Brian-Chaniov, Nicholas, 191
Brinton, Crane, 201
Britain, 5; royal ritual in, 25, 53–54, 66, 97,
    175–76; and Chinese emperor, 87–88;
    relations with Switzerland, 89; in North-
    ern Ireland, 123–24; and cricket, 129;
    American colonies of, 162; colonialism in
    India, 169–70; and South Africa, 173
Brou, France, 147
Brown, Judith, 202
Brutus, 118
Bryant, Lawrence, 197
Bucci, P. Vincent, 198
Buddhism, 123
Budget making, 49–50
Bundy, MacGeorge, 193
Bunyoro, 35–36
Burden, Hamilton, 202
Burgundy, France, 146
Burial: of Chinese emperor, 105–06
Burke, Kenneth, 4, 16, 101, 185, 188, 196
Bwiti, 68

Caesar, Julius, 118
Calder, P. R., 199
Calendar: political use of, 20; in French
    Revolution, 157–58
Cannadine, David, 203
Cannibalism, 180
Canterbury, Archbishop of, 176
Cantor, Nancy, 195
Cape Town, South Africa, 172

Caraffa brothers, 145
Cargo systems, 51–52
Carlyle, Thomas, 5, 185
Carnival, 144–50, 153; as safety valve, 55
Carter, Jimmy, 178, 182–83; and Iranian crisis, 86
Cassirer, Ernst, 25, 67, 181, 185, 187, 189, 194, 204
Caste ritual, 110, 112–14, 131
Catechism: in Italy, 116–17
Categorization, 4, 81, 82–83, 84
Catholic: rites of Carnival, 144
Catholic-Protestant conflict, 32, 130
Chad, 47
Chagnon, Napoleon, 126, 198
Chanting, 99, 102; in black power movement, 24
Charles IX, King, 27; royal tour of, 22–23
Charles the Bald, King, 190
Charles V, King, 31, 77–78
Charles, Prince of Wales, 66
Chastel, André, 194
Chatham, Lord, 168, 202
Chelkowski, Peter, 168, 202
Cherniavsky, Michael, 190
Children: political education of, 12–13; political conceptions of, 16; impact of ritual on, 83
China: political philosophy in, 13; and imperial rites, 20; political use of calendar in, 29–30; imperial accession in, 46; emperor's burial in, 105–06
Christian Democratic party, 71, 116, 117, 135–40, 184
Christianity: in India, 113
Christmas, 46, 166
Christmas tree, 86
Chuang Tzu, 13
Church: role in coronation, 27–28; absorption of pagan ritual, 45; and Bastille Day, 71; and rites of passage, 114–18; and ritual competition, 177
Churchill, Winston, 5
Civil religion, 65, 66
Civil rights protest: in U.S., 122–23
Clans, 130
Class conflict: in Britain, 176
Clement VII, Pope, 78
Cleveland, Les, 194
Clothing, 40; of European royalty, 5, 41, 78, 106–07; and self-identity, 16; and organizational identity, 21; among Monhegan Indians, 21; in Black Power movement, 24; in funerary ritual, 26–27; in African movements, 35, 36, 170, 171; in Hawaii, 52; in protest demonstra-

tions, 103, 121, 122, 148; in India, 112–13, 143; at Soviet rites, 116; inversion through, 149; in French Revolution, 151, 156, 158; in Iranian Revolution, 168. See also Bodily adornment
Coat of arms: Brazilian, 74
Coburg, Germany, 164
Cockade, 158
Cognition: and emotion, 82, 99–101; conservatism of, 83
Cognitive characteristics, 82–83
Cognitive dissonance, 97–98
Cohen, Abner, 185, 186, 187, 188, 189, 191, 192, 194
Cohen, William, 197
Collioure, France, 147, 148
Colonialism: responses to, 19, 169–71; and defining new nation, 20; in Africa, 23, 33, 36, 41; in India, 112–13; Dutch, 179
Colorado, 18
Commencement, 129
Committee on Un-American Activities, 188
Communication: through ritual, 29–34, 85, 104–07, 128, 180; between nations, 31–34; between organizations, 31–34; economy of, 136
Communitas, 72
Community ritual, 104, 145
Concentration camps, 94–95
Condensation, 11
Conflict: and ritual, 62–63
Conflict theory, 38–39
Conformity, 39–40
Congress party (India), 143
Congress, U.S., 6, 37, 107–08, 163
Congressional hearings, 91, 107
Connors, Bull, 92
Conrad, Geoffrey, 191
Constitution: of United States, 64–65, 69, 133
Constitutional Revolution, 167
Construct accessibility, 80
Conventions, 74, 122–23
Converse, Philip, 194
Cook, Rhodes, 198
Corneilla-la-Rivière, France, 148
Coronation: in Britain, 66, 176
Corporations, 42
Corpus Christi Day, 130, 147
Counter-revolution, 158
Counter-ritual, 121
Counter-rites, 121; in India, 141
Court ritual, 132; in France, 32, 106–07
Cramp rings, 54
Crick, Malcolm, 48, 192
Cricket, 129

Crisis, 134–44
Crocker, J. Christopher, 195, 199
Cross, 78, 118, 158; flaming, 15
Crowd behavior, 100
Cultural consensus, 68
Cultural management, 179
Culture, 51, 68, 174; relation to individual,
   3–4; defined, 79; as categorization, 84; of
   U.S. Senate, 91
Curtis, Kenneth, 50
Curtis, Richard, 189, 204
Cushing, Richard Cardinal, 60

D'Aquili, Eugene, 187, 190, 195
Da Matta, Roberto, 87, 186, 194, 195, 201
Dahl, Robert, 74, 192, 194
Dance, 40, 99; among Monhegan Indians,
   21; in Swaziland, 89–90; Yanomamo, 126
Dandi, India, 169
Dani, 199
Davis, Marvin, 113, 197
Davis, Natalie Zemon, 130, 199, 200
De Quincy (French assemblyman), 156
De'Medici, Catherine, 22, 32
De-Stalinization, 28–29
Deal, Terrence, 42, 188, 191
Declaration of Independence, 161
Declaration of the Rights of Man, 155, 157
Delegitimation, 161, 169, 178
Delhi, India, 141
Demarest, Arthur, 191
Denver, Colorado, 18, 21
Descent, 19
Descent groups, 110–12
Diadem, 27
Dijon, France, 146
Di Maggio, Paul, 188
Dini ya Msambwa, 170–71
Diplomacy, 87–88, 104–05
Distinctiveness, 82–83
Divination, 133–34
Divine king, 48, 50, 52–54
Dommanget, Maurice, 201
Douglas, Mary, 12, 84, 188, 195
Doutte, E., 67, 194
Dowd, David, 201
Draft card protest, 102–03, 121–22, 178
Drama, 92, 88–89, 135, 138; human need
   for, 14; staging of, 40–41; in American
   politics, 108; defined, 187
Dramatization, 90; of conflict, 120
Dress. See Clothing
Duke of Kent, 89
Duncan, Hugh, 186, 192, 197
Dunn, Seymour, 201
Durham Miner's Gala, 201

Durkheim, Emile, 91, 186, 191, 193; on
   defining ritual, 9; on legitimation, 37–39;
   on solidarity, 61–66, 76, 153; on belief,
   68–69, 86; on emotion, 100
Duvignaud, Jean, 201

East Africa: Shilluk rites in, 25–26; Ankole
   kingdom in, 46
Easter, 166
Eastern Europe, 115
Eckardt, A. Roy, 196
Edelman, Murray, 42, 84, 90, 96, 131, 186,
   191, 193, 195, 196, 199
Edward IV, King, 54
Effigy: among Shilluk, 25–26; in Northern
   Ireland, 124; in India, 141; of French
   official, 148; in American Revolution,
   161, 162
Egalitarianism, 48; symbols of, 41
Egypt, 53
El Salvador, 49
Elba, 183
Election ritual; in the United States, 11, 49,
   86; in the Soviet Union, 49; in El Sal-
   vador, 49
Elias, Norbert, 197
Elites, 176
Elizabeth, Queen (of Russia), 28
Emotion, 10, 11, 41, 97, 144, 180; political
   importance of, 14; in coronation rites,
   28; and symbols, 40; and solidarity, 64;
   caused by national anthem, 73; influ-
   ences on perception, 67, 86, 99–101, 182;
   impact of rallies on, 119
Emotions: and cricket, 129; in Iranian Rev-
   olution, 168; in South African funerals,
   172; stirred by "Marseillaise," 174
Enemy: image of, 84, 91
Engell, Ivan, 192
England. See Britain
Enlightenment, 181
Epilepsy, 54
Eritrea, 178
Esprit de corps, 72
Etampes, France, 154, 155
Ethiopia, 178
Ethnic identity, 20–21
Ethnocentrism, 37
Ethology, 128
Etruscan, 29
Europe. See Eastern Europe; individual
   countries and cities
Evans-Pritchard, E. E., 26, 62, 189, 190,
   193
Evolution, 128, 174–75

Factions: in Tunisia, 110–11; in India, 114
Fairbanks, James, 193
Fairman, H. W., 192
Faith, 96, 188
False consciousness, 48
Fang cult, 68
Fascism: in Italy, 70, 119
Faure, Alain, 150, 201
Fear: generated by ritual, 180
Feast: in Tunisia, 111; Yanomamo, 125
Fédérés, 151–52
Fernandez, James, 68, 187, 194, 204
Festinger, Leon, 98, 196
Festival of Liberty, 154–55
Festival of Love, 131
Festival of National Brotherhood, 166
Festival of Simonneau, 154–56
Festival of the Federation, 151–52, 159
Festival of the Supreme Being, 157
Fetish, 46–47
Fetishism, 64
Fire, 103, 104 05, 121–22, in South Africa,
    36–37; as symbol of ruler, 53; in India,
    143; in American Revolution, 162, 163
First Communion: in Italy, 116–17
First Ladies, 109
Firth, Raymond, 186
Fishwick, Duncan, 189
Fiske, Susan, 194
Flag, 32, 174, 184; United States, 6, 15, 57,
    59, 66, 86, 90, 92, 102, 120, 134, 162;
    defining nation, 7; as country, 16; in
    South Africa, 20, 172–73; in Iran, 24;
    red, 45, 183; Brazilian, 74; saluting, 83,
    Vietnamese, 102, 121; Italian, 118, 139;
    Thai, 123; British, 124; of Red Brigades,
    136; Indian, 143; French, 147, 183; of
    Communism, 164; Nazi, 164, 165, 166;
    Ethiopian, 178, in Soviet Union, 183
Foner, Anne, 192
Food: taboos, 47; symbolism of caste, 114
Force: used in politics, 2
Fortes, Meyer, 62, 189, 192, 193
Fox, Richard, 175, 186, 203
France: and national identity, 17; political
    use of calendar in, 20; Montagnard so-
    cieties in, 21; royal rites in, 22–23, 26–
    27, 32, 77; revolution in, 23, 151–61;
    king's two bodies in, 26; rites of healing
    in, 53–54; rites of rebellion in, 55; histo-
    ry of social theory in, 63; festival for Joan
    of Arc in, 71–72; national anthem in, 73;
    war commemoration in, 93; ritual strug-
    gle in, 106; Catholic-Protestant conflict
    in, 130; Carnival in, 145–48; popular
    rites in, 177; and symbols of nation, 183

Francis I, King, 148, 190
Franco, Francisco, 149, 150
Frazer, James, 55, 192
French Revolution, 151–60, 172, 183; use
    of simultaneity in, 23
Freud, Sigmund, 182, 187
Frey, Frederick, 188
Fry, Peter, 189
Fu I (Grand Astrologer), 20
Fuenmayor, Spain, 149–50
Functionalism, 54–55
Funeral, 100, 184; among French royalty,
    26, 190; among Bunyoro, 35; in Soviet
    Union, 116; in Italy, 118, 119, 139–40; of
    Indira Gandhi, 142–44; of Simonneau,
    155; in South Africa, 171–73, 180; of
    Bunyoro king, 190
Fustel de Coulanges, 189, 191, 192

Gagarin, Yuri, 38
Galbraith, John K., 182, 204
Gandhi, Indira, 140–44
Gandhi, Mahatma, 143, 169–70
Gandhi, Rajiv, 142–44
Garfinkel, Harold, 190, 196
Garrow, David, 196
Geertz, Clifford, 86, 185, 186, 189, 192,
    195, 202, 203; on interest theory, 7–8; on
    Javanese king, 22; on Moroccan mon-
    archy, 23; on demystification, 48
George III, King, 97, 161
George IV, King, 176
Georgia, 15
Gerlach, Luther, 189
Germany: and NATO anniversary, 120; and
    Nazism, 5, 163–67; Bitburg rites in, 77,
    93–95, 121; and red flag, 99
Ghost Dance, 170
Giesey, Ralph, 190
Gillespie, Joanna, 197
Gilmore, David, 149, 201
Gluckman, Max, 54–55, 133, 177, 186, 192,
    194, 199, 204
"God Save the Queen," 89
Goffman, Erving, 187
Goldberg, Robert, 189
Golden Temple, 140–42
Goldschlager, Alain, 70, 194
Goody, Jack, 187
Gorbachev, Mikhail: in Iceland, 32, 109
Government: personification of, 7
Graham, Victor, 189
Gramsci, Antonio, 96, 186, 188, 196
Granvelle, Cardinal, 146
Great Trek, 36–37, 173
Green Berets, 59

Greisman, H. C., 192
Gronbeck, Bruce, 190, 196
Grosvenor, Melville, 193
Guanajuato, Mexico, 85
Guillotine, 148, 159
Gusii, 170

H.M.S. Pinafore, 182
Habermas, Jürgen, 94, 196
Hahn, Dan, 195, 204
"Hail to the Chief," 28, 59, 60, 90
Hall, Peter, 191
Hamill, Hugh, 185, 195
Hamilton, David, 194
Hanley, Sarah, 190, 197
Hardgrave, Robert, 197
Hart, C. W. M., 199
Hart, Gary, 108
Hawaii, 47, 52
Hayes, Carlton, 191, 193, 194
Hegemony, 96, 175
Heider, Karl, 199
Henry II, King, 190
Henry IV, King, 53
Henry VI, King, 54
Henry VII, King, 54; coronation of, 25
Herzl, Theodore, 109, 174
Heuristics, 81
Hicks, George, 189
Hidalgo, Miguel, 1
Hidalgo's revolt, 23, 85
Hierarchy, 48, 51, 104
Higgins, E. Tory, 195
Hilberg, Raul, 196
Hindu: anger at Sikhs, 142
Hindu kingdoms, 47
Hine, Virginia, 47
Historians, 159
Hitler, Adolf, 5, 163–67, 181, 202; and Nazi
    salute, 98
Hitler Youth, 166
Hobsbawm, E. J., 196, 201
Hocart, A. M., 52, 192
Hogan, Dennis, 198
Holtom, Daniel, 191
Hooglund, Mary, 189, 202
House of Burgesses, 162
Hunt, Eva, 131, 191, 199
Hunt, Lynn, 158, 201, 202
Hussein (7th c.), 168
Huxley, Julian, 128, 190, 198

Iceland, 32, 109
Icon: of legitimacy, 46; revolutionary, 136;
    Hitler as, 163

Ideology: of legitimacy, 39; of indi-
    vidualism, 108
Immortality: of political leaders, 18
Inaugural address, 59
Inauguration: in the Philippines, 25; of
    U.S. President, 57–58
Inden, Ronald, 192
Independence Day: Brazilian, 73–74; U.S.,
    83; Swazi, 89–90
India: caste ritual in, 112–14; Festival of
    Love in, 131; and assassination of I.
    Gandhi, 140–44; and the salt march,
    169–70
Indians: American, 20–21, 170
Indonesia, 179
Inglis, K. S., 202
Interest group theory, 174–75
International relations, 32
Iran: revolution in, 24, 167–68; and taking
    of U.S. embassy, 85–86, 134; U.S. hear-
    ings on, 91
Isaac, Rhys, 202
Islam: and revolution, 167–68
Islamic: saint, 110–11; ritual and politics,
    45
Israel, 109–10
Italian Communist Party, 55, 136, 138–40,
    184; and peace demonstration, 32; sym-
    bols of, 45; and Resistance, 71
Italy: political use of calendar in, 20; politi-
    cal parties in, 32; and Resistance sym-
    bolism, 70–71; palio in, 74–75; rites of
    passage in, 135–40; and Fascism, 183.
    See Italian Communist Party; individual
    cities

Jabotinski, V., 110
Jackson, Andrew, 163
Jackson, Richard, 190
Jacobins, 154, 155
Jaffna, Sri Lanka, 178
Japan: emperor's sacred power in, 47; ritu-
    al suicide in, 88
Java, 22
Jefferson, Thomas, 163
Jesus, 147
Joan of Arc, 71–72
Johnson, Hayes, 194
Johnson, Lyndon, 57–58
Johnson, W. McAllister, 189
Johnson, Willis, 192
Jordan, 202
Judicial ritual, 132, 137
Jupiter (Roman god), 30

Kahneman, Daniel, 80, 195
Kanouse, David, 195
Kantorowicz, Ernst, 190
Kao-tsu (Chinese emperor), 29
Kaplan, Temma, 200
Katz, Robert, 199
Kelly, Raymond, 189
Kennedy, Allan, 42, 188, 191
Kennedy, Jacqueline, 58–59
Kennedy, John F., 142; funeral of, 57–61
Kennedy, John, Jr., 61
Kenya, 170–71
Kertzer, David, 186, 189, 191, 192, 193, 198
Kessler, Clive, 5, 185, 191, 199
Khomeini, Ayatollah, 24
Kidnapping: in Iran, 86; of Aldo Moro, 135–40
Kinder, Donald, 194
King's two bodies, 26
King, Gillian, 195
King, Martin Luther, Jr., 24, 102, 123
Kinship, 19, 110, 132
Knauft, Bruce, 189
Kohl, Helmut, 77, 93–95
Kohn, Hans, 201, 202
Koran, 172
Kowalewski, David, 204
Kowtowing, 87–88
Ku Klux Klan: ceremony in Georgia, 15; in Colorado, 18, 21; membership allure of, 72; use of flag, 92
Kuper, Hilda, 187, 196
Kurtz, Donald, 191, 192

Labor party (Israel), 110
Lafayette, Marquis de, 151, 154
Laitin, David, 186
Lane, Christel, 55, 178, 180, 187, 188, 190, 191, 192, 193, 194, 196, 197, 198, 203, 204
Lanternari, Vittorio, 202
Lassalle, Ferdinand, 99
Laughlin, Charles, 187, 190, 195
Leach, Edmund, 67, 186, 187, 191, 194
Leader: as symbol of group, 18
Lee, Alfred, 198, 199
Legitimacy: borrowing of, 42–46; use of icons for, 46; of rulers in Brazil, 74; of Italian government, 139; Nazi, 166
Legitimation: through ritual, 37–42, 53; of inequality, 50–52
Lenin, Vladimir, 16, 138
Lenin: body of, 18, 45; worship of, 38; and Christian ritual, 46; statue of, 116; death of, 199–200
Leo X, Pope, 31

Lepeletier, Louis-Michel, 158, 201
Lerner, Max, 64, 186, 193; on power of symbols, 5
Levée, 106
Lévi-Strauss, Claude, 186
Lewis, Gilbert, 187, 188
Lewis, Ioan, 99, 187, 196
Liberty tree, 162
Libro Cerimoniale, 105
Light, Ivan, 181, 204
Likud party, 109–10
Liminality, 137
Lincoln, Abraham, 58
Lincoln Monument, 120, 122
Linton, Ralph, 133, 199
Lipsitz, Lewis, 204
Local level: relation to national, 21–24
London, England, 57
Longley, James, 50
Lorenz, Konrad, 128–29, 190, 198
Louis the Stammerer, King, 190
Louis XIII, King, 27, 106; healing ritual of, 53
Louis XIV, King, 106; and personification of nation, 17; death of, 27; healing ritual, 53
Louis XV, King, 155; accession to throne, 27
Louis XVI, King, 152, 159
Love, Minnie, 18, 21
Lowe, David, 194
Loyd, Sir Francis, 89
Luckmann, Thomas, 199
Luhya, 171
Lukes, Steven, 69, 187, 192, 194, 195
Luther, Martin, 103
Lyly, John, 32

Machiavelli, 181
Mackenzie, W. J. M., 185
Madagascar, 133–34
Magic, 177
Maine, 50
Malan, Daniel, 191
Malaysia, 199
Malinowski, Bronislaw, 132, 177, 199, 203, 204
Manchester, William, 193
Mann, Michael, 194
Mao Tse-tung: body of, 18
Marat, 158
Marcos, Ferdinand, 50
Mardi Gras, 146
Margadant, Ted, 188
Marie-Antoinette, 106–07

Marriott, McKim, 131, 199
"Marseillaise," 157, 174
Martin, Joanne, 188
Marx, Karl, 138, 186; on modern politics, 8
Marxian perspectives: on ritual, 38–39; on false consciousness, 48
Masaniello, leader of the Neapolitan revolt, 145
Masinde, African leader, 171
Masquerade, 147
Mass: in Italy, 116, 117; in French Revolution, 151
Mass media, 120; election coverage, 11; and organizational distinctiveness, 19; and Bitburg, 121; and Aldo Moro, funeral of, 140; in India, 141, 143, 169
Mass protests, 132
Mass psychology, 165
Massacre of the Champ de Mars, 154
Material effects, 140
Material forces: and politics, 2; and ritual, 39
Material interests: as basis of motivation, 7–8
Material resources, 174–75
Material world, 175–76; constraints on symbolic, 170
Mathiez, Albert, 201
Mau Mau, 181
Maundy Thursday, 147
May Day, 201; in Vienna, 10; in Moscow, 54; in Germany, 166; in Soviet Union, 180; in Italy, 183
Mayes, Sharon, 192
Mayor, 50
McDowell, Jennifer, 197
McGuire, Claire, 195
McGuire, William, 195
McManus, John, 190, 195, 196
McPhee, Peter, 189, 200, 204
Mead, Margaret, 187, 188
Medici princes, 75
Meeker, Michael, 190
Meetings, 42
Mein Kampf, 164
Memorial Day, 65–66
Mengitsu, Haile Mariam, 178
Metaphor: of journey, 108; in political thought, 6–7, 84
Methods: of political study, 7
Mexico: celebrating Hidalgo's revolt in, 1, 23; cargo systems in, 51–52; Hidalgo's revolt in, 85
Michelet, Jules, 63, 64
Military: ritual in Roman Empire, 29–30; glorification of, 166; in Brazil, 73–74

Minister of cults, 160
Mishima, Yukio, 88
Missionaries, 177; in India, 113
Mitterand, Francois, 93, 94
Mock battles, 130
Mock burial, 161
Monhegan Indians, 20–21
Montagnard movement, 17, 147; and organizational identity, 21
Montezuma, 34
Montepellier, France, 146
Mooney, James, 202
Moore, Sally, 187, 188, 189, 192, 195
Moro, Aldo, 135–40, 184
Moro, Eleonora, 139
Morocco: royal rites in, 23
Moscow, 18, 38; demonstrations in, 30, 54, 104
Moss, David, 136, 199
Mosse, George, 159, 164, 187, 201, 202, 203
Motolinia, 191
Moundang, 47
Mount Herzl, 110
Mourning: in France, 26; Jewish, 110; rites among Sikhs, 141
Muhammad, 97
Muir, Edward, 105, 197, 199, 200, 204
Multivocality: of symbols, 11
Mumbo, cult of, 170
Munich, Germany, 165
Munn, Nancy, 63, 187, 188, 193
Music, 40, 103; in Soviet ritual, 180
Muslim: community in South Africa, 172
Mussolini, Benito, 47, 181, 183; political use of the calendar by, 20; and rites of allegiance, 118
Myerhoff, Barbara, 10, 187, 188, 192, 195
Mystification, 48–50
Myth: political, 12, 13, 84, 174; in organizations, 17–18; relation to ritual of, 67

Nadel, S. F., 186
Names, 113
Nancy, France, 154, 155
Naples, Italy, 145–46, 148
Napoleon, 160–61, 183
Narbonne, France, 147
Nation: creation through symbols, 6, 16, 20; personification of, 17; allegiance to, 6, 175; symbolic construction of, 160, 178–79; need for ritual in, 64; defined by flag, 7
National Assembly (France), 151–52, 155–56
National Front (Iran), 168

Nationalism: in France, 63; role of ritual in, 69, 73–74; in Ukraine, 181
Nations: establishment of, 23
Nazi: salute, 98, 180; book burning, 122
Nazism, 70, 93–95, 163–67
Ndembu, 63, 132–33
Needham, Rodney, 84, 195
Nehru, Jawaharlal, 143
Neighborhood, 75
Neisser, Uri, 80, 194
Nelson, Janet, 190
Netherlands, The, 146
Neurotic ritual, 187
New Delhi, India, 142
New Guinea, 19, 199
New Year's Day, 46
New York City, 122, 161, 162
New Zealand, 194
Newburyport, Massachusetts, 65
Newton, Huey, 24
Nicaragua: U.S. hearings on, 91
Nieburg, H. L., 186, 187, 192, 194, 195
Niemi, Richard, 186
Nièvre, France, 177
Ninety-Five Articles, 103
Nisbett, Richard, 82, 194, 195
Nixon, Richard, 28, 91
Norbeck, Edward, 185, 192, 199
Norman, Ross, 196
Northern Ireland, 69, 130, 179; divisiveness of ritual in, 65; Orangemen's parade, 69, 123–24; and U.S. demonstration, 120; demonstrations in, 121
Norway, 192
Nôtre Dame (Paris), 193
Novak, Michael, 65, 108, 186, 197, 202
Nuremberg, Germany, 165

Oath: of Ku Klux Klan, 15; of induction in France, 17; in French Revolution, 23, 151, 152, 159, 180; of coronation in Europe, 27
Oberg, K., 191
Olsen, Johan, 192
Olympics, 129
Orangemen's parade, 69, 123–24
Organization: symbolic representation of, 15–21; of revolt, 168–69
Organizational: communication, 29–34; distinctiveness, 17
Ortner, Sherry, 187, 199, 196
Ozouf, Mona, 159, 189, 201, 202; on use of simultaneity, 23

Pacific islands, 170
Packard, Randall, 189

Palace of Festive Events, 116
Palestinians, 76
Palio, 75
Paris, France, 154, 155, 157, 158, 190
Parlement, 26, 106
Parliament, Italian, 137
Patron-client relations, 31
Patron saint, 146, 148
Patterson, Orlando, 199
Paul VI, Pope, 140
Peace marches: in Northern Ireland, 132
Perception: selectivity of, 79–80
Perrot, Michelle, 201
Persia, 53
Personification: of nation, 17, 178
Peters, Emyrs, 197
Pfaffenberger, Bryan, 197
Pfeffer, Jeffrey, 188
Pharaoh, 53
Philip V (of Macedonia), 190
Philippines: inauguration rites, 25; election, 50
Philosophy, 96
Pike, 156
Pilgrimage: in Italy, 139; in India, 141, 144, 169; of Dini ya Msambwa, 171
Pilling, Arnold, 199
Pioneer Monument, 173
Piven, Francis Fox, 39, 191
Pocock, J. G. A., 188
Poison ordeal, 134
Poland, 99, 153
Political parties: in the United States, 74
Political science, 186
Political study, 7
Politics: as rational, 2, 3, 6, 7–8; as self-interest, 12
Polynesia, 2
Powell, Walter, 188
Power: sacralization of, 2
Prayer, 97
Presidency: ritualization of, 163, 182–83; American, 6
President, U.S.: as symbol-maker, 6; sacred power of, 47, 48; enforcing authority, 53; as symbol manipulator, 90
Presidential campaign, 108–09
Presidential seal, 90
Price, S. R. F., 189, 190
Primacy effect, 83, 86
Primo di Rivera, Miguel, 149
Prince of Wales, 41
Protest marches, 134
Protestants: in Northern Ireland, 69
Protocol, 32, 104–05
Provence, France, 148

Psychological: function of ritual, 131–32; reductionism, 63
Psychology: of parade, 72; of commitment, 72; cognitive, 79
Punjab, 140, 142, 179
Pythian-Adams, Charles, 192

Quebec, 179
Quinet, Edgar, 159

Radcliffe-Brown, A. R., 62, 186, 193, 204
Rain rites, 177
Ranger, Terrence, 191
Rappaport, Roy, 68, 187, 194
Rasnake, Roger, 193
Rationality: in politics, 3, 6, 7–8, 12, 13, 95–96, 182–83; Soviet views of, 100
Reagan, Nancy, 109
Reagan, Ronald: at Iceland, 32, 109; at Bitburg, 77, 90, 93–95, 121, 178; on "Peacekeeper," 70
Reality: perception of, 3–4; construction of, 5, 48, 51, 95; representation of political, 84–92
Rearick, Charles, 193, 201
Reay, Marie, 199
Rebellion, 39, 168–73
Red Brigades, 135–40
Red Square, 38, 45, 104
Reformation, 148
Regalia: imperial (China), 46; royal (in India), 47
Reichsparty-day rallies, 165–66
Reification, 186
Reign of Terror, 154
Religion, 62, 65, 71; and ritual, 8, 9
Remembrance Day, 166
Representativeness, 81
Republic Day, 173
Resistance, 138
Resistance Day, 122
Resistance movement: in Italy, 70–71
Revolt: led by ritualists, 19
Revolution: rituals of 151–73; importance of ritual to, 153
Revolution. See also American Revolution; French Revolution; Iran
Reykjavik, Iceland, 32
Reynolds, Frank, 198
Rhetoric, 70, 101
Rhodesia, 19, 33, 41
Richards, Audrey, 189, 190
Riefenstahl, Leni, 202
Rites of allegiance: in Roman Empire, 22
Rites of degradation, 28
Rites of delegitimation, 2

Rites of obeisance, 38, 54, 118, 161, 183
Rites of passage, 51; battle over, 114–19; sponsored by state, 115–16; in Soviet Union, 115–16; in Italy, 116–19; in kidnapping, 137; in French Revolution, 157; in Nazi Germany, 167; in political organizations, 17; in New Guinea, 19; in political office, 24–25
Rites of Reason, 183
Rites of rebellion, 54–56, 144
Rites of resistance, 167, 168–69
Rites of reversal, 55, 132; in India, 131
Rites of transition, 100
Rites of violence, 130
Ritual: and religion, 2; in industrial society, 2; creation of reality, 2, 10, 12, 14, 79, 84–92; political importance of, 2–3, 12–14, 67, 159–60, 178–81; used to communicate, 29–34, 90, 104–07; and religion, 8, 9; defined, 8–9, 128; and symbolization, 9; and belief, 9, 67–69, 91; and cognition, 9, 83–84; links past to present, 9–10; characteristics of, 9–12; psychological bases of, 10; conservative aspects of, 10, 12, 112; physiological bases of, 10, 40; creation of, 10, 12, 20, 87, 160; dramatic quality of, 10–11; change in, 12, 39, 67; and myth, 12–13; secrecy, 15, 17, 21; of membership, 17; of purity, 18; hostilities, 19, 126–27; used to define boundaries, 21–22, 62; tying periphery to center, 21–24; investiture of power, 24–28; divesting of power, 28–29; use of space, 30; used to note status, 30–31; of address, 31, 45; used to instill fear, 33, 172; and material forces, 39; in corporations, 42; of political continuity, 45; pagan, 45; of democratic participation, 50; of sacrifice, 52; of royalty, 53, 54, 66; as a safety valve, 55, 127, 131–34, 146, 149–50, 172, 173; of equality, 56; producing solidarity, 61–67; of communion, 62; negative, 64; rationalization of, 67; fosters division, 69; and self-importance, 72; promoting group attachment, 72; emotional potency of, 73; of nationalism, 73; reinforcing division, 74–76; fosters solidarity, 75–76; ambiguity in, 83; artificiality of, 85, 88; cognitive effect of, 94; poles of, 100; as rhetoric, 101; and political change, 104; struggle for power through, 107–10, 119–24; of caste groupings, 110, 112–14; of community, 110–11, 150; of descent groups, 110–12; of hierarchy in India, 113–14; of allegiance, 118; sponsored by govern-

ment, 129; standardization of, 122; used to make alliance, 125; of law court, 132–34; response to crises, 134–44; of justice, 137, 145; as weapon of the powerless, 144, 181; of degradation, 145–46; in revolution, 151–73; of revolt, 162, 168–73; of self-flagellation, 168; and sophistication, 177–78; of new nations, 178; routinization of, 179–80

Ritualization: of conflict, 127–30, phylogenetic, 128; spontaneous, 158; of the presidency, 163; of social relations, 177

Roberts, John, 199

Robespierre, Maximilien, 156–57, 164

Rockhill, William, 195

Rodger, Ian, 201

Roehm, Ernest, 202

Roman Empire, 22, 78

Romano, France, 145

Rome, 135, 139, 140; political use of calendar in, 20; triumphal entrances in, 29–30; Senate rites in, 37; festival in, 55

Roosevelt, Franklin D., 5, 58

Rosaldo, Renato, 192

Roscoe, J., 199

Rosenfeld, Alvin, 196

Ross, Lee, 82, 194, 195

Rousseau, Jean-Jacques, 153

Royal: excreta, 47; entries, 153;

Royal regalia: in France, 26; among Bunyoro, 35; in Swaziland, 89

Royal tour: in Java, 22; in France, 22–23; in Morocco, 23

Ruiz, Teofilo, 192

Russia, 177; coronation in, 27–28. See also Soviet Union

Russian Orthodox Church, 115, 177

Sacralization: of power, 28, 37, 52

Sacred ruler, 47

Sacrifice: among Bunyoro, 35; rituals of, 52, 171

Sacrilege, 38

Safety valve, 55, 127, 131–34, 144, 146, 149–50, 172, 173

Sahlins, Marshall, 185, 186, 192

Salt tax, 169–70

Salute: Nazi, 164, 167, 180; Roman, 183

Sanskritization, 112

Sanson, Rosemonde, 191, 194, 201

Savannah, Georgia, 161

Schema, 79–82

Schematic thinking, 79–82

Schultz, Alfred, 83–84, 195

Schutzstaffel (SS), 94–95

Science, 177

Scott, James, 192

Scribner, Bob, 197

Scrofula, 53–54

Scullard, H. H., 190

Secrecy, 15, 17, 21

Self-crowning, 190

Selma, Alabama, 92

Semiotic analysis, 188

Semites, 67

Senate, U.S., 91

Seneviratne, H. L., 191

Senin-Artina, Giovanna, 198

Shafer, Boyd, 194, 201

Shah of Iran, 86, 168

Shaw, Peter, 202

Shilluk, 25–26

Shils, Edward, 66, 185, 194

Shiva, 144

Shrovetide, 177

Siegel, James, 194

Siena, Italy, 74–75

Sikhs, 140–43

Silverman, Sydel, 75, 187, 194, 195

Simonneau, Jacques, 154–56

Simplification: of reality, 4

Simultaneity, 23, 122

Singer, Milton, 186

Singh, Khushwant, 141

Singh, Zail, 143

Situational pressure, 96

Skinner, Quentin, 188

Skulls, 85, 145

Slavery, 49

Smith, Bardwell, 191

Smith, W. John, 198

Smith, W. Robertson, 67, 193, 194

Snyder, Mark, 74, 96, 194, 195, 196

Soboul, Albert, 201, 202

Soccer, 74, 129

Social consensus, 68

Social theory, 61

Solidarity: theory of, 61–67; without consensus, 66–69; and belief, 75–76; of working class, 149; created by ritual, 153

Song, 40, 99, 184; in Black Power Movement, 24; in Italy, 45, 71; in Tunisia, 111; Thai, 123; in French Revolution, 151, 157, 158; in South Africa, 171

South Africa, 49, 169; defining nation in, 20; rites of Great Trek in, 36–37; funerals in, 171–73, 180

Soviet Union: early political ritual in, 14; state rites in, 16, 178, 179, 180; de-Stalinization in, 28–29; parade rites in, 30; Lenin rites in, 38; Christian ritual in, 45; mausoleums in, 45; election ritual in,

Soviet Union (*continued*)
49; rites of rebellion in, 55; symbolism of World War II in, 70; view of ritual in, 100; demonstrations in, 104; summit meeting, 109; and rites of passage, 115–16. *See also* Russia
Spain: Carnival in, 149–50; royal rites in, 48, 190
Spatial symbolism, 30
Sperber, Dan, 188
Spock, Benjamin, 102
Sproull, Lee, 194
Sri Lanka, 197
Srinivas, M. N., 112, 197
St. Petersburg, Russia, 121
Stalin, Joseph, 28–29; body of, 45; on statistics, 82
Stalingrad, 28
Stamp Act, 162
Stanley, Sir Herbert, 41
Starkey, David, 192
State. *See* Nation
Strassburg, France, 152
Strike, 138
Strong, Roy, 189, 191, 194
Struve, Nikita, 179, 204
Subhuza, King (of Swaziland), 89–90
Sudan, 179
Suicide, 88
Summit meeting, 109
Sun worship, 177
Supek, Olga, 197
Supernatural: and ritual, 9
Swann, William, 96, 196
Swaziland, 54, 89–90
Swiss regiment, 154–55
Switzerland, 99, 146
Symbolic inversion, 137
Symbolism: importance to politics, 2, 8; of death, 65; of enemy, 70; vividness of, 88; of Nazism, 94–95; spatial, 105, 112, 187; of family, 108; of mass protests, 120; of simultaneity, 122; borrowing of, 123; battle of, 130; of Moro kidnapping, 135–36; revolutionary, 138; Communist, 138; in India, 141, 169–70; of class conflict, 147; of blood, 148; in American Revolution, 161; in Iranian Revolution, 168; diversity of, 175; and nationalism, 181
Symbolization of hierarchy, 145
Symbols: political importance of, 3; as shield against terror, 4; and reality, 4, 182; change in, 4–5, 175; power of, 5; properties of, 7, 11; in ritual, 12; relation to the material world of, 13; of political allegiance, 17; of identity, 18, 81; re-ligious, 45; conflict between, 51; of national unity, 64; ambiguity of, 69–75, 83, 129, 177; meaning of, 70; battle over, 71; influence belief, 85, 86; power of, 92–93; emotional impact of, 99–100; in diplomacy, 104–05; of legitimization in Israel, 109–10; of subordination, 112; in mass rallies, 119; of protest, 121; derogatory, 130; Hindu, 142; of authority, 144; of treachery, 145; of revolutionary France, 147; of law and order, 156; creation of, 158, 160; of democracy, 160; of American presidency, 90, 163; of Nazism, 164, 166; Christian, 171; vulnerability of, 176; definition of, 185

Taboo, 18; defining group, 19; on contact with rulers, 46–48; in Hawaii, 47; in Australia, 64
Tallensi, 18
Talleyrand, Bishop of Autun, 151
Tamil, 178
Tanala, 133
Tanzania, 23
Tarring and feathering, 162
Taylor, Simon, 189, 192, 198, 202
Tedeschi, James, 195
Teheran, Iran, 134, 168
Terlinden, Vicomte, 194
Tesser, Abraham, 194, 195, 196
Thailand, 123
The Golden Bough, 55
Thermidorians, 157
Third Reich, 166, 167
Thompson, Leonard, 189, 191
Three Sacred Treasures, 47
Times Square, 60
Tire, 172
Tito, Marshal, 178
Tiwi, 199
Tonkin, Elizabeth, 187
Totems, 64
Tourzel, Duchess of, 155
Town council, 49
Trexler, Richard, 187
Trial by ordeal, 133–34
"Triumph of the Will," 202
Trobriand Islanders, 132
Trotsky, Leon, 14
Tsar, 27–28, 121
Tudeh Party, 168
Tumarkin, Nina, 189
Tunisia, 110–11
Turkey, 31
Turner, Bryan, 191
Turner, Victor, 40, 63, 72, 100, 132, 186,

187, 188, 189, 191, 193, 194, 195, 196, 199, 203
Tversky, Amos, 80, 195

Uganda, 35, 134
Ukraine, 181
Ulster, Northern Ireland, 123
Unger, Aryeh, 192, 197, 202
Uniforms, 81
United States: sacralization of power in, 2; and political ritual, 3, 70, 73, 90–91, 100; presidential ritual in, 6, 57–61, 182–83; and hostage crisis in Iran, 6, 85–86, 134; election campaigns in, 11, 49, 74, 182; political socialization in, 12–13; congressional ritual in, 37, 107–08; civil rights movement in, 23–24, 92; rites of degradation in, 28; Constitution, 64–65; Memorial Day rites in, 65–66; and Bitburg ritual, 77, 93–95, 121; antiwar movement in, 92, 102–03, 119–20, 121, 122; reception for queen of England in, 120

Valeri, Valerio, 192
Values, 69
Van Gennep, 189, 197
Vatican, 33
Venezuela, 125
Venice, 105, 130, 145
Verba, Sidney, 204
Versailles, France, 158
Victoria, Queen (of Britain), 176
Vienna, Austria, 10
Vietnam war, 178
Violence: produced by ritual, 130
Virginia, 162
Vividness, 82
Vogt, Evon, 185
Voortrekker Monument, 36

Wagner-Pacifici, Robin, 199
Walzer, Michael, 6, 8, 186
War, 105, 129; as dependent on nationalism, 6; role of ritual in, 69, 74, 130; symbolism of, 70
Warner, W. Lloyd, 65, 193
Warsaw, Poland, 57

Washington Monument, 120
Washington, D.C., 58–61, 120, 122
Washington, George, 163
Watergate, 28, 91
"We Shall Overcome," 122–23
Weatherford, J. McIver, 91, 196, 197
Weber, Eugen, 203
Weber, Max, 51, 189
Wechsler, Howard, 189, 190, 191, 197
Weddings: in India, 114; Italian Communist, 117–18; Nazi, 167
Weinstein, Eugene, 188
Weizmann, Chaim, 109
West Africa, 18, 68, 132
West Berlin, West Germany, 57
West Indies, 129
White House, 58, 60, 86
Whitman, Walt, 67
Wicklund, Robert, 196
Wilder, David, 195
Wilentz, Sean, 186
William IV, King, 176
William of Orange, King, 123
Williamsburg, Virginia, 162
Winthrop, Robert, 64, 193
Winton, Ward, 195
Wipper, Audrey, 202
Witches, 52
Witch-hunts, 91–92
Wittenburg, Germany, 103
Wooley, Reginald, 190
World War I: commemoration of, 93; Nazi symbolism of, 165
World War II: as symbol, 69; commemoration of, 70, 93
Worship: of state, 65
Worsley, Peter, 202

Yanomamo Indians, 125–27
Yazid, 168
Yeta (Barotse leader), 33
Young, Michael, 66, 194, 195
Yugoslavia, 115, 178

Zaccagnini, Benigno, 138, 140
Zinacantan Indians, 51–52
Zionism, 109–10